D1188213

Always among us

Images of the poor in Zwingli's Zurich

Always among us

Images of the poor in Zwingli's Zurich

LEE PALMER WANDEL

Yale University

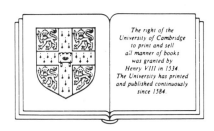

The right of the
University of Cambridge
to print and sell
all manner of books
was granted by
Henry VIII in 1534.
The University has printed
and published continuously
since 1584.

CAMBRIDGE UNIVERSITY PRESS

Cambridge

London   New York   Port Chester   Melbourne   Sydney

Published by the Press Syndicate of the University of Cambridge
The Pitt Building, Trumpington Street, Cambridge CB2 1RP
40 West 20th Street, New York, NY 10011, USA
10 Stamford Road, Oakleigh, Melbourne 3166, Australia

© Cambridge University Press 1990

First published 1990

Printed in the United States of America

This book was published with the assistance of the Frederick W. Hilles Publication Fund of the Whitney Humanities Center of Yale University.

Library of Congress Cataloging-in-Publication Data
Wandel, Lee Palmer.
Always among us : images of the poor in Zwingli's Zurich / Lee
Palmer Wandel.
p. cm.
Includes bibliographical references.
ISBN 0-521-39096-6
1. Poor – Switzerland – Zurich – History–16th century. 2. Church
and the poor – Switzerland – Zurich – History – 16th century.
3. Zwingli, Ulrich, 1484–1531. 4. Poor laws – Switzerland –
History – 16th century. I. Title.
HV4130.Z87W36   1990
362.5'09494'57 – dc20   90–31038
CIP

British Library Cataloguing in Publication Data
Wandel, Lee Palmer
Always among us : Images of the poor in Zwingli's Zurich.
1. Switzerland. Zurich. Poverty
I. Title
362.50949457

ISBN 0-521-39096-6 hardback

Contents

Acknowledgments

This book has been written in a number of places over a number of years. It began in Tübingen at the Institut für Spätmittelalter und Reformation, under the direction of Heiko A. Oberman, who introduced me to the pamphlets, with their title-page prints, of the Sonderforschungsbereich Z1. The members of SFB-Z1, especially Dr. Hans-Joachim Köhler, were enormously generous with their time, their resources, and their knowledge. In Zurich, the staffs of the Zentralbibliothek and the Staatsarchiv, and in particular the archive's director, Dr. Otto Sigg, and his assistant, Dr. Thomas Schärli, provided invaluable information and assistance, enhancing the project as a whole with their detailed knowledge of Reformation Zurich. Libraries in Europe and here in the United States have facilitated my research. I am particularly grateful to the Universtätsbibliothek Tübingen; the Herzog August Bibliothek, Wolfenbüttel; the Bayerische Staatsbibliothek, Munich; the British Library; the University of Michigan Libraries, especially the staff of the Interlibrary Loan Office; Green Library, Stanford University; and the University Libraries of Yale University. I wish to thank the following institutions for permission to reproduce prints from their collections: the Zentralbibliothek Zürich; the Graphische Sammlung of the Albertina, Vienna; the Beinecke Rare Book and Manuscript Library, Yale University; the Schlossmuseum, Museen der Stadt Gotha, Gotha; the Kupferstichkabinett of the Staatliche Museen Preussicher Kulturbesitz, Berlin; The Art Institute of Chicago; and the Oeffentliche Kunstsammlung Basel, Kupferstichkabinett.

My research was funded by the Deutscher Akademischer Austauschdienst and the History Department of the University of Michigan. The book was published with the assistance of the Frederick W. Hilles Publication Fund of Yale University.

John Boswell, Ron Delph, Thomas Green, Diane Owen Hughes, Rudi Lindner, Sabine MacCormack, Thomas Tentler, Charles Trinkaus, and Nathan Whitman have all enriched my thinking on the issues in Zurich through their insightful reading of chapters of the manuscript. Though she was not able to read the manuscript, Christine Bornstein taught me much about reading images; Chapter 3 is better for her guidance. Three people, in particular, have given generously of their fine knowledge of the people of sixteenth-century Europe and shared the fruitful ways of thinking about the past that they have developed in their own research. Thomas A. Brady, Hans-Christoph Rublack, and Bob Scribner have been both teachers and friends. What they have given this book has made it far better.

My husband, Laurence H. Winnie, has lived with this book graciously and generously, contributing his skills as an editor and his acuity as an historian. He, more than any other, has made this book possible.

Introduction

> You always have the poor with you, but you will not always have me. (Matthew 26:11)

The poor had indeed been among the peoples of Europe always. Numbers and relative proportions of the poor fluctuated, as did the kinds of people who were poor, but their presence was a constant. The poor were familiar, a point of reference in people's lives.

> For you know the grace of our Lord Jesus Christ, that though he was rich, yet for your sake he became poor, so that by his poverty you might become rich (II Corinthians 8:9).

And since at least the time of Christ, the condition of poverty was not understood solely in economic terms.[1] The life of Christ had brought to the physical condition of poverty a religious value, complex and ambivalent connotations. Christ had connected himself to the poor in two ways: as their shepherd, who offered them the Kingdom of God; and as their brother, whose life was akin to theirs in its lack of property, of fixed abode, of wealth. He had renounced not only wealth, but all that wealth brought: power in political life, influence in social relations, and the worth of the self. His poverty was total. Christ's life posed a central paradox for Christians: his spirituality was anchored in his poverty and his poverty was a metaphor for his spirituality.

> If you would be perfect, go sell what you possess and give to the poor, and you will have treasure in heaven (Matthew 19:21).

---

[1] J. LeClercq "Aux origines bibliques du vocabulaire de la pauvreté," *Etudes sur l'Histoire de la Pauvreté,* vol. 1, ed. Michel Mollat, Publications de la Sorbonne, vol. 8, (Paris, 1974), pp. 42–3.

For the greater number of Christians who followed Christ's call to poverty during the next 1,500 years, however, that poverty meant solely material dispossession.[2] From its earliest forms in the deserts of Egypt through the many reforms at Cluny, Cîteaux, Chartreuse, and elsewhere, monasticism found sanctity in the abdication of all private wealth. The twelfth-century Lyonnais merchant, Waldes, found in Matthew 19:21 the precise form he would give to his piety. The defining characteristic of his piety and of his movement was not an abject humility, but the lack of property.[3]

The person who most completely captured the fullness of Christ's poverty and, in doing so, the imagination of Europeans prior to the Reformation, was Francis of Assisi.[4] Seeking to imitate Christ, Francis wed "Lady Poverty." Like Christ, Francis renounced not only gold, silver, possessions, and shelter, but all the values his society associated with them: power, influence, and the worth of the self. For Francis, the physical condition of poverty corresponded to man's spiritual and eschatological condition.[5] Man was as a beggar before God: destitute and powerless. Indeed, all men were beggars before God; for Francis the poor were essentially no different from other men. They shared in the glory of God's creation[6] and the poverty of man's condition.[7]

> He who curses a poor man, does an injury to Christ, because he bears the noble sign of him, 'who made himself poor for us in the world' (Francis, in *I Celano*).[8]

[2] Ray C. Petry, *Francis of Assisi, Apostle of Poverty* (Durham, N.C., 1941), p. 4. On the debates about the nature of Christ's poverty from the patristic age to the thirteenth century, see J. LeClercq, "Les controverses sur la pauvreté du Christ," *Etudes*, vol. 1, pp. 45–56. On the religious connotations of poverty in the Middle Ages, see especially *Etudes*, vol. 1, entire; Lester Little, *Religious Poverty and the Profit Economy in Medieval Europe* (Ithaca, 1978); and Michel Mollat, *The Poor in the Middle Ages*, trans. Goldhammer (New Haven, Conn., 1987).

[3] Little, pp. 121ff.

[4] The literature on Francis and his notion of poverty is enormous. See, especially, Kajetan Esser, "Die Armutsfassung des Hl. Franziskus," in *Poverty in the Middle Ages*, ed. David Flood (Werl/ Westf., 1975), pp. 60–70; M. D. Lambert, *Franciscan Poverty* (London, 1961); Little; Petry; and *La povertá del secolo XII e Francesco d'Assisi* (Assisi, 1975). Although the person and personality of Francis differ markedly from those of Dominic, Little, pp. 158–9, finds that the "purpose and many of the approaches to achieving that purpose," as well as the "geographic spread, social composition, forms of ministry, or style of life" of the orders founded by the two men are fundamentally alike. It is not clear to me if later medieval perceptions of the two orders were as unified.

[5] Esser, p. 69. Bonaventure made the fullest statement of the Franciscan notion of poverty in the thirteenth century in the *Apologia pauperum*, especially chaps. 7–12.

[6] Canticle of the Sun; Mollat, pp. 70–1.

[7] Esser, pp. 69–70.

[8] Cited in Lambert, p. 59.

If the monks, the Humiliati, the Waldensians, and the canons found religious value in a life of poverty, Francis transvaluated the religious meaning of the poor themselves. For him, the distinction between involuntary and voluntary poverty was far less significant than the nature of the poverty one lived.[9] The poor who lived on the streets of towns, who were destitute and humiliated, who had not chosen to live in such harsh conditions, were not merely Francis's brothers, his fellow creatures. Francis found in the poor, in their wretchedness, their powerlessness, their dependency, the poverty Christ had preached. The fullness of their poverty brought them dignity and the promise of divine love.[10] Francis located religious meaning and value not in the simple condition of material deprivation, but in the complex situation of the poor themselves. And that relocation enabled him and the early Franciscans to look to the poor, to care for them, and to live among them.

Francis left his followers a difficult legacy. The complete poverty he embraced was difficult to emulate. And yet, the story of the Franciscans to the time of the Reformation is one of the struggle to keep Francis's notion of poverty viable and vital. In the early fourteenth century, that struggle centered on the question of Christ's poverty. Pope John XXII had opposed the absolute poverty certain friars had pursued and, in 1318, had four Spiritual Franciscans burned at the stake for their "heretical" adherence to total poverty.[11] In 1323, in the papal bull *Cum inter nonnullos,* he declared that it was heretical to hold contrary to Scripture that Christ and his apostles had had or owned no property.[12] With this bull, he sought to sever the Franciscan notion of poverty from its biblical foundation. That he failed in his effort bespeaks not only the centrality of Francis's notion of poverty to many of those who chose to follow him, but also its wider importance to the laity, who supported the more radical Franciscans in their pursuit of Christ's poverty throughout the fourteenth and fifteenth centuries.

[9] Rule of 1221, Section 8; Rule of 1223, Section 6, both in *St. Francis of Assisi Writings and Early Biographies; English Omnibus of the Sources,* ed. Marion A. Habig (Chicago, 1973), pp. 31–64.
[10] Petry, p. 53.
[11] John Moorman, *A History of the Franciscan Order from its Origins to the Year 1517* (Oxford, 1968), p. 311.
[12] "Quod Redemptori nostro eiusque Apostolis quae ipsos habuisse scriptura sacra testat nequaquam ius ipsis utendi competerit nec illa vendendi seu donandi ius habuerint; aut ex ipsis alia acquirendi," quoted in A. G. Ferrers Howell, *S. Bernardino of Siena* (London, 1913), p. 39. See also Moorman, p. 317.

And so, firmly established in the Catholic faith, we may live always according to the poverty, and the humility, and the Gospel of our Lord Jesus Christ, as we have solemnly promised (Rule of 1223).

For the Franciscans, the late fourteenth and fifteenth centuries were dominated by the conflict between the Conventuals, those who pursued a moderate and cloistered life,[13] and the Friars of the Strict Observance, or Observants.[14] The Observant movement began in 1334, when a group of five friars received permission from the Minister General to found a hermitage, in order to live according to the strictest interpretation of the Rule. The Observants sought to recover the quality of Francis's life of poverty: its instability, its insecurity, its lack of provision. In its early years, the movement met with much opposition from the Conventuals and from some of the Popes. In the last quarter of the century, however, the Conventuals and the Popes came to support it, as its form of piety grew in popularity and validity among the peasants and patricians of northern Italy. In the fifteenth century, the fate of the Observant movement was secured and advanced by a series of extraordinary preachers, among them Bernardino da Feltre, John of Capistrano, James of the March, and Bernardino of Siena.

> In the name of blessed Jesus, I began with a mouthful of sow-thistle, and, putting it into my mouth, set about chewing it. Chew! chew! It would not go down. ... And so, with a bit of sow-thistle I got rid of temptation; for I know well enough now that it *was* temptation. ... But how about S. Francis who fasted forty days and ate nothing? He might do it, but I can't. And I tell you I would not do it, and would not like God to make me want to do it (Bernardino of Siena, Sermon).[15]

The life of the best known among these preachers, Bernardino of Siena, suggests some of the dimensions of the Franciscan ideal of poverty in the fifteenth century.[16] It was a life less dramatic than Francis's, expressed not in gestures of mortification or brutalization of the body.[17]

---

[13] The Conventuals comprised that part of the Order who chose to live in cloisters, hold property that often was rent producing, and keep stores of food in excess of daily needs.

[14] For the following, see Moorman, pt. 4, and Howell, pp. 53–61.

[15] *Le Prediche Volgari* II, 351, 352, quoted in Howell, pp. 93–4.

[16] On the life of Bernardino of Siena, see Moorman, pp. 457–66; Howell.

[17] "To take up the cross in a way that the body cannot bear, is not an inspiration of God, but a temptation of the devil; and the reason is, that God hates none of the things He has made; wherefore He hates not our body, but loves it, and would have us love it, and preserve it for His honour, and not destroy it, nor give it a burden it cannot bear," quoted in Howell, p. 94.

It was, nonetheless, a life that mirrored Francis's in specific moments and gestures. Early in his pursuit of the religious life, Bernardino abandoned the stability and comfort of a Conventual house, moving into an Observant house, where he was permitted to beg his food and to work among the poor. In 1405, he was commissioned as a preacher, a vocation he was to follow until his death in 1444. It was in his life as a preacher that he most closely approached the quality of Francis's life: He lived on the gifts of others, making no provision for future needs; he was itinerant, and after 1418, had no fixed abode.[18] He preached against luxury and extravagance, effecting bonfires of "vanities" throughout northern Italy. But his fiercest polemic was reserved for the economic practice that created money from money, that was in its essence artificial and inorganic, that was concerned exclusively with money, and that created wealth by impoverishing others – usury.[19]

In 1418, when the friar's preaching was bringing him a dangerous popularity in Milan, the duke, Filippo Maria Visconti, sought to test the most dramatic and visible attribute of Bernardino's sanctity: his poverty. The duke sent the friar a messenger bearing a gift of gold coin. Following Francis's Rule precisely, Bernardino refused even to touch the money. And when the duke's messenger would not be turned away, Bernardino had him apply the money to free local prisoners. In both gestures, Bernardino evoked and invoked Francis himself; in both, his life imitated Francis's with striking precision.[20]

According to his contemporary, John of Capistrano, when Bernardino first joined the Order, perhaps twenty communities of Observants were to be found in Italy. By his death, the number had grown to 230 communities.[21] The image of the gaunt friar moved many to either join or support the Observants. In recognition of this, in 1437, the Minister

[18] Raymond DeRoover asserts that Bernardino "took a rest at the small friary of La Capiola near Siena" during the years 1431–3, in *San Bernardino of Siena and Sant'Antonino of Florence; Two Great Economic Thinkers of the Middle Ages* (Boston, 1967), p. 3.

[19] The Observants were to develop this position into a program of relief for poor citizens, the Monti di Pietá, in the later fifteenth century. Moorman, pp. 529–32; Brian Pullan, *Rich and Poor in Renaissance Venice* (Oxford, 1971), pt. 3, especially pp. 449–75; Reinhold Mueller, "Charitable Institutions, the Jewish Community and Venetian Society. A Discussion of the Recent Volume by Brian Pullan," *Studi Veneziani* 14 (1972): 37–82. On the importance of San Bernardino for Florentine communal ideals of charity, see Phillip Gavitt, "Economy, Charity, and Community in Florence, 1350–1450," in *Aspects of Poverty in Early Modern Europe*, ed. Thomas Riis (Alphen aan den Rijn, 1981), pp. 109–11.

[20] Moorman, p. 458; Howell, pp. 109–11.

[21] Quoted in Moorman, p. 465.

General of the Franciscans made him Vicar of the Observants in Italy. In 1440, together with another friar, Bernardino wrote the "Exposition of the Rule," the Observant interpretation of Francis's Rule. The Exposition defined the nature of Franciscan poverty for the fifteenth century: It regulated against owning money and called for the renunciation of all goods that were not essential to daily survival. It reasserted the instability and dependency of Francis's life.

Bernardino's reform movement, the Observants, triumphed in the early sixteenth century. By the end of the fifteenth century, the reform party, or *reformati*, which comprised the Observants and a number of smaller, equally rigorous groups,[22] had come to represent the majority of Franciscans, outnumbering the Conventuals in most countries.[23] In 1517, Pope Leo X gave the *reformati* the right to determine the leadership and the direction of the Order of Friars Minor; the Conventuals were required to submit or establish a separate Order.

In 1517, those who had sought to shape their lives in strict accordance with Francis's Rule, who had placed a notion of poverty at the center of the Order's identity, were triumphant in the Franciscan Order. That notion was no longer precisely Francis's, but it shared many of the qualities Francis had attributed to true poverty. The notion of poverty shaping Franciscan piety in 1517 retained its characteristics of instability, insecurity, its lack of fixed location, of provision – its dependency and humility. And for those who followed that ideal, the line dividing those who chose poverty from those who were involuntarily poor remained pale. The condition of true poverty brought to both a life devoid of many qualities their contemporary society valued.

It may be that for those who saw the most devout *reformati*, that line was equally difficult to trace. Portraits of Bernardino present a man emaciated, his cheeks sunken, without the shaping presence of teeth.[24] Others portrayed his head as skull-like, his hair sparse, eyes sunken.[25] In his person his audience could see poverty – not mere austerity – in all its deformity. Like Christ and Francis, he had no fixed abode, no

[22] Moorman, chap. 43.
[23] Ibid., pp. 581ff.
[24] See, for example, the portraits by Sano di Pietro, in the Palazzo Pubblico, Siena, and Fiorenzo di Lorenzo, in the Pinacoteca Vannucci, Perugia.
[25] For example, the head of Bernardino by Lorenzo Vecchietta, in the Palazzo Palmieri-Nuti, Siena; the portrait by Pietro di Giovanni Ambossi in L'Observanza, Siena; and the "Glorification of San Bernardino," by Pintoricchio, in Santa Maria in Aracoeli, Rome.

wealth, no property, no political or social status. His face bore the marks of deprivation, of homelessness, of insecurity. He looked, because he was, a poor man, a beggar.

Social, as well as religious, evaluations were applied to the material condition of poverty.[26] The poverty practiced by Christ, Francis, Bernardino, and the Observant Franciscans played upon contemporary social definitions of poverty. Indeed, well into the sixteenth century, the terms by which poverty was defined were social: The poor were understood first in relation to other parts of society. They were defined according to categories that enabled late medieval society to place individuals in relationship to others, hierarchically and vertically, and to give each a place, a status – relative social worth.[27] The poor lacked precisely those attributes that gave social value and significance to certain of their contemporaries.

First among those attributes was power: the ability to exercise authority over others. In late medieval towns, power was most visibly and frequently expressed through membership in the town council and the guild. The key criteria in determining that membership were property ownership and citizenship.[28] Symbols and rights reinforced distinctions of status and worth.[29] Clothes and access to public festivals, in particular, were important marks of social status and influence.[30] So, too, was place of residence symbolic of social place: Those who lived just outside the town walls, in the Vorstädte, had less status, a lesser place than those who lived within the walls.[31]

Each of these attributes had been rejected by Francis and his followers.

---

[26] On the social values attached to poverty, see Karl Bosl, "Potens und Pauper: Begriffgeschichtliche Studien zur gesellschaftlichen Differenzierung im frühen Mittelalter und zum 'Pauperismus' des Hochmittelalters," in *Frühformen der Gesellschaft im mittelalterlichen Europa* (Vienna, 1964), 106–34; *Etudes*, vol. 2; Little; Mollat; and Erich Maschke, "Die Unterschichten der mittelalterlichen Städte Deutschlands," in *Städte und Menschen*, Vierteljahrschrift für Sozial– und Wirtschaftsgeschichte, Bd. 68 (Wiesbaden, 1980), pp. 306–79.

[27] Maschke has traced in great detail the categories by which late medieval society designated the lower, and poorer, ranks.

[28] For the towns of Freiburg im Br. and Basel, Thomas Fischer finds that these criteria were not as central. See *Städtische Armut und Armenfürsorge im 15. und 16. Jahrhundert*, Göttinger Beiträge zur Wirtschafts– und Sozialgeschichte, Bd. 4 (Göttingen, 1979), pp. 74–82.

[29] See, for example, John Martin Vincent, *Costume and Conduct in the Laws of Basel, Bern, and Zürich, 1370–1800* (Baltimore, 1935; reprint, New York, 1969) on the regulation of dress.

[30] Servants, for example, were not allowed to attend a wedding in late thirteenth-century Augsburg. Maschke, p. 316.

[31] Ibid., p. 321.

They placed "power" in relation to the omnipotence of God and found all men lacking. They avoided all public symbols of status: property, clothes, access to festivals. So, too, their itinerant life denied them both citizenship and permanent place of residence – they had no social place. Finally, Francis and his followers defined themselves in contradistinction to an essential social value: "honor."[32]

Of particular importance in identifying the poor was the application of this value to professions: the distinction made between "honorable" and "dishonorable" professions.[33] Those who practiced "dishonorable" professions lived at the margins of society; most of them also lived at the margins of subsistence. Honor had no clear principle of application among professions. It did not correspond directly with guild membership. Butchers and leatherworkers belonged to guilds; the one retained its honorable status through its association with food, the other did not.[34] The work of millers was often considered dishonorable, perhaps because mills were located on the edge, the margin, of towns, perhaps because millers themselves lived at the edges of society, belonging fully neither to the town nor to the countryside.[35] Servants, both male and female, because they were dependent upon the households of others, having no home of their own, held dishonorable status.

Although some dishonorable professions were organized into guilds, most were not. Those not belonging to any guild had less identity within the town, less influence, less status. Membership in a guild provided certain protections not available to most dishonorable professions.[36] Urban day laborers comprised the largest group of nonguild workers. Because they belonged to no guild, their skill was not regulated. They had no stable place of work. They received the lowest wages among artisans. In an Augsburg tax census of 1475, day laborers ranked immediately above beggars in income.[37]

Other professions were "dishonorable" for more obvious reasons. Gamblers and prostitutes shared the loss of dignity brought by work

---

[32] Werner Danckert, *Unehrliche Leute* (Bern, 1963), Introduction, on the notion of "honor" in late medieval society.

[33] Danckert; Maschke, pp. 318ff.

[34] Maschke, p. 320.

[35] Danckert, pp. 125–45.

[36] Fischer found that guild membership was the single most important criterion in delimiting poverty for Basel and Freiburg, pp. 59ff.

[37] Maschke, p. 331.

considered immoral. Work that concerned the dead, that of executioners and gravediggers, was dishonorable. Lacking in honor, too, was the work surrounding prisons and criminals: tower guards, caretakers. Itinerant professions, such as miming, acrobatics, and juggling, were all dishonorable. A last and separate category of dishonorable people, whose dishonor lay not in their profession, but in their person, comprised all those who were considered truly outsiders for late medieval society: Jews and gypsies, bastards and moral deviants.

The social value of honor had direct and material repercussions for certain economic functions. Dishonorable professions were much more vulnerable economically. Guild membership provided a number of protections; its absence meant insecurity on a number of fronts. There were no fixed wages for many dishonorable professions, most prominently, both urban and rural day laborers. Their employment was sporadic; permanent employment was problematic at best. Their lives as well as their livelihoods depended upon the demands of others.

That so many of those who practiced dishonorable professions lived near the line of poverty may well have led people to view some poor as lacking in honor. Yet, as we shall see, poverty and dishonor were not inextricably intertwined. Certain poor were known as "honorable poor."[38] Perhaps more important, many more people were poor or potentially poor than those who belonged to dishonorable professions. As early as 1340 in Florence, *pauper* and *laborator* were becoming interchangeable.[39] Among the crafts, and among their guilds, a wide disparity of income and property existed.[40] A number of professions could not ensure for themselves stability in their standard of living.[41] Many people were vulnerable to wage and price fluctuations and to shortages; many were forced to ask for support from others in order to ensure a basic subsistence.[42]

---

[38] Richard Trexler, "Charity and the Defense of Urban Elites in the Italian Communes," in *The Rich, the Well Born and the Powerful*, ed. Frederic Cople Jaher (Urbana, 1973), pp. 64–109; Amleto Spicciani, "The 'Poveri Vergognosi' in 15th Century Florence," in *Aspects of Poverty in Early Modern Europe*, p. 129, 129n. 42.

[39] Catherina Lis and Hugo Soly, *Poverty and Capitalism in Early Modern Europe* (Bristol, 1982 [1979]), p. 51.

[40] See Maschke's figures for Breslau, p. 329; Fischer, pp. 59–79.

[41] Fischer found poverty occurring most often in three professional sectors: textile workers, construction, and the urban agrarian workers, pp. 67ff. Spicciani found relief programs in Florence specifically designed for the temporarily poor, pp. 136ff.

[42] "In a broad sense the term 'the poor' was often, and correctly, used to designate the majority of the working population," Carlo Cipolla, "Economic Fluctuations, the Poor, and Public Policy

I had hoped to become rich
Over my own on this earth
Many enterprises I've begun
None of which got off the ground
Indeed it's true as men often say
Ah, handwork brings new bad luck...
And the fine people think not
That tomorrow may be for them as today is for me
So turns the wheel
Where luck shifts early and late
Quickly over itself, then suddenly down
Luck reigns today, bad luck again tomorrow...
Therefore let no one ridicule me
Who knows yet who will be the last
Who will go down just like me
When in the day many hours still remain
(Peter Flettner, *The Fallen Artisan*, c. 1535)[43]

The line dividing the poor from the rest of society was less and less stable.[44] It fluctuated according to larger, structural changes, such as climate, economy, and the contours of political jurisdiction. Agricultural production depended more and more upon the labor not of property-owning peasants, but of day laborers, who had come to comprise roughly 50 percent of the rural population in New Castile.[45] The organization of the textile industries led increasingly to the impoverishment of the textile workers.[46] In Leyden, the town secretary stated that the few

(Italy, 16th and 17th Centuries)," in *Aspects of Poverty in Early Modern Europe*, p. 65. See also Fischer, pt. A.

[43] "Ich han gehoffet reich zu werden/ Uber mein gelich auff disen erden/ Hab vil hendel gefangen an/ Der mir keyner von stat wolt gan/ Ist noch war wie man saget dick/ Acht handwerck pringen neun ungluck/ Das ist mir eben auch geschehen/ ... Und dencken nicht die dollen lewt/ In sey morgen wie mir ist hewt/ So in gee ubern pauch ein radt/ Wan glück bewegt sich fru und spat/ Schnell uber sich, dann plotzlich nider/ Regiert hewt gluck morgen ungluck wider/ ... Darumb darff niemant spotten mein/ Wer waiss wer noch der letzt will sein/ Wann in dem tag sand yezt d fl stundt," from *Der zugrunde gerichtete Handwerker* (ca. 1535), by Peter Flettner, reprinted in Max Geisberg, *Der deutsche Einblatt Holzschnitt* (Munich, 1923–30), vol. 20, p. 828.

[44] W. P. Blockmans and W. Prevenier, "Poverty in Flanders and Brabant from the Fourteenth to the Mid-Sixteenth Century: Sources and Problems," *Acta Historiae Neerlandicae* 10 (1978): 1–58; Cipolla.

[45] Lis and Soly, pp. 73, 62. On the decline in agricultural real wages, see Wilhelm Abel, *Agricultural Fluctuations in Europe; From the thirteenth to the twentieth centuries*, trans. Olive Ordish (New York, 1980 [1978]), pp. 116–46.

[46] Fischer, pp. 67ff.; Lis and Soly, p. 69; Spicciani, pp. 157ff; Gavitt, pp. 93ff.

drapeniers entirely dominated those who lived from spinning, weaving, fulling, and other wool processes.[47] So, too, individual shifts of fortune could move a family from financial stability to dependency. Increasingly in the late fifteenth and early sixteenth centuries, urban artisans and peasants left their towns and villages, their crafts and their land, in search of a means of existence.[48]

By the late fifteenth century, the faces of the poor were many in kind and in number. The poor included not only the traditional groups: widows, orphans, the blind, the lame. They also comprised newer kinds as well: artisans temporarily out of work, urban wage earners, day laborers between harvests, peasants whose holdings had been ravaged by natural disaster or war.[49] Their number was growing. In Lübeck, the percentage of the population comprised in the lower, and therefore vulnerable, strata, rose from 42 percent in 1380 to 52 percent in 1460.[50] In ten Württemberger villages, the number of poor, of those people permanently dependent on others for their subsistence, comprised at least 65 percent of the population in 1544.[51] In Memmingen, the number of "Have-nots" on the tax registers leapt from 31 percent to 55 percent in 1521.[52] Thomas Fischer has estimated that roughly one-fifth of the population received no regular nourishment.[53] The faces of the poor were many. They were also diverse, and they may well have been familiar.

> Irides. To these rags we owe our happiness.
> Misop. But I'm afraid you're going to lose a good deal of this happiness
>   before long.
> Irides. How so?
> Misop. Because citizens are already muttering that beggars shouldn't
>   be allowed to roam about at will, but that each city should support
>   its own beggars and all the able-bodied ones forced to work.
> Irides. Why are they planning this?

---

[47] Lis and Soly, p. 69.
[48] Ibid., p. 78.
[49] Fischer finds six basic categories of poor – craftsmen with houses and small workshops; journeymen and maids; day laborers; alms recipients; dishonorable professions; the asocial – which he has divided according to their willingness and ability to work, pp. 83ff.
[50] Lis and Soly, p. 74. In 1475, 66 percent of Augsburg's taxable population belonged to the category "Habnits," Maschke, p. 323.
[51] Lis and Soly, p. 74.
[52] Ibid., p. 78.
[53] Fischer, p. 57.

Misop. Because they find prodigious crimes committed under pretext of begging. In the second place, there's not a little danger from your order

(Erasmus, "Beggar Talk," *Colloquies.*)[54]

In the years between Francis's death and the beginning of the Reformation, the precise religious and social values associated with poverty, as well as the prosopography of the poor, changed.[55] Michel Mollat has argued, and much of the scholarship on sixteenth-century poor relief seems to concur, that the social evaluation of the poor eclipsed religious connotations by the beginning of the sixteenth century.[56] They were perceived, Mollat and others argue, after the social revolts of the fourteenth and fifteenth centuries, as a disruptive and periodically violent presence – as a source of social unrest and consequently, a focus for social control.[57]

However, for the people of sixteenth-century Europe, poverty was not so easily severed from its religious connotations. The story of the Franciscans suggests that as late as 1517, poverty retained at least some of the complexity that Christ, Francis, and Bernardino had brought to it. And their effort to return to an original form of Franciscan religious life true to the intent of the founder echoed the much broader movement to return to an original Christianity – a Christianity whose historical dimensions could be mapped with precision in its liturgy, its practices, its doctrine – that emerged in the first decades of the sixteenth century. At the same time that the Franciscans were defining the form of their life, all forms of religious life were called into question, examined, reevaluated against the lives of Christ and His apostles. It may be no

---

[54] *The Colloquies of Erasmus*, trans. Craig R. Thompson (Chicago, 1965), pp. 253–4.

[55] Bosl; Mollat; Little; *Etudes*, vols. 1 and 2.

[56] Two exceptions to this are Elsie McKee, *John Calvin on the Diaconate and Liturgical Almsgiving* (Geneva, 1984); and Brian Pullan, "Catholics and the Poor in Early Modern Europe," *Transactions of the Royal Historical Society*, 5th ser., 26 (1976): 26–34, especially.

[57] Mollat, chap. IV; Lis and Soly, pp. 51ff. and 82–96; Jean-Pierre Gutton, *La société et les pauvres en Europe (XVIe–XVIIIe siècles)* (Paris, 1974); André Vauchez, "Le peuple au Moyen Age: du 'Populus Christianus' aux classes dangereuses," in *Aspects of Poverty in Early Modern Europe II*, ed. Thomas Riis (Odense, 1986), pp. 9–18. Richard Gascon places the shift in evaluation of the poor in the seventeenth century, "Economie et pauvreté aux XVIe et XVIIe siècles: Lyon, ville exemplaire et prophétique," *Etudes*, vol. 2, pp. 747–60. On the theme of social control, see especially Robert Jütte, "Poor Relief and Social Discipline in Sixteenth-Century Europe," *European Studies Review* 11 (1981): 25–52. As John Boswell pointed out to me, the Bull *Cum inter nonnullos* suggests that the association between poverty and social instability and rebellion came much earlier.

coincidence that among the most vocal critics were mendicants.[58] It should not be surprising that they brought to their vision of religious practice some of the values they had sought to establish in their own order: simplicity of piety and a direct engagement with the poor.

Nor were the mendicants alone in their concern for the poor in the early sixteenth century; indeed, humanists and civic leaders are more often credited with a concern that translated into action.[59] It has long been acknowledged that poor relief and religion were reformed simultaneously in a number of towns, among them, Nuremberg, Wittenberg, Zurich, Strasbourg, Basel, and Geneva.[60] In each urban community, a range of influences, of ideas, values, and attitudes, came to play in that reform. In each, reform assumed an identity slightly different from those of other towns. But for all, poverty and reform were linked.

As each civic community sought to redefine what constituted true Christian practice and liturgy, it also sought to define its relation with its poor. In Leisnig, Wittenberg, and Nuremberg, town councils called upon their citizens to care for the poor out of Christian love.[61] In Strasbourg, the first administrator of poor relief, appointed in 1523, was a former chaplain.[62] In Geneva, the *procureurs* placed in charge of poor relief were equal in authority to the elders of consistory, who supervised

---

[58] Among the best known were Martin Bucer, a Dominican, and Eberlin von Günzberg and Francis Lambert, Franciscans. In Zurich, two of the earliest and most outspoken proponents of reform were the Franciscans Sebastian Meyer (1465–1545) and Sebastian Hofmeister (1476–1533).

[59] Natalie Zemon Davis, "Poor Relief, Humanism, and Heresy," in *Society and Culture in Early Modern France* (Stanford, 1975), 17–64; Paul Fideler, "Christian humanism and poor law reform in early Tudor England," *Societas* 4 (1974): 269–85; Pullan, "Catholics and the Poor in Early Modern Europe."

[60] The modern discussion was initiated by Franz Ehrle, *Beiträge zur Reform der Armenpflege* (Freiburg im Br., 1881) and Georg Ratzinger, *Geschichte der Kirchlichen Armenpflege* (Freiburg im Br., 1884). On Nuremberg and Wittenberg, see Harold Grimm, "Luther's Contributions to Sixteenth-Century Organization of Poor Relief," *Archiv für Reformationsgeschichte [ARG]* 61 (1970): 222–34; and Carter Lindberg, "There Should Be No Beggars Among Christians," *Church History* 46 (1977): 313–34. On Zurich, see Alice Denzler, "*Geschichte des Armenwesens in Kanton Zürich im 16. und 17. Jahrhundert*," *Zürcher volkswirtschaftliche Studien*, N.F. 7 (1920): 1–215. On Strasbourg, Miriam Usher Chrisman, "Urban Poor in the Sixteenth Century: The Case of Strasbourg," *Social Groups and Religious Ideas in the Sixteenth Century*, Studies in Medieval Culture, XIII (Kalamazoo, Mich., 1978), pp. 59–67. On Basel, see Fischer. On Geneva, see Robert Kingdon, "Social Welfare in Calvin's Geneva," *American Historical Review* 76(1971), reprinted in *Church and Society in Reformation Europe* (London, 1985), section VI, pp. 50–69; and McKee.

[61] Grimm, "Luther's Contributions to Sixteenth-Century Organization of Poor Relief," 227–33. See, for example, the poor ordinances of Nuremberg and Kitzingen, in Otto Winckelmann, "Die Armenordnungen von Nürnberg (1522), Kitzingen (1523), Regensburg (1523), und Ypern (1525)," *ARG* 10 (1913): 259, and 11 (1914): 8, respectively.

[62] Chrisman, p. 61.

the beliefs and morals of the community.[63] The *procureurs* were among Calvin's most ardent supporters; along with their colleagues, the *hospitalliers,* they became among the most powerful officials in Geneva.[64]

> What else, I ask you, is a city than a great monastery? (Erasmus, Letter to Paul Volz)[65]

One by one, towns and cities sought to shape themselves in accord with a vision of true Christian life. One by one, they delineated what was to be the relation of a true Christian community to the least powerful, the most vulnerable among its inhabitants. Why did Zurich, Geneva, and other towns place men of status and importance in charge of programs of relief? Was the reform of poor relief primarily a reaction of anxious governments to increasing numbers of poor?[66] Was religious reform merely the opportune moment for exerting social control over the local poor? The religious commitments of the men placed in charge of the programs and the language in which that reform was articulated suggest not.[67] What, then, did the poor mean to reforming communities?

This is a study of one town's relationship to its poor during the Reformation. It is not, fundamentally, a contribution to the debate about Catholic as opposed to Protestant forms of relief. Brian Pullan and Natalie Zemon Davis have shown that the sources for notions of charity were not so much Catholic or Protestant as humanist and civic.[68] And Fischer and Robert Jütte have delineated in detail the similarities and divergences in urban Catholic and Protestant programs of relief.[69] Rather, its point of departure is one point of consensus among scholars:

---

[63] Kingdon, "Social Welfare in Calvin's Geneva," 56–7.

[64] Robert Kingdon, "The Deacons of the Reformed Church in Calvin's Geneva," *Melanges d'histoire du XVIe siècle offerts a Henri Meylan; Travaux d'Humanisme et Renaissance* 110 (Geneva, 1970), reprinted in *Church and Society*, section VII, pp. 83–5.

[65] Dated 14 August 1518. *Collected Works of Erasmus*, Vol. 6: *The Correspondence of Erasmus*, Letters 842 to 992, trans. R. A. B. Mynors and D. F. S. Thomson, annotated Peter G. Bietenholz (Toronto, 1982), p. 89.

[66] Lis and Soly; Chrisman.

[67] Grimm, "Luther's Contributions to Sixteenth-Century Organization of Poor Relief"; Lindberg, "There Should Be No Beggars Among Christians."

[68] Brian Pullan, *Rich and Poor in Renaissance Venice* and "Catholics and the Poor in Early Modern Europe"; Davis, "Poor Relief, Humanism and Heresy."

[69] Fischer; and Robert Jütte, *Obrigkeitliche Armenfürsorge in deutschen Reichstädten der frühen Neuzeit,* Kölner Historische Abhandlungen, Bd. 31 (Cologne, 1984).

that the reform of poor relief took place at the local, for the most part civic, level.[70]

Zurich offers a promising locus for study for a number of reasons. Reform in Zurich was guided by Huldrych Zwingli, one of the most active and important reformers of the first generation. Zurich was among the first communities to reform its religious life and the care of its poor. Although itself relatively small, Zurich's influence extended to larger cities in southwest Germany, in particular, Strasbourg and Augsburg, to Basel and Geneva, shaping the religious life of each in specific and important ways. And in the early sixteenth century, it was to Zurich that peasants, artisans, and some rulers throughout southwestern Germany looked for the shape of the true Christian community, the form of human relations.[71]

Zurich is also a promising locus of study for another compelling reason. In Zurich, the poor appear in more than one aspect of the town's culture; they appear in more than one kind of source material. As the focus of institutions delineated by the town council in the reorganization of relief, the poor were addressed in legislation. Zwingli spoke of them in sermons and wrote of them in pamphlets. In both spoken and printed word, the poor were given a place within Zwingli's theology, in his construction of Christian ethics. And the poor appeared in printed images on the title pages of some of those pamphlets: In two woodcuts and one engraving, the poor were represented to the eyes of Zurich. In the 1520s, the people of Zurich heard about the poor, those who could, read about the poor, and they saw the poor, not only in the streets, but in their homes as they looked at pamphlets of Zwingli's writings.

Each of these sources constitutes a distinct medium of expression, of communication, of definition. Each represents a separate language[72] within the culture of the town. They were languages in which the town's civic identity had been articulated and the reform of its religious life was being delineated: sermons and pamphlets, visual images, laws. Each

---

[70] The one major exception to this is England, where the reform of poor relief took place under the monarch at the national level.

[71] Thomas A. Brady, *Turning Swiss; Cities and Empire, 1450–1550* (Cambridge, 1985); Peter Blickle, *The Revolution of 1525*, trans. Thomas A. Brady, Jr. and H. C. Erik Midelfort (Baltimore, Md., 1981), especially pt. 2.

[72] Although language is at the heart of debates in both literature and history (most recently, in *American Historical Review* 93 [June 1989]), the term, "language," it seems to me, best conveys the complexity, the fluidity, the ubiquity of the cultural forms that are the focus of this study.

language possessed its own vocabulary, its own linkages of meaning. Each brought to consideration of the poor particular associations of values drawn from its own tradition. Each brought different nuances of meaning to perceptions of the poor. Together they provided the people of Zurich with vocabularies for discussion of the poor, who they were and what social and religious values were to be attributed to them. And they gave particular resonance in Zurich to "the poor" [*die Arme*] at a time when various groups, predominantly peasants and less powerful artisans, increasingly referred to themselves as "poor."

Much of the scholarship on the poor in early modern Europe has focused on the institutions of relief. This focus may help to explain why modern scholars have viewed the poor of early modern Europe primarily in terms of civic regulation and social control. Yet these institutions were formulated within the context of a particular urban or regional culture. The poor were discussed in languages other than that of legislation: sermons and pamphlets, testimonies and recorded conversations among peasants and artisans, visual traditions. These languages give dimension to the context within which institutions were formulated. They provide a fuller picture of the culture that created those institutions, that gave them not only their structure, but also their meaning.

Analysis in this study is structured according to the different cultural languages. Following a brief chapter describing the town of Zurich, individual chapters address the spoken and printed word (Chapter 2), the printed image (Chapter 3), and the language of legislation (Chapter 4). Such a structure is, of course, artificial – the languages were interwoven in the lives of each resident of Zurich, providing a multilingual, yet coherent expression of commonly understood values and attitudes. It allows us, however, to discover some of the allusions, associated meanings, "word plays" that each language brought from its own medium of expression to the perception of the poor in Zurich. In the end, it allows us to discover in its fullness and in its complexity the perception of the poor articulated by those who spoke, who wrote, who printed – to see the perception that, I suggest, shaped the values and attitudes of the community as a whole and determined the parameters of the community's responses to the poor.

The city on the Limmat

Zurich's treatment of its poor bore the distinctive imprint of the town's religious, political, social, and moral identity. It was an identity rooted in Zurich's past, its origins as a crossing, a Roman customs station, at the mouth of the Limmat,[1] and its early development under the Carolingians as a locus for piety. That treatment was shaped by the town's political identity, both in its role as major city of the canton and member of the Swiss Confederation, and as it was articulated in its governing institutions and in the allocation of authority and influence. It was shaped by the forms of association that delineated relations among its residents. Finally, that treatment was shaped by Zurich's moral identity: as a Christian civic community.

In 1576, Jos Murer drew a map of Zurich. The town walls form a border for his detailed representation of the physical town: its buildings, its public squares, its marketplaces, its gardens, its graveyards. The ancient settlement at the mouth of Lake Zurich was then, as now, defined by water. Open on one side to the lake, the town received traders from Italy and pilgrims from across its waters. The river divides the town into two sides, right and left, north and south. Fishing nets mark the tentative advance of the town on the river, an advance that had not yet solidified into the extension of the banks onto the river. Bridges and boats link the two halves of the town, but the division carved by the river runs deeper; to this day, the two banks of the river differ in economic and social composition (Figure 1).

Within the walls of the town, the buildings and spaces that were religious in 1520 dominate: the Grossmünster, the Fraumünster, St.

---

[1] Anton Largiadér, *Geschichte von Stadt und Landschaft Zürich* (Ehrlenbach-Zurich, 1945), vol. 1.

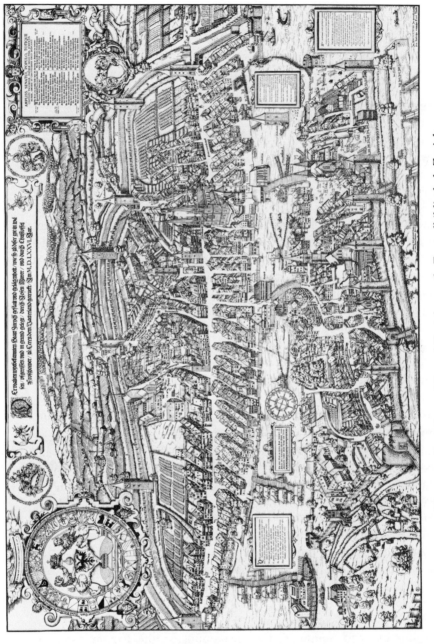

Figure 1: Jos Murer, Map of Zurich, 1576. Zentralbibliothek Zurich

Peter's Church, the Franciscan, Dominican, and Augustinian cloisters. Since 1480, these, along with the Waterchurch, marked the seven holy places pilgrims were to visit in order to receive the same indulgences as a pilgrim could receive in Rome. In 1520, the map of Zurich was dominated by water and sacred spaces.

Like the water, Zurich's sacred spaces had been present since its very beginnings as a town. The town's origins were interwoven with the legend of two Christians, the brother and sister, Felix and Regula, martyred by Roman soldiers. Little is known of the settlement on the Limmat until the consecration of the graves of Felix and Regula on the right bank, first recorded in the early ninth century.[2] The graves of the two saints gave to the settlement on the Limmat an anchor, and the first of its sacred places. Legend has it that Charlemagne built the first Grossmünster over their graves at the behest of a hermit.[3] Some of their relics were later moved, and a second location in the town received remnants of their sanctity. The relics were carried in a procession across the Limmat to the Benedictine convent, the Fraumünster, and placed under its high altar.[4]

The two Münster formed the two loci for lay piety in early Zurich. Facing each other across the Limmat, they competed for prominence in the religious and economic life of the town. At its foundation, the Grossmünster had been entrusted with the rights of baptism, burial, tithing, and with the care of souls; as such, it served as a second parish church in Zurich. The Fraumünster was given the important right of minting coinage. Both Münster had royal origins: the men's convent traced its founding charter to Charlemagne; the women's was endowed by his nephew, Ludwig the German. In both, the close ties between the German kings and Zurich's nobility were made explicit.[5] The Fraumünster retained its noble identity right up to its dissolution in the Reformation. Each of its abbesses was of high social rank: Ludwig's daughter, the Princess Hildegard, was the first abbess,[6] and subsequent abbesses were of either royal or noble descent. Their convent's royal origins, noble patronage and clientage, and right of coinage brought the

[2] Rudolf Pfister, *Kirchengeschichte der Schweiz*, vol. 1 (Zurich, 1964), pp. 24–5.
[3] Ibid., pp. 150–1. The present church dates from the twelfth century.
[4] Ibid., p. 92.
[5] Hans Nabholz, "Die soziale Schichtung der Bevölkerung in der Stadt Zürich bis zur Reformation," in *Festgabe für Max Huber* (Zurich, 1934), p. 311.
[6] Pfister, p. 224.

abbesses great political as well as social authority in the town. In the twelfth and thirteenth centuries, the town's political life was directed by the abbess and her ministers, and under her patronage, the central civic political institution, the town council, was created.[7] And both convents came to be landlords with extensive holdings in the Zurich countryside.

When the chronicler Otto von Freising described Zurich in the early eleventh century as one of the most beautiful cities in Swabia, he noted the two Münster. He did not include St. Peter's parish church, whose oldest altar dates from the twelfth century. St. Peter's, nonetheless, was the oldest parish in Zurich, the parish church probably the oldest in Zurich and in all of Switzerland. In the thirteenth century, it provided sanctuary for Zurich's Beguines. In the sixteenth, it was a center for Reformation preaching and iconoclasm. The Waterchurch was built in 1479–84 on an islet in the Limmat, where judgments and executions had taken place, to mark the spot where Felix and Regula had been martyred.

The mendicants arrived very early in Zurich, the Dominicans in 1229 and the Franciscans in 1238.[8] Their churches were the oldest in Switzerland for each Order. The Dominican church was built between 1230 and 1240, the Franciscan, between 1240 and 1250.[9] The Franciscans quickly developed close ties to the citizens, who held their services and ember days [*Jahrzeiten*] in the friars' church. Many Zurichers were buried in the church or its cloister. In the late thirteenth-century conflict between Emperor and Pope, the Franciscans took the imperial side and were, alone among the religious houses, therefore allowed to remain in the town. As the first friars to arrive in Zurich, the Dominicans met with resistance from the older religious foundations, especially the canons of the Grossmünster. Their papal loyalties did not increase their popularity with the laity; they never achieved the same integration into the life of the town.[10] The third cloister, the Augustinian, was not as much a presence in the town. The Augustinian hermits arrived about 1270 and began building in 1274.

Religious life in Zurich was anchored to these seven spots. It was also

---

[7] Nabholz, pp. 310ff.

[8] Pfister, pp. 237–8 and 263–6, on the Franciscans and Dominicans, respectively.

[9] Ibid., pp. 414–15. Although the Franciscan church was taken down in the nineteenth century, the Dominican stands today, attached to the Zentralbibliothek.

[10] Ibid. In the first two centuries of their existence, both houses provided the town with preachers of enormous power. On the endowment of preachers, see pp. 447–9.

mobile. Various feast days were marked by processions. On Pentecost Wednesday, the town's religious and guild members carried the relics of Felix and Regula through the town to the Lindenhof, where divine services were held.[11] In 1504, a Felix and Regula play was held in the town.[12] On Palm Sunday, an ass was led into the plaza before the church, where palms were scattered. On Corpus Christi, the host was carried "with great pomp and splendor" in a monstrance through the town.[13]

The most famous Swiss pilgrimage site, Einsiedeln, lay a day's journey from Zurich.[14] On September 14, 948, an angel is supposed to have consecrated a spot near the abbey; celebration of that event can be traced to the thirteenth century. By the fifteenth century, thousands of pilgrims from places as distant as Rome, Denmark, and Sweden visited the shrine annually; in 1466, more than 130,000 were recorded. The celebration became ever more elaborate. In the fifteenth century, the festivities lasted two weeks every seven years. The procession began on Pentecost Monday in Zurich, where the pilgrims boarded a ship and sailed toward Richterswil, whence they disembarked and proceeded on foot to the shrine. Their goal: the honor of God, for the most holy Virgin Mary and all saints, for the consolation of faithful souls, and for divine protection for town and countryside.

In his map of Zurich, Jos Murer delineated spaces designated for that activity that gave urban life its form, its identity: the marketplace, the locus of sustenance and commerce. Some marketplaces were permanent: the grain market [*Kornmarkt*], the fish market [*Fischmarkt*], the market and the new market [*Neumarkt*]. Others appeared perhaps once a week, holding a location only so long as the produce or products were sold: the fruit market, held on the Limmat quay; the chicken, egg, and milk market, held on the lower bridge; the butter and cheese market, held before the Kerzhaus. Salt, fish, beef, pork, leather, grain, linen cloth, wool, and wine were each sold at its own market. The cycles of season and liturgy set the rhythm for markets: Residents of the town enjoyed special markets on May 1, during the outgoing Pentecost week, on the

[11] Heinrich Bullinger, *Reformationsgeschichte*, vol. 1, ed. J. J. Hottinger and H. H. Vögeli (Frauenfeld, 1838), p. 160.
[12] Pfister, pp. 362–3.
[13] Bullinger, p. 160.
[14] Pfister, pp. 362–3.

day of Zurich's parish fair (September 11), and St. Martin's Day. Markets served as a locus for the exchange of products and produce, among which were pamphlets, and for commerce between town and land, a commerce of ideas as well as objects. As such, the market was a central symbol of Zurich's civic identity.

Within the town walls, social and political forms of association were shaped by ideals of fraternity, ideals that had their origin in the guild struggles of the fourteenth century, and were anchored in the realities of the distribution of wealth in the town. From the mid-thirteenth century, when "citizen of Zurich" [*Bürger von Zürich*] became the most common form of identification for official business, Zurich defined itself in terms of crafts and trade. In 1336, the importance of crafts to that identity was given institutional form. The artisans, in allegiance with the patriciate, overthrew the merchants' regime and restructured the government of the town. They organized all crafts into thirteen guilds, giving definition and structure to the artisanate within the town.[15] Those who had previously dominated civic politics – the "knights, nobles, rentiers, merchants, mine owners, moneychangers, goldsmiths, and salt merchants"[16] – were united into one corporation, the Constaffler, thereby restricting the number who could participate in government at any one time. The town council was divided equally between the guilds and the former rulers: twenty-six seats for guildmasters and twenty-six for the Constaffler. In 1336, the crafts acquired a substantial, if not yet determining, voice in political life. By the end of the fifteenth century, the guilds acquired the deciding voice in Zurich's political life: The Charters [*Geschworene Briefe*] of 1489 and 1498 gave them structurally the majority in the town council. Political relations were to be shaped according to the craft guild, rather than the patriciate. By the sixteenth century, families of artisans had come to be numbered among the ruling elite; and in the 1520s and 1530s, many of those who gave their support early to the cause of reform acquired political and social prominence.[17]

Zurich was a town of middling size. The enormously wealthy merchants and entrepreneurs who made their home in urban centers like

---

[15] The number of guilds was reduced to twelve in 1440, with the unification of the two weavers' guilds, the wool and linen.

[16] Paul Guyer, "Die soziale Schichtung der Bürgerschaft Zürichs vom Ausgang des Mittelalters bis 1798," *Schweizerische Zeitschrift für Geschichte* 2 (1952): 573.

[17] Guyer, p. 576.

Augsburg or Florence were not to be found in Zurich. The contrast between rich and poor was not as marked.[18] Not until after the Thirty Years' War would wealth become polarized, a divisive element in civic life. Wealth was, moreover, not a birthright, but a product of craft for most residents of Zurich. With the exception of a very few families, such as the Göldli, wealth was earned, not inherited, primarily from one's own labors,[19] though those successful artisans who could give up their craft to join the rentiers did. Differences of wealth were far less marked between members of the wealthier guilds, such as the *zur Meisen*, and members of the patrician Constaffler, than between crafts such as the goldsmiths and the shoemakers or fishers.[20] Many members of the poorer guilds, the fishers and sailors, the shoemakers, the weavers, and the men and women in service [*Zimmerleuten*], were vulnerable to fluctuations of market and fortune. They, along with widows, journeymen, and wage laborers, lived on the margins of subsistence and would be, after 1525, among the most likely candidates for civic poor relief. And if wealth divided, kinship, neighborhood, guild membership, and, sometimes, participation in political life linked the men and women of Zurich.

In the sixteenth century, after the institutional reforms of 1489 and 1498, the town was governed by 210 councillors, who were divided into two Councils, the Great and Small, and two Burgermeisters.[21] The Great Council consisted of 162 citizens, twelve members elected from each of the twelve guilds, and eighteen drawn from the patrician Constaffler. The Small Council comprised twenty-four guild masters, two from each guild; four Constafflers; twelve town councillors, one from each guild elected for life from the Great Council; two town councillors from the Constaffler, also elected for life from the Great Council; six councillors, freely elected, also for life, from the Great Council; and the two Burgermeisters, for a total of fifty members.

At any one time the town council reflected about 4 percent of the urban population and 20 percent of the households. The pool from which it drew its members was in theory large: in law, anyone who belonged to

---

[18] Ulrich Schlüer, *Untersuchungen über die soziale Struktur von Stadt und Landschaft Zürich im fünfzehnten Jahrhundert* (Zurich, 1978), p. 49. Although Schlüer's figures are for the fifteenth century, the general contours he draws continue into the sixteenth century.

[19] Ibid., p. 51.

[20] Ibid., p. 106.

[21] Walter Jacob, *Politische Führungsschicht und Reformation*, Zürcher Beiträge zur Reformationsgeschichte, Bd. 1 (Zurich, 1970).

a guild could become a town councillor.[22] Access to the Great Council was not difficult, once one was a citizen [*Bürger*]. Most of the members of the Great Council continued to live from their craft; they were not so wealthy that they could give up their profession.[23] The men who held key offices in the Small Council and the office of Burgermeister were drawn from a much narrower pool;[24] they were "wealthy," (possessing at least five hundred gulden), and belonged to one of perhaps a dozen families.[25] Even among the most powerful, however, the craft guilds were represented.[26] As the career of Hans Rudolf Lavater (d. 1557) demonstrates, it was possible to rise from a lesser profession, glazier, and a less powerful guild, the *Gerwe*, to become one of the most influential men in Zurich.[27] Lines of influence and authority in Zurich were not solely determined by wealth or status; access to political life was restricted, but not closed.

The events of 1336 marked the beginning of the political ascendancy of the guilds, an ascendancy that was to last until 1798. Guilds dominated the life of the town, both ideologically and structurally. They provided the unit of organization within the two councils. Membership in the town council was dependent upon guild membership; guilds represented the sole access to political life. Legislative and judicial decisions, therefore, were made solely by guildsmen. Some of the town council's concerns reflected the immediate concerns of craftsmen. In addition to jurisdictional and administrative concerns, the council's legislation addressed issues of trade regulation, currency, and citizenship, a central form of access to the town's economic life.

Guild membership provided a framework for the social stratification of the town: Membership in the more powerful and wealthy *zur Meisen* or *Safran* guild brought status and prestige to most, if not all. Few of even the most successful and wealthy members of the lesser *Schiffleuten*, *Schuhmachern* or *Zimmerleuten*, on the other hand, were able to achieve

[22] There were 1,000 citizens in a population of 5,700 (Guyer, p. 576). Toward the end of the century, Zurich closed its citizenship with increasing frequency. See Guyer, pp. 576ff.; Nabholz, p. 328.
[23] Hans Morf, *Zunftverfassung und Obrigkeit in Zürich von Waldmann bis Zwingli*, Mitteilungen der Antiquärischen Gesellschaft in Zürich, Bd. 45.1 (Zurich, 1969), p. 60.
[24] Ibid., p. 3. On the distribution of power among the guilds, see Morf in general.
[25] Jacob, pp. 4–5.
[26] Largiadér, pp. 266–9.
[27] Heinzpeter Stucki, *Bürgermeister Hans Rudolf Lavater 1492–1557*, Zürcher Beiträge zur Reformationszeit, 3 (Zurich, 1973).

any rank in the town. So, too, the social place of journeymen, widows, and wage laborers reflected each group's relative worth within the structure of the guild. And those who worked outside of a guild, such as day laborers, had the least status of all within the town.

Guilds also offered a structure for lay piety. By the end of the fifteenth century, at least two guilds, the bakers and millers' guild, *zum Weggen*, and the shoemakers', were also religious confraternities, placing themselves under the spiritual direction of the Dominicans and Franciscans, respectively.[28] At least two other confraternities were craft related, if not based in a guild: that of the tailors' journeymen and that of the furriers.[29] Only one confraternity, the Brotherhood of St. Lux and Loyen, crossed over guild lines,[30] and even here, the professions were all related.[31] Guilds sponsored processions on feast days, donated stained glass windows and belltowers, and endowed the construction and maintenance of altars in the town's seven churches.[32]

The town of Zurich was the major city in the canton that bore its name. It rested within a number of spheres of ecclesiastical and political authority, both as subject and as lord. It lay in the diocese of the powerful bishop of Constance. With 1,800 parishes, 350 cloisters, and 15,000 priests, the bishopric of Constance was the largest in the Holy Roman Empire.[33] By law, Zurich lay within the jurisdiction of the Empire, until the Treaties of Westphalia in 1648 acknowledged the independence of the Swiss cantons. In practice, however, the Treaty of Basel in 1499 had acknowledged the independence of the Confederation of Swiss Cantons. The Confederation had originated as a defensive alliance, to which Zurich had been admitted in 1351, as one of the urban cantons. In the 1520s and 1530s, as Zurich chose a path divergent from that of the original cantons, all of which remained faithful to Rome, the nature of membership in the Swiss Confederation, its delimitations and privileges, would be called into question.

---

[28] Pfister, p. 360; Largiadér, p. 294.
[29] Largiadér, p. 296.
[30] Paul Schweizer, "Die St. Lux– und Loyen-Bruderschaft von Zürich," *Anzeiger für Schweizerische Altertumskunde* 1884, no. 1, Supplement, pp. 1–5.
[31] According to Largiadér, p. 295, members included "Goldschmiede, Maler, Glasmaler, und verwandte Berufe wie Färber, Glaser, Schreiber, Musikanten, Seidensticker und Münzmeister."
[32] Staatsarchiv Zürich [StAZ]: A 73, 1–2: Zunftwesen: Verschiedene Handwerke.
[33] *1484–1984; Zwingli und die Zürcher Reformation* (Zurich, 1984), p. 15.

To sixteenth-century observers, the Swiss Confederation represented a form of political organization that offered its citizens unusually extensive participatory powers.[34] The power of the lords seemed less dramatic, less articulated than their northern counterparts, in part because the peasants were so much more visible. The Confederation itself had begun with the allegiance of three "rural" or "forest" cantons, Uri, Schwyz, and Unterwalden, in 1291, three cantons whose populations were predominantly, if not exclusively agricultural. The military ability of Swiss peasants, moreover, was a source of both pride and profit. Their victories at Morgarten in 1315, Sempach in 1386, Nancy in 1477, Dornach in 1499, and Novara in 1513, were famous and the crowns of Europe, Emperor, Pope, and king, vied for Swiss peasant mercenaries. In Zurich, as elsewhere, the peasants held military service not merely as a duty, but as a right.[35] And Swiss peasants were fiercely protective of their rights. Zurich witnessed numerous revolts throughout the fifteenth century; in 1515, especially outraged by a corrupt civic government, the peasants looted the city.[36]

If the peasants appeared unusually independent to outsiders, they were nonetheless under siege from the urban regimes. One by one, in the late Middle Ages, cantonal cities took over the blood ban [*Blutbann*], the right of coining and of setting customs tolls, labor and tax restrictions. By the Reformation, Zurich had acquired dominion of some kind over all the territory, some 1,700 square kilometers, that comprises the modern canton.[37] Until 1798, the town would seek to expand and solidify its jurisdiction in the countryside.[38] Early on, it placed residents and citizens of the town, rather than local villagers or rural inhabitants, to govern the *Vogteien*, or administrative units, of the canton. But the town council sought more than administrative and juridical authority over the canton. Beginning in the fourteenth century, the town council also sought

---

[34] Thomas A. Brady, *Turning Swiss; Cities and Empire, 1450–1550* (Cambridge, 1985), especially pp. 28–42; and Peter Blickle, *The Revolution of 1525*, trans. Thomas A. Brady, Jr. and H. C. Erik Midelfort (Baltimore, 1981) especially pp. 128–9.

[35] Walter Claassen, "Schweizer Bauernpolitik im Zeitalter Ulrich Zwinglis," *Socialgeschichtliche Forschungen*, vol. 4 (Berlin, 1899), p. 33.

[36] *Johannes Stumpfs Schweizer– und Reformationschronik*, ed. Ernst Gagliardi, Hans Müller, and Fritz Büsser, *Quellen zur Schweizer Geschichte*, vol. 5 (Basel, 1952), pt. 1, pp. 137ff.

[37] Guyer, p. 570.

[38] Elisabeth Raiser, *Städtische Territorialpolitik im Mittelalter*, Historische Studien, Bd. 406 (Lübeck, 1969); Anton Largiadér, "Die Anfänge des zürcherischen Stadtstaats," in *Festgabe Paul Schweizer* (Zurich, 1922), pp. 1–92.

to extend its moral authority onto the countryside. At first, those efforts failed. In the sixteenth century, however, the town council's campaign was far more successful.[39]

Peasants comprised by far the largest portion of the cantonal population; during the Reformation, the number of peasants was proportionately greater than at any other time. In 1529, the entire population of the canton numbered some 73,400, of which 5,700 were residents of the town of Zurich and another 2,500, of the town of Winterthur.[40] There were 193 rural communes [*Landesgemeinden*], villages varying in size from a dozen to a few hundred inhabitants. At most, 5 percent of the rural population was engaged in trade, such as milling, or crafts, such as shoemaking or weaving, and most of them pursued those trades and crafts in addition to their agricultural work.[41] Eighty-five percent of the canton's population were engaged exclusively in agriculture.

Relative to other peasant populations to the north and east, the peasants of Zurich were economically and socially homogeneous. Probably the most significant division in the countryside was that between propertied peasants, peasants who leased or owned the land they cultivated, and day laborers, who worked the land of others for wages. In Zurich, the great majority of peasants held some land of their own; their ratio to day laborers was roughly 8.5 to 1 throughout the canton.[42] Before the 1520s, the peasants were not divided among themselves by great diversity of wealth or possessions. Only in the second half of the century did a fall in real wages produce a rise in the number of wage laborers, of the poorest kind of agricultural worker, and an increasing polarization of property ownership and wealth in the countryside.[43] In the 1520s, peasant political demands were made from a position of solidarity defined according to jurisdictional, rather than social or economic boundaries:

---

[39] Peter Huber, "Annahme und Durchführung der Reformation auf der Zürcher Landschaft in den Jahren 1519 bis 1530," (dissertation, Zurich, 1972); Kurt Maeder, "Die Bedeutung der Landschaft für den Verlauf des reformatorischen Prozesses in Zürich (1522–1532)," in *Stadt und Kirche im 16. Jahrhundert*, ed. Bernd Moeller, Schriften des Vereins für Reformationsgeschichte, no. 190 (Gütersloh, 1978), pp. 91–8.

[40] Claassen, p. 25; Werner Schnyder reckoned the rural population in 1529 to be between 48,100 and 58,790, *Die Bevölkerung der Stadt und Landschaft Zürich vom 14. bis 17. Jahrhundert* (Zurich, 1925), p. 108.

[41] Claassen, p. 30.

[42] Ibid., p. 121.

[43] Otto Sigg, "Bevölkerungs-, Agrar- und Sozialgeschichtliche Probleme des 16. Jahrhunderts am Beispiel der Zürcher Landschaft," *Schweizerische Zeitschrift für Geschichte* 24 (1974): 1–25.

as subjects of the abbot of Rüti, the abbot of Thoss, or the governor [*Vogt*] of Eglisau.

In 1525, the town council of Zurich bid "those from all communes from the town and the countryside, to remain by God's word and the received evangelical teaching, . . . just as they would, as obedient people, present their bodies, honor, and goods to their lords of Zurich."[44] The relation of the town council to the rural population in the 1520s was neither simple imperialism nor unalloyed beneficence.[45] On the one hand, as the peasants' Catholic lords, the abbots, and their religious allies, the Catholic cantons, recognized, the town council, as the one Protestant authority in the region, represented an alternative locus of authority.[46] The council presented the peasants with an alternative kind of legitimacy, one that claimed its basis in Scripture, and offered them the means and the language to change lords.[47] In the eyes of the Catholic cantons, especially during the Ittinger riot of 1524, the town council's motives were almost impossible to separate from those of the peasants.[48]

Indeed, for a brief time, the peasants looked to the town council for a reformation of social and economic ties. On June 22, 1523,

> The officers of the communes of Zollikon, Riesbach, Fällenden, Hirslanden, Unterstrass, and Wytikon file complaint against the Provost and Chapter of the Grossmünster in Zurich on account of the tithe. They were now informed and instructed by the holy Gospel that the tithe was nothing other than alms, and the canons of the Grossmünster were using those tithes for unnecessary and frivolous things, as one knew.[49]

[44] "Daruff inen von allen gmeinden uss statt und land zu antwort geben ward und sy gebetten, by gottes wort und angenomner evangelischer ler zuo blyben, . . . alsdan wöltend sy als gehorsam lüt zu iren hern von Zürich setzen ir lyb, eer, und guot," in response to Confederation charges of complicity in the Ittingersturm of 1524, Stumpf, pp. 233–4.

[45] On the transactions between the Zurich town council and various peasant communes, see Stumpf, pp. 137ff., 203–33, 252–61; Bullinger, pp. 265ff.; *Aktensammlung zur Geschichte der Zürcher Reformation in den Jahren 1519–1533*, ed. Emil Egli (Zurich, 1879; reprint, Aalen, 1973) (Hereafter EAk).

[46] Philip Broadhead, "Rural Revolt and Urban Betrayal in Reformation Switzerland: The Peasants of St. Gallen and Zwinglian Zurich," in *Religion and Rural Revolt*, ed. Janos Bak and Gerhard Benecke (Dover, N.H., 1984), p. 165.

[47] See, for example, Stumpf, pp. 233–4, 253ff.

[48] On the correspondence between the Zurich town council and Catholic authorities, see, for example, Stumpf, pp. 207–8 and 233–4.

[49] "Juni 22 (Montag 10,000 Ritter). BM. Schmid, RR. und B. 1. Die Verordneten der Gemeinden Zollikon, Riesbach, Fällenden, Hirslanden, Unterstrass, und Wytikon beschweren sich gegen Probst und Capital zum Grossmünster in Zürich wegen des Zehnten. Sie würden 'jetz durch das heilig Evangelium bericht(et) und underwist, dass der zechend nüt anders dann ein almuosen wär, und bruchtind etlich chorherrn solichen zechend zuo unnütz(en) und liechtfertigen dingen, als man wüsste.' " EAk, no. 368.

The tithe was probably the primary issue around which the relation of the town council to the countryside formed in the 1520s. Again and again during the years 1523–5, various communes in the canton and beyond petitioned the council for the abolition of the tithe.[50] The tithe provided a focus for rural grievances against ecclesiastical and secular lords; it was the institution in which economic and political injustices were most clearly defined and articulated. Paid both in kind and in coin and often comprising far more than 10 percent of a household's income, it placed a serious financial burden on the rural population. In particular, the tithe made precise what was so terribly wrong in the peasants' relations with their ecclesiastical lords. As the peasants learned when they listened to their evangelical preachers, the tithe, which had drained wealth from the countryside and poured it into the coffers of mendicants and Rome for so long, had no basis in the Gospels.

> The many sorts of people are to give in rents and tithes all that which has been owed in the past and customarily, also the small tithe, excepting those acres in which two crops a year are grown, such as spelt after hay, turnips after hemp, millet after the winter barley, and the like: the first fruit (harvest) alone should be tithed and those following should be left free (Mandate on the Tithe, July 1, 1525).[51]

But as the peasants discovered to their great disillusionment, the town council did not wish to abolish economic practices that reinforced disparity of wealth, to reform society – it was not seeking to facilitate an aggregate of independent Protestant congregations modeled on the Swiss Confederation. The tithe, the town council asserted, would serve Protestant purposes, instead of Catholic.[52] As the peasants learned in the 1520s, the council was guided by a very different vision of a Protestant political association. That vision was also evident in other of its actions: directing rural congregations to enforce sumptuary and marriage laws it promulgated; delineating precisely the limits of each congrega-

---

[50] See EAk nos. 351, 365, 368, 370, 375–6, 391, 397, 452, and 477 for 1523; nos. 558, 568–9, and 577 for 1524. See below, Chapter 2, on Zwingli's position on the tithe.

[51] "mencklichem an zinssen und zehenden alles das ze geben, das man vonn althar und gewonlicher pflicht schuldig were, ouch die kleynen zehenden, usgenommen, in welchen ackeren zum jar zweyerley nutzung gwachsend, als nach dem hew das eombt, nach dem hanff die rüeben, nach der wintergersten der hirsch und derglychen: so solt allein die erst frucht verzendet werden und die nachfolgend fry gelassen syn." Stumpf, p. 261.

[52] On Zwingli's justification of the tithe, which provided a basis for the town council's position, see Chapter 2.

tion's autonomy in choosing a pastor and in determining the extent of their churches' decoration; and suggesting the structure for poor relief in each of the congregations.

The peasants figure obliquely in this study. They were probably included among the poor about whom Zwingli spoke in his sermons, but the town council excluded most, if not all of them, when it formulated its program of relief. Their grievances, especially concerning the tithe, led Zwingli and the town council to formulate positions which directly affected the poor, and may well have helped to shape both Zwingli's and the town council's responses to the poor in the town.[53] Some of the poor who begged in the streets of Zurich probably came from the countryside. Droughts, flooding, hailstorms, long winters, cold summers, all noted by the chroniclers, rhythmically brought ruin to peasant families throughout the period. Beginning in the 1470s, the rural population increased markedly, tripling in size by 1585.[54] After the 1520s, rises in the price of grain and land, combined with a freeze in wages, led to a fall in real wages and the growth of the numbers of day laborers in the countryside.[55] Like most of the population of Zurich, both urban and rural, the peasants were never secure against disaster; they did not have the resources to survive a bad harvest or the destruction of their crops or property. As a group, however, they seem not to have been particularly impoverished before 1525; if the winter of 1512 witnessed a severe drought, 1522 was, exceptionally, a good year for wine on Lake Zurich.[56]

It was not until May, June, and July of 1525, after the Poor Ordinance was passed, that the peasants assumed central importance for the town council in Zurich. In those months, rural communes throughout the canton presented the council with lists of grievances; in some areas, riots erupted.[57] These actions mirrored the actions of "the common man" throughout the southwest German lands, Thuringia, Tyrol, and northern Switzerland. In an area stretching from Alsace to Styria, Trent to Goslar, thousands of peasants and artisans presented governments, princes and town councils alike, with demands: for the right to choose their own pastors, for the rights to common lands and forests, for the

---

[53] See below, Chapters 2 and 4.
[54] Sigg, pp. 1–2.
[55] Ibid., pp. 2–4, 19ff.
[56] Stumpf, pp. 105, 182.
[57] Stumpf, pp. 253–73; EAk, nos. 702–71. The list of the Zurich peasants' grievances is recorded in Stumpf, pp. 255–8.

abolition of tithes and rents, and for the reformulation of political relations in accord with a notion of "Christian freedom."

The meaning of those lists, and of the violence that ensued, has been the subject of much debate.[58] In his work, Peter Blickle has called attention to the language of community, of "brotherly love," drawn from the Gospels, that the peasants and artisans employed to articulate their claims.[59] A product, Blickle argues, of the "new biblicism," that language was not embraced either by the reformers Luther and Zwingli, or by the town councils that supported them. Yet, as this study seeks to show, Zwingli and the Zurich town council were also guided by Christian ideals of community, which overlapped, but were not identical. These ideals, too, were anchored in the Bible, but in Paul, as well as in Matthew, and were shaped by collective life, but that of the town, rather than of the rural commune.

At the beginning of the sixteenth century, Zurich did not seem poised to take the lead in reforming religious life in the southern reaches of the Empire. It was not a university town, where the hard kernels of theology captured men's imagination or the new philology could lead men to a fresh reading of Holy Scripture. It was not a center of preaching; no Geiler von Kaisersberg or Bernardino was to be found among the canons of the Grossmünster. It was a city of ancient sacred spaces and marketplaces, of some two hundred religious and of guildsmen.

> The work of reformation, or the improvement of faith took its beginning, following God's help, from M. Ulrich Zwingli (Hans Heinrich Bluntschli, *Memorabilia Tigurina*).[60]

Late in the fall of 1518, these guildsmen chose a new people's preacher for the Grossmünster to replace the one who had died. They

---

[58] Blickle provides a review of the literature to 1981 in *The Revolution of 1525*, Introduction. Robert Scribner, "The German Peasants' War," in *Reformation Europe: A Guide to Research*, ed. Steven Ozment (St. Louis, Mo., 1982), pp. 107–33, also discusses the extensive literature on the rebellion. See also *The German Peasant War 1525: New Viewpoints*, ed. Bob Scribner and Gerhard Benecke (London, 1979); and most recently, Peter Blickle, *Gemeindereformation; Die Menschen des 16. Jahrhunderts auf dem Weg zum Heil* (Munich, 1985), especially pp. 28–33 on Zurich; *Bauer und Reformation*, Vol. 1: *Zugänge zur bäuerlichen Reformation*, ed. Peter Blickle (Zurich, 1987).

[59] See especially, Blickle, *The Revolution of 1525*, chaps. 5 and 9.

[60] "Reformations-Werk. Oder Glaubens-Verbesserung, hat nächst Gottes hülff ihren Anfang genommen von M. Ulrich Zwingli," *Memorabilia Tigurina oder Merkwürdigkeiten der Stadt und Landschaft Zürich* (Zurich, 1742; facsimile reprint, Winterthur, 1975), p. 338.

chose a man whose talents would lead him and them to reform. The Toggenburger Huldrych Zwingli was an impressive preacher – his preaching had first brought him to the attention of the Zurich town council.[61] He was also a biblical scholar. He had been reading the Greek New Testament for some three years, since learning Greek, and had begun the study of Hebrew. He had read the Latin and Greek Church Fathers and the medieval masters, and had studied with Erasmus at Basel. His conversion to that which we now call Protestantism occurred not in a moment of revelation, as it did with Luther, but over time.

> This Master Ulrich Zwingli repudiated and annihilated all the Doctors, who did not form themselves in accord with the Gospel, but rested on human acts, such as Thomas Aquinas, Scotus, Nicholas of Lyra, and the like. He would have nothing of cloisters and confraternities, for he thought … that it was a retreat from Jesus Christ, who is for us all the single head; that we should all be brothers and following him, also call ourselves Christians…. He also struck down petitions and prayers to Mary and the saints – who are in heaven – proved from many texts that one should pray to no creature other than God alone (Bernhard Wyss, *Chronicle*).[62]

In 1519, Zwingli began preaching the "pure word of Scripture" to his Zurich congregation. By 1520, when he gave up his pension from Rome, he had come to judge the strictures of Rome – canon law, papal bulls, the pronouncements of Schoolmen – against the word of Scripture.[63] By 1522, Zwingli was preaching against pilgrimages, the penitential system and indulgences, processions, clerical vows, especially of celibacy, the cults of Mary and the saints, and calling for a return to a

---

[61] On the following, see Bullinger; EAk; Walter Köhler, *Huldrych Zwingli*, 4 vols. (Leipzig, 1943–54); Gottfried Locher, *Die Zwinglische Reformation im Rahmen der europäischen Kirchengeschichte* (Göttingen, 1979); G. R. Potter, *Zwingli* (Cambridge, 1976); Stumpf; *Die Chronik Bernhard Wyss 1519–1530*, ed. Georg Finsler, Quellen zur Schweizerischen Reformationsgeschichte, vol. 1 (Basel, 1901).

[62] "Diser meister Ulrich Zwingli verwarf und vernichtet alle doctores, wo si sich nit nach dem evangelio gstaltetend, sonder nun uf menschlichem tant lagend als Thomas de Aquino, Scotus, Nicolaus de Lyra, und derglichen. Er hat gar nüt uf allen clöstren und bruoderschaften, dann er meint – als ouch was ist und am tag ligt –, es were ein abzug von Christo Jesu, der aller unser einigs houpt ist; des brüder soltend wir all sin und uns nach im ouch Christen nennen. Er hat ouch nüt uf den romferten, walferten und ablass, den man um gelt koufen muoss und vil us Paulo herfür bracht, das nun der gmein man vor nie gehört hat, wie, das alles opfer und gelt, so man uf den altar legt, nun ein almuosen were und wenn es ein uppiger unnützer pfaff vertäte, so wer es wäger eim armen noturftigen menschen geben. Er schluog ouch ab Mariae und aller heiligen – so im himel sind – fürbitt und gebätt; probiert das us vil gschriften, dass man kein creatur sonder allein Gott anbetten solt," pp. 10–12.

[63] See Potter, chap. 4.

simple practice of Christianity.[64] In 1522, Zwingli's evangelicalism, his insistence on the test of Scripture, was echoed among some of the people of Zurich. In March of that year, a group of citizens, including Zwingli's close friend, the publisher Christoph Froschauer, ate wurst during Lent, breaking the traditional fast, because "a Christian life rests not in food, nor in drink, indeed in no outward works, but alone in a right belief, trust and love, by which we live with one another truthfully, rightly, in friendship and simply; in Scripture I believe."[65]

> Zwingli has created much turmoil in this city, where once more unity existed than now with their preaching. And those who made the images in the churches were more pious than those who would remove them (Thomas Kleinbrötli, 1523).[66]

Others among the people of Zurich, such as the canon Conrad Hoffmann, the chaplain Hans Widmer, and Kleinbrötli, found Zwingli's message dangerous, perhaps heretical. These angry voices and the ensuing rancor and divisiveness within the town and the canton, perhaps more than Zwingli's expressed desire for a public discussion of faith, led the town council to call a formal Disputation, to be held on January 29, 1523. Invited were "each and every people's priest, pastor, minister and preacher, who holds benefices and resides in our city, counties, domains, high or low jurisdictions and regions," as well as the Bishop of Constance or his representative.[67] All discussion of the Christian religion, both liturgy and theology, was to be grounded in "the true divine Scripture" and held "in the German tongue and language."[68]

At the opening of the Disputation, Zwingli presented to the assembly, some six hundred priests, pastors, canons, friars, monks, and lay people,

---

[64] He was joined in 1523 in Zurich by Leo Jud, who was appointed the pastor of St. Peter's and was a close friend and colleague of Zwingli.

[65] "denn nüt hat uns Gott uf ertrich gelassen, domit wir uns trösten mögen, denn das heilig Evangelium.... ein christlich leben nit in spis, nach in trank, ja in kein usswendigen werken, dann allein in einem rechten glouben, vertruwen und liebe, domit wir mit einander warhaftig, rechtlich, früntlich, einfaltig leben, stande; der geschrift gloub ich," Froschauer's testimony before the town council, EAk, no. 234.

[66] " 'der Zwingli hat vil unruow in diser statt gmacht; und wärent vor bas eins gewesen, dann jetz mit irem predigen. Und die, so die bild in der kilchen gemacht, sind frömmer gewesen, weder die, so sie herus tuon wöllent,' " testimony of Nicholas Spreng at an investigation of Kleinbrötli, EAk, no. 416.

[67] "allen und jeden lütpriestern, pfarrern, seelsorgern und prädicanten, so in unseren städten, grafschaften, herrschaften, hochen oder nidern gerichten und gepieten verpfrüendt und wonhaft sind," EAk, no. 318.

[68] "mit warhafter göttlicher gschrift in tütscher zungen und sprach anzöigend," EAk, no. 318.

33

sixty-seven Conclusions, derived from his reading of Scripture. Two themes dominate the Conclusions: the exclusive authority of Scripture in determining matters of Christian faith and practice, and the significance of Christ. Christ was for Zwingli, more than for Luther, the keystone: He was the sole mediator between man and God, the voice of the Gospel, the means by which God made possible human righteousness, the embodying of God's loving nature, the physical reassurance of divine mercy. Christ made unnecessary the cult of saints, indulgences, purgatory, the penitential system and the powers it allotted the priests.

Zwingli's Conclusions were not successfully challenged. The bishop's representative, Johannes Faber, withdrew from debate after his initial efforts were poorly received. Zwingli prevailed in the first formal public discussion of evangelical theology in Zurich. The First Disputation was also a victory for the town council, which became, with its confirmation of Scripture as the sole authority in determining religious practice, a major force in defining religious life in Zurich.

The First Disputation marks the beginning of the public and collective reform of religious life in Zurich.[69] From then on, the form and content of religion would be held to the test of Scripture. The public debate in Zurich would no longer center on whether to reform, but on the precise nature of that reform and its pace. Some, such as Simon Stumpf and Ludwig Haetzer, were to call for a more pronounced and rapid break with past practice, but the community of Zurich had agreed that religious life as people had known it would be formed anew in the image of the early church.

> [Zwingli] would also have nothing of the pilgrimages, to Rome or elsewhere, of indulgences, which men must purchase with money and on which Paul has much to say, that the common man had never heard before, how all the offerings and money, which one lays upon the altar, was in fact alms, and if an arrogant useless priest used them, it were better to give them to a poor needy person (Bernhard Wyss, *Chronicle*).[70]

As reform was being addressed in the town's various cultural languages, that very culture, its forms and its function, was itself the subject of intense scrutiny and reevaluation. A panel of four censors, which

---

[69] Which is not to suggest that reform was endorsed by all individuals in Zurich. As the case of Kleinbrötli reminds us, some in Zurich found the old ways much more pious than the new.
[70] See note 62.

included Zwingli, was appointed in January 1523 to oversee publishing in Zurich: to screen which words entered into print.[71] Much more dramatically, a number of people in Zurich questioned the nature and function of the visual images in the churches in the years 1523–4. The images were a central topic for debate in the Second Disputation, held in October 1523.[72] During the same time, Ludwig Haetzer published a pamphlet in Zurich listing all the biblical references to and prohibitions of images.[73] Leo Jud began preaching against them in St. Peter's Church in September 1524. And, as we shall see, residents of the town and surrounding villages became increasingly violent and public in their physical attacks on the objects in the churches. By the time the Poor Law was passed in January 1525, no images remained in any of the churches, lay or religious; the town council, in reaction to extraordinary popular action, had legislated to cleanse the churches of their idols. The language of legislation had been turned to the definition and evaluation of religious culture.

[71] EAk, no. 319.
[72] The text of the Second Disputation is reproduced in *Corpus Reformatorum*, vol. 89: *Huldreich Zwinglis Sämtliche Werke*, vol. 2, ed. Emil Egli and Georg Finsler (Leipzig, 1908), pp. 664–803.
[73] *Ein urteil gottes unsers ee gemahels wie man sich mit allen gotzen und bildnussen halte sol* (Zurich: Christoph Froschauer, 1523). Haetzer was present at the Second Disputation in Zurich and may well have written the pamphlet in preparation for the debate on the images in the churches.

∞∞∞∞∞∞∞∞∞∞∞∞∞∞∞∞∞∞∞∞∞∞∞∞∞∞∞∞∞∞∞∞∞∞∞∞∞∞

The people's preacher and
the living images of God

Words – printed, read aloud, repeated, preached, spoken in the streets – filled the ears and eyes of Europeans in the sixteenth century as they had never done before. The words of Holy Scripture in particular caught the attention of thousands of people. From the search for the exact meaning of each word, most fully pursued in Erasmus's Greek New Testament, to the efforts to convey those words to the unlearned, captured in Luther's German Bible and Tyndale's English Bible, the words of Scripture were scrutinized, their histories uncovered, their definitions mapped with terrible precision, their connotations delineated and delimited. As never before, these words entered into printed culture, as Bibles, exegeses, and commentaries, and into oral culture, as lectures, sermons, and readings. For many, the key to Christian practice and faith could be found alone in the specific words of Scripture.

For the "evangelicals," for Luther and Zwingli, Carlstadt and Bucer, words were the primary source and medium for reform. Printed, their words appeared in single-page broadsheets and in pamphlets ranging in length from a few pages to hundreds; printed, the Word appeared in Bibles of many languages and sizes. In these forms, which emerged in the fifteenth century, written words were able to reach new kinds of readers.[1] With no binding or expensive illustrations, smaller in size (usually octavo) and printed on paper, pamphlets and broadsheets cost less than the manuscripts of previous generations or the costly hand-colored and bound volumes commissioned by princes and courts.[2] They

---

[1] On the origins of printed books, Lucien Febvre and Henri Martin, *The Coming of the Book*, trans. David Gerard (London, 1976; 1984); Rudolf Hirsch, *Printing, Selling and Reading 1450–1550* (Wiesbaden, 1967) and *The Printed Word: Its Impact and Diffusion* (London, 1978); Elizabeth Eisenstein, *The Printing Press as an Agent of Change* (Cambridge, 1979).

[2] The special form of the pamphlet or Flugschrift has been the focus of a great deal of study in

The people's preacher

were accessible to men and women who were neither wealthy, nor scholars who were willing to sacrifice the bulk of their income to printed texts: to men such as the artisan Ulrich Schmid, the shoemaker Hans Sachs, or the peasant Karsthans. Small and light, they could travel, from hand to hand, across geographical, political, and social boundaries.[3]

Nor were printed words accessible only to the literate.[4] Reading aloud was the prevalent form of engagement with a text. In rural houses and urban workshops, in inns and spinning rooms, one reader could make a printed text accessible to all within hearing, could read aloud the words of Scripture, of Luther or Zwingli, of Eberlin von Günzburg or Karsthans. Texts were sometimes printed with explicit instructions for the purchaser who could not read, to take the work to a "brother who can." Reading aloud could be spontaneous and public as well.[5] Texts could be heard in marketplaces, in village squares, and before church doors.

Reading aloud was not limited to semiliterate circles. It served readers of a wide range of skills for a variety of purposes. Even the most learned circles found reading aloud an important exercise. In 1527, Zwingli formed the Prophezei, a group of scholars and preachers, to read Scripture aloud in the original Hebrew or Greek, which Zwingli or Leo Jud then translated into Latin.[6] Such an exercise allowed the men in Zwingli's Prophezei not only to appreciate the qualities of tone and rhythm, the poetry, of the original text, but to grapple with the problems of the

the last decade. Hans-Joachim Köhler published the preliminary findings of the Sonderforschungsbereich Z1 in Tübingen, "Die Flugschriften des frühen 16. Jhts.," in "Die Flugschriften. Versuch der Präzisierung eines geläufigen Begriffs," in *Festgabe Ernst Walter Zeeden*, ed. Horst Raabe, Hansgeorg Molitor, and Hans-Christoph Rublack (Münster Westphalen, 1976), pp. 36–61. For a review of the literature on pamphlets to 1978, see Hella Tompert, "Die Flugschrift als Medium religiöser Publizistik," in *Kontinuität und Umbruch. Theologie und Frömmigkeit in Flugschriften und Kleinliteratur an der Wende vom 15. zum 16. Jahrhundert*, ed. Josef Nolte, Hella Tompert, and Christof Windhorst (Stuttgart, 1978), pp. 211–21. Papers from a symposium on the function of pamphlets in the Reformation has been published in *Flugschriften als Massenmedium*, ed. Hans-Joachim Köhler (Stuttgart, 1981). Most recently, Miriam Usher Chrisman has investigated the kinds of pamphlets and of readerships different kinds of pamphlets engendered, in *Lay Culture, Learned Culture* (New Haven, Conn., 1982).

3 As Chandra Mukerji has argued, books and pamphlets were also objects, discrete units, that were therefore portable. *From Graven Images: Patterns of Modern Materialism* (New York, 1983), Introduction.

4 On the relation between literacy and accessibility of texts, see Robert Scribner, "Oral Culture and the Diffusion of Reformation Ideas," *History of European Ideas* 5 (1984): 237–56.

5 Scribner has found record that in 1524, a clerk read one of Carlstadt's works aloud in the Nuremberg market square. Ibid., p. 241.

6 Heinrich Bullinger, *Reformationsgeschichte*, ed. J. J. Hottinger and H. H. Vögeli (Frauenfeld, 1838/40), vol. 1, pp. 289f.

translator: syntax, structure, context, and the exclusivity of each language.

Among all the forms words took, preaching was the most dramatic. Among the cultural forms of the Reformation, it was preeminent.[7] Preaching had the broadest potential audience. It could reach the illiterate – the peasants, the day laborers, journeymen, wage earners – at the same time as the shopkeepers, the masters, and the town councillors. The men who gave shape and direction to the evangelical reform movement were all preachers. They were able to give words an aural presence – an immediacy, a weight, a force – that carried them beyond the printed page into the hearts of the audience. As villagers and artisans understood, it was the preacher alone who could make the words of Scripture accessible to all.[8]

> On Saturday, New Year's Day, 1519, Huldrych Zwingli preached his first sermon and announced that on the following Sunday morning he would begin to expound the holy gospel of Matthew, through and with divine truth and not with human hands. Soon there was a remarkable flocking of all kinds of people, especially of the common man, to these evangelical sermons (Heinrich Bullinger, *Reformationsgeschichte*).[9]

At the age of thirty-four, Huldrych Zwingli was called to Zurich to be the People's Pastor [*Leutpriester*]. This role, as preacher to the laity, the people, was to be his primary identity for the rest of his life. As a preacher, he was gifted, eloquent and effective.[10] He took seriously his role, crafting his sermons in simple and familiar language, avoiding unnecessary and pretentious words, making the content of his sermons aurally understandable and "landtlich."[11] Beginning with the Gospel of Matthew in 1519 and preaching weekly on the New Testament texts of

---

[7] On preaching, see Robert Scribner, "Practice and Principle in German Towns: Preachers and People," in *Reformation Principle and Practice: Essays in Honor of A. G. Dickens*, ed. P. N. Brooks (London, 1980), pp. 95–117.

[8] The First Article of *The Twelve Articles* requests "the authority and power for the whole community to elect and appoint its own pastor. We also want authority to depose a pastor who behaves improperly. This elected pastor should preach to us the holy gospel purely and clearly, without human additions or human doctrines or precepts." English translation from Peter Blickle, *The Revolution of 1525*, trans. Thomas A. Brady, Jr. and H. C. Erik Midelfort (Baltimore, 1981), Appendix 1, p. 196.

[9] Bullinger, p. 12.

[10] Ibid., p. 306.

[11] Ibid.

Acts, Paul's Epistles, I Timothy, Galatians, and II Timothy, Peter's First and Second Epistles, and Paul's Epistle to the Hebrews, Zwingli drew his audience into a careful and detailed consideration of the word of God.[12]

Zwingli employed a number of approaches and all forms of verbal expression to convey the message of Scripture to as broad an audience as possible. He had been appointed to the largest church in Zurich, the Grossmünster; he chose to preach not only inside the church, but before it, in the open space of the churchyard. In addition to preaching on Sundays, Fridays, and feast days, he held a kind of open house on Fridays, in order to reach those who came into Zurich for the markets.[13] If preaching was his most successful medium, his words acquired permanence in print. In printed form, Zwingli's words travelled beyond the boundaries of Zurich, entering the libraries and vocabularies of other Swiss and south German reformers. In printed form, his words recalled to the people of Zurich the ephemeral performance of the sermon and the force of his voice as he challenged them to embrace his message, a message which included the poor.

> ... one should clothe the living images of God, the poor Christians, not the wooden and stone idols, for the honor of God (*The Shepherd*).[14]

On October 28, 1523, during the Second Disputation in Zurich, Ulrich Zwingli preached the sermon, "The Shepherd" [*"Der hirt"*]. In it he outlined the responsibilities of the pastor of a Christian community, the primary of which was preaching the word of God. Among the secondary responsibilities Zwingli placed the care of the poor. When the sermon was published on March 26 the following year, the engraved border on the title page portrayed Christ with His apostles, which was not unusual, and detailed images of poor people, which was.[15] The

---

[12] Zwingli, *Apologeti/cus Archeteles* (Zurich: Christoph Froschauer, August, 1522).

[13] Peter Heinrich Huber, "Annahme und Durchführung der Reformation auf der Zürcher Landschaft in den Jahren 1519 bis 1530," (Ph.D. dissertation, Zurich, 1972), p. 20.

[14] "das man die läbenden bilder gottes, die armen Christen, nit die hültzinen und steininen götzen zuo der eer gottes bekleiden sol," *Der hirt,* originally published by Christoph Froschauer in Zurich, reprinted as *Der Hirt* in the *Corpus Reformatorum,* (hereafter *CR*), vol. 90: *Huldreich Zwinglis Sämtliche Werke,* (hereafter *ZSW*), vol. 3, ed. Emil Egli, Georg Finsler, and Walther Köhler (Leipzig, 1914), p. 51. All quotations of Zwingli's works are taken from the *CR* edition.

[15] In addition to *Der hirt*, this border appears on the title page to *De vera et falsa religione commentarius* (March 1525), and to *Uber Doctor Balthazars Touffbüchlein* (November 5, 1525). According to the catalogue, *Zürcher Kunst nach der Reformation; Hans Asper und Seine Zeit* (Zurich, 1981), p. 144, this title page border appeared for the first time with *Der hirt.* Paul Leemann-van Elck,

publisher, Christoph Froschauer, was a close personal friend of Zwingli.[16] That he chose this particular motif suggests that the poor, or what they represented, had acquired greater significance in the intervening five months.

Similarly, the description of the poor from *The Shepherd*, which Luther and other reformers also invoked, was more than a simple polemical device for Zwingli.[17] Within the thirteen months following the publication of *The Shepherd*, Zwingli addressed the subject of the poor in three more major treatises, in detail in two of them. In a treatise dealing in large part with tithes and rents, entitled *Who is the Source of Sedition* and published on December 28, 1524, Zwingli articulated the relationship he envisioned between the poor and the Christian community.[18] In the spring of 1525, in his long treatise on the mass and images, the *Reply to Valentin Compar*, published April 27, 1525, he returned to the metaphor of the poor as the image of God and gave it depth and substance.[19] These three works are linked by their concern with the poor. On the title page of each, moreover, was a different woodcut or engraving, presenting an image of Christ with poor folk.

These works appeared at a critical time in Zurich, a time of change and of confrontation. They all appeared within one year, framing Zurich's Poor Law with their publication dates. *Who is the Source of Sedition* was published three weeks before, and the *Reply to Valentin Compar* three months after the town council enacted the Poor Law on January 15, 1525. They also appeared at the time when the Anabaptists were emerg-

who identifies this border with the one used with Froschauer's 1524 edition of the New Testament, also states, "Die stillvolle Titelrahmen fand erstmals in Zwinglis Schrift *Der Hirt* Verwendung." *Die zürcherische Buchillustration von den Anfängen bis um 1850* (Zurich, 1952), p. 28.

[16] On Froschauer, see Paul Leemann-van Elck, *Die Offizin Froschauer*, Mitteilungen der antiquarischen Gesellschaft in Zürich, vol. 33.2 (1940); Joachim Staedtke, *Christoph Froschauer der Begründer des Zürcher Buchwesens* (Zurich, 1964); E. Camillo Rudolphi, *Die Buchdrucker Familie Froschauer in Zürich, 1521–1595* (Zurich, 1869; reprint, Nieuwkoop, 1963); and S. Vögelin, "Christoph Frochauer, erster berühmter Buchdrucker in Zürich nach seinem Leben und Wirken," *Zur vierten Säkularfeier der Erfindung der Buchdruckerkunst* (Zurich, 1840).

[17] Martin Luther referred to the poor as the "living images of God" in 1522 (Weimar edition 10 III, 334, 25f.). I am grateful to Hans-Christoph Rublack for this reference.

[18] *WElche ursach gebind ze ufruoren*, originally published by Froschauer in Zurich. All citations from this work are from the edition, entitled *Wer Ursach gebe zu Aufruhr usw.*, in *CR* vol. 90: *ZSW* vol. 3, pp. 355–469.

[19] *EIn Antwurt Huldrychen Zwinglis Valentino Compar alten Landt/schrybern zuo Ure ggeben...*, originally published by Hans Hager in Zurich. All citations are from the modern edition, entitled *Eine Antwort, Valentin Compar gegeben*, in *CR* vol. 91: *ZSW* vol. 4, ed. Emil Egli, Georg Finsler, Walther Köhler, and Oskar Farner (Leipzig, 1927), pp. 35–159.

ing as a divisive force in Zurich. Equally important, these works appeared in the early months of the primarily rural revolt that became the Peasants' War of 1525: at a time when peasants were increasingly resistant to the economic and social injustices they perceived.[20]

Zwingli intended each text to have a wide audience. All three were published in German, the language of the council chamber, the marketplace, and the village. Even his reply to Valentin Compar, who knew Latin, was published in German. We do not know how large each text's edition was, the number of copies that might have been available to urban and rural readers; we can only approximate.[21] As texts intended for a popular readership, each of the works would have had an edition of more than five hundred copies. As texts less important than Bibles or major theological treatises, none would have had an edition reaching fifteen hundred copies.[22] Of the three, *The Shepherd* received the largest publication; it was printed in two editions on March 26, 1524.[23] Zwingli also seems to have sent the texts to friends beyond the borders of the canton: his texts on the poor were read, and possibly heard, in Martin Bucer's Strasbourg, and in Basel, where his friends Oecolampadius and Myconius furthered his work publicly.[24] The three title page prints, too,

---

[20] Blickle has argued in *The Revolution of 1525*, I think convincingly, that the so-called Peasants' War of 1525 was more broadly based, that it was a "revolution of the common man." See also Heiko A. Oberman, "The Gospel of Social Unrest," in *The German Peasant War of 1525 – New Viewpoints*, ed. Robert Scribner and Gerhard Benecke (London, 1979), pp. 39–51. In the canton of Zurich, however, the revolt was predominantly rural; peasants most often voiced the sense of injustice and the demand for a more Christian community that Blickle found among both rural and urban societies farther north.

[21] There is no record of the size of the editions extant for either of the two Zurich publishers, Froschauer or Hager.

[22] Febvre and Martin, pp. 214–19.

[23] Georg Finsler, *Zwingli Bibliographie* (reprinted Nieuwkoop, 1968), p. 23.

[24] See Bucer's letters to Zwingli of April 19, 1524 and January 29, 1526, found in *CR* vol. 95: *ZSW* vol. 8; *Zwinglis Briefwechsel*, ed. Emil Egli, Georg Finsler, and Walther Köhler (Leipzig, 1915), nos. 333 and 446. The earlier letter dwells at some length on Bucer's uneasiness with Zwingli's position on images: "Qui igitur non liceat habere imaginem aut statuam, si sine iactura id fiat tam fidei quam charitatis?" Oecolampadius had translated Gregory of Nazianzus' sermon on the poor into Latin in 1519. In 1521, a German translation of his work appeared in Mainz. In 1523 Oecolampdius published his own treatise on poor relief, *De non habendo pauperum delectu*, with the Basel house of Cratander. This work was translated into German in 1524, and published in Basel by Cratander, Ernst Staehelin, *Oekolampad Bibliographie*, Verzeichnis der im 16. Jahrhundert erschienen Oekolampaddrücke, (Nieuwkoop, 1963), nos. 10, 11, 49, 70, 77, and 94. I am grateful to Hans-Christoph Rublack for this reference. Oecolampadius, then, had written extensively on the problem of poor relief before his friend Zwingli had begun to address it. Zwingli apparently did not own a copy of any of these works; he was, however, frequently in contact with Oecolampadius after 1522 and could well have been acquainted with their contents.

may intimate how broad an audience Zwingli sought to reach: in each, Christ is reaching out to the poor and common folk.

It is no accident that the three works share a common motif in their title page prints: The prints mark the three works among all Zwingli's sermons and treatises that address the care of the poor most fully. None of his texts has the poor and their care as its central theme. His statements on the poor were not organized in a single treatise, a single argument, but scattered, articulated in relation to his larger themes of social ethics, of brotherly love, and of community. It is only in relation to these themes that his perception of the poor gains dimension and definition. Zwingli discussed the poor most explicitly in relation to his larger themes in the three works of 1523–5. Let us begin with these three works, then, to delineate the place of the poor within the pattern of Zwingli's thought and to discover the value that the people's preacher of Zurich gave to the living images of God.

The Shepherd

The first of the three works to be published, *The Shepherd*, contains the fewest number of passages dealing with the poor. In part, the reasons for this lie in the broader historical context: the condition of poverty was not as politically volatile an issue in the spring of 1523 as it was to become by late 1524. In part, too, the reasons lie in the development of Zwingli's thought. At the time of the publication of *The Shepherd*, the fall of 1523 through spring 1524, Zwingli was still primarily concerned with establishing the basic principles of his reform.[25] Not until after the Second Disputation did he turn to applying his principles to specific problems within the community of Zurich. Among the basic principles of his reform was the special place he assigned to the preacher, who was to make the Divine Word heard and foster its realization.[26] This role extended into the realm of politics and economics; the preacher functioned to strengthen the Christian conscience of the leaders and to

---

[25] Siegfried Rother, *Die religiösen und geistigen Grundlagen der Politik Huldrych Zwinglis* (Erlangen, 1956).

[26] This is most evident in *Der Hirt*. See Rother, pp. 63–72. Hans-Christoph Rublack underlined the role for the preacher that Zwingli envisioned and the place of the Prophezei in Zurich in "Zwingli und Zürich," *Zwingliana* 16/5 (1985/1), 393–426.

oversee the proper use of the community's wealth.[27] It is in the context of this latter responsibility that the passage cited above was spoken:

> If they only knew, that the holding of mass [in expectation of] a reward pleases God so poorly; and that one should clothe the living images of God, the poor Christians, not the wooden and stone idols, for the honor of God; ... that it is so shameful that among the Christian people exist so many idlers, priests, monks, and nuns; ... and that what is applied to the walls should be given to the protection of the piety of poor daughters and wives, whose beauty, through poverty, leads them into danger.[28]

This passage, which is unique in *The Shepherd*, is the first instance of Zwingli's use of the metaphor for the poor as the "images of God."[29] In arguing that the proper use of the wealth traditionally invested in church decoration was the care of the poor, Zwingli was voicing an ancient criticism of church art, a criticism Luther and the Zurich iconoclasts were also to express.[30] In framing that opposition in terms of true and false images of God, Zwingli also chose a metaphor that touched the wellsprings of popular social values and piety.

Zwingli did not expand upon the metaphor here; its impression was fleeting, its challenge momentary. He returned to it in later works, however, and developed it. Its function in *The Shepherd*, therefore, was transitory, but it was a metaphor that received depth and strength in the

---

[27] See, for example, *Der Hirt*, p. 66. There have been a number of studies of Zwingli's social and political thought that touch upon his position on rents and tithes. Most helpful among them are Leonhard von Muralt, "Zwingli als Sozialpolitiker," *Zwingliana* 5 (1931): 276–96; Arthur Rich, "Zwingli als sozialpolitischer Denker," *Zwingliana* 13 (1969): 67–89; and Joachim Rogge, "Zwingli und Luther in ihren sozialen Handlungsfeldern," *Zwingliana* 13 (1969–73), 625–44. Alfred Farner's study, *Die Lehre von Kirche und Staat bei Zwingli* (Tübingen, 1930), although exaggerated in parts, provides an extended analysis of Zwingli's ethics. Norman Birnbaum has sought to place Zwingli's reform in the social, economic, and political context of Zurich in "The Zwinglian Reformation in Zurich," in *Toward a Critical Sociology* (New York, 1971), pp. 133–61.

[28] "Wenn sy aber wüsstind, das gott das verlonet messhalten so übel gefalt; und das man die läbenden bilder gottes, die armen Christen, nit die hültzinen und steininen götzen zu der eer gottes bekleiden sol; ... das es so schädlich ist under dem christenen volck so vil muessigenger, pfaffen, münchen, nonnen halten; ... und das, so an die muren verwendet wirdt, zuo bewarung der frommgheit armer dochtren unnd frowen, dero schöne durch armuot inn gefärd gfeuert, ussgeben wirt ... " *Der Hirt*, pp. 51–2.

[29] This metaphor, which originates in Genesis 1:26–7, has a long history. See Gerhard Ladner, *The Idea of Reform* (Cambridge, Mass., 1959).

[30] "Und insofern steht er in der Kontroverse zwischen Luther und den aufrührischen Bauern diesen näher als jenem." Rich, "Zwingli als sozialpolitischer Denker," p. 71. On the position of the Zurich iconoclasts, see my "Iconoclasts in Zürich," to be published in a volume on Iconoclasm by the Herzog August Bibliothek Wolfenbüttel.

recalling. The remaining passages in *The Shepherd* dealing with the poor are brief and equally threads of a theme to which Zwingli returned: "Those who do not give shelter to the poor are false shepherds."[31] And again: "Whoever does not watch over the poor, lets them be oppressed and burdened, are false shepherds."[32]

The Shepherd was addressed to the pastors, of the parish and of the diocese. It was a call to return to the pastoral duties Christ defined for His apostles. These two statements tell us more by their silences, by what they do not say about the pastor and his poor, than by their assertions. There is no suggestion of a personal or direct tie between the preacher and the poor; he is their caretaker, no more, no less. In contrast to the relationship between the preacher and the political leaders that Zwingli outlined in this work, the preacher does not chastise, nor address the motives or conscience of the poor, nor is he to challenge the poor to work and to become active in the Christian community. In this sermon, Zwingli dealt narrowly with the relation of the Christian pastor to the poor. He did not move beyond that relationship to address the broader one between the Christian community and its poor. The principle upon which those relationships were founded, however, was present; it had not yet been applied specifically to the care of the poor.

Brothers and neighbors

The second of the three works, *Who is the Source of Sedition,* was published on December 28, only three weeks after Zwingli began writing it.[33] Zwingli probably never delivered it aloud. It was not addressed to one audience, but two, who opposed one another and threatened to become or had become deaf to his reform: those "who with their sedition want to be good Christians," and those "true seditionists who do not want to be named as such."[34] For Zwingli, the first group comprised

---

[31] "Die nit ze herberg nemend die armen, sind valsche hirten," *Der Hirt,* p. 54.

[32] "6. Welche der armen nit achtend, sy vertrucken lassend und beschwären, sind valsch hirten," Ibid., p. 59.

[33] On the dating and the context of this work, see Walther Köhler's Introduction to the text, *CR* vol. 90: *ZSW* vol. 3, pp. 361–6.

[34] "Zum ersten von den ufruerigen sagen, die damit guot Christen wellend sin.
"Zum andren von den rechten ufruerigen, die dess doch ghein wort wellend haben." Ibid., p. 380. Köhler suggests in the Introduction that this text is Zwingli's counterpart to Luther's *An den christlichen Adel deutscher Nation,* although Zwingli's work addresses a wider number of issues and is more economic in orientation.

those peasants who protested tithes and ecclesiastical rents, and the Anabaptists, who were becoming increasingly alienated from Zwingli.[35] The second group comprised the papal hierarchy – "the high bishops," "the clamoring priests, monks, nuns, foremost the abbots" – and the "princes, the powerful and the rich of this world."[36] This work addresses an audience that is politically and economically polarized, and focuses on issues of community, public economy and authority.[37] It also deals most specifically with the care of the poor, suggesting, as we shall see more fully below, that for Zwingli, the poor were a public and communal issue, to be understood in reference to the economy and ethics of the Christian community.

Walther Köhler has suggested that *Who is the Source of Sedition* is a continuation of many points Zwingli first made in his major treatise, *On Divine and Human Justice.*[38] At the center of the former work is the argument that the rebellious peasants and the religious and secular authorities, each in their own way, falsely understood the relationship between the divine realm and the human. Zwingli had already presented his conception of that relationship in detail in *On Divine and Human Justice.*[39] He returned in *Who is the Source of Sedition* to make explicit the implications of his larger argument with regard to individual

---

[35] It is not clear from the text of *Wer Ursach gebe zu Aufruhr* whether the Anabaptists were in fact one of Zwingli's primary targets. Studies of Anabaptism have suggested that this work is concerned solely with the Anabaptists. See, for example, Claus-Peter Clasen, *Anabaptism: A Social History, 1525–1618* (Ithaca, N.Y., 1972), p. 10; and James M. Stayer, *Anabaptism and the Sword* (Lawrence, Kans., 1976[1972]), p. 99. The Anabaptists shared many positions with the peasants, moreover, such as the rebellion against tithes and interest. See Conrad Grebel's letter to Thomas Müntzer, in *Quellen zur Geschichte der Täufer in der Schweiz*, ed. Leonhard von Muralt and Walter Schmid (Zurich, 1952), pp. 13–21.

[36] "Die ersten sind die hohen bischoff," *Wer Ursach gebe zu Aufruhr*, p. 412; "Die andren sind die übrigen zal der widerbefftzenden pfaffen, münchen, nonnen, voruss der äbten," ibid., p. 420; "Die dritten warlichen ufruorer sind die fürsten, gewaltigen und rychen diser welt," ibid., p. 423.

[37] This may help to explain why it is the least studied of all of Zwingli's works. See, for example, Ulrich Gäbler, *Huldrych Zwingli; Leben und Werk* (Munich, 1983), pp. 87–9; Von Muralt, "Zwingli: als Sozialpolitiker," pp. 289–90; and Rich, "Zwingli als sozialpolitischer Denker," pp. 76–80. Oskar Farner deals in some depth with the problem of the Anabaptists and the peasants for Zwingli, yet he used *Wer Ursach gebe zu Aufruhr* only once. *Huldrych Zwingli*, Vol. 4: *Reformatorische Erneuerung von Kirche und Volk in Zürich und in der Eidgenossenschaft, 1525–31* (Zurich, 1960), pp. 102–58. See also, Clasen, p. 10; and Stayer, p. 99.

[38] Walther Köhler, Introduction to *Wer Ursach gebe zu Aufruhr*, p. 353.

[39] *Von göttlicher und menschlicher Gerechtigkeit*, in *CR* vol. 89: *ZSW* vol. 2, ed. Emil Egli and Georg Finsler (Leipzig, 1908), pp. 458–525. Oskar Farner argues that this was Zwingli's first response to the "radicals," in *Huldrych Zwingli*, Vol. 3: *Seine Verkündigung und ihre ersten Fruchte* (Zurich, 1954), pp. 389–96.

"abuses," abuses of the peasants, of the nascent Anabaptists, and of the ecclesiastical and secular authorities.

One problem of particular significance, both for us and for Zwingli, was that of tithes and rents. Again, Zwingli's two audiences form the two poles between which he formulated his argument. On the one hand, peasants, both individuals and entire villages, and Anabaptists were questioning the legitimacy of tithes and refusing to pay them. For the peasants, tithes had come to represent an unjust and overbearing financial burden, and a symbol of their oppression by both lay and ecclesiastical lords.[40] We shall hear their voices in Chapter 4. For the Anabaptists, tithes were no more than usury, the unjust and sinful profit at the expense of others.[41] If Zwingli was to retain the support, or at least the sympathy, of the rural populace and the urban Anabaptists, he had to reach a position of accommodation.

On Zwingli's other hand stood the ecclesiastical and secular authorities, who collected the tithes, who were financed by them, and who had come to see them as their personal property.[42] The leaders of the Peasants' War in 1525 were not the first to voice their conviction that lay and ecclesiastical lords were abusing the tithe. In the fifteenth century, Conrad Summenhart had given voice to the popular view that both lay and ecclesiastical lords were abusing the tithe, in its estimation, in its collection, and in its use.[43] Yet, Zwingli could not afford to alienate those secular authorities, many of whom were members of the town council, who were supporting his reform in Zurich.

The problem for Zwingli, and for the town council, when they were confronted with the peasants' position on tithes, was that the New Testament contained no justification for tithes. If they were to support the imposition and collection of tithes, they had to turn to the traditional position of the church – which was ultimately unsatisfactory – or to

---

[40] On the peasants' attitudes toward ecclesiastical tithes, see Henry Cohn, "Anticlericalism in the German Peasants' War 1525," *Past and Present* 83 (1979): 3–31; and toward secular tithes, see Lawrence P. Buck, "Opposition to Tithes in the Peasants' Revolt: A Case Study of Nuremberg in 1524," *The Sixteenth Century Journal* 4 (1973): 11–22.

[41] See Grebel's letter, pp. 13–21.

[42] Catherine Boyd traces the transformation of tithes in Italy from a form of ecclesiastical dues to an institution of extraordinarily confused and confusing purposes and justifications. See her *Tithes and Parishes in Medieval Italy* (Ithaca, 1952). There is no comparable study for Germany, but it seems that the general contours were similar.

[43] On the place of tithes in the social thought of the university masters, see Heiko A. Oberman, *Werden und Wertung der Reformation* (Tubingen, 1979), pp. 146-56, especially.

reasons of custom. Zwingli chose an approach that reflected some of his deeper concerns with the Christian community and with the poor.

Zwingli constructed his argument against the position of the peasants and the Anabaptists on a number of levels. He did not begin with an explanation for tithes, but turned to the opponents themselves, and to their refusal to pay rents, interest, or other debts, as well as tithes.[44] He chose a line of approach that at first glance seems to echo Summenhart's: to apply Romans 13:7 – "You should give all men what you owe them."[45] Yet, he did not invoke Paul merely to justify authority. He was concerned, rather, with something internal, with social bonds. He chose to emphasize the notion of debt present in Romans 13 and to explore its meaning for the Christian community.

It is theft, Zwingli argued, to keep what you owe, whether or not the demand for payment is justified.[46] In calling the refusal to pay tithes theft, even though the debtor perceived those tithes as unjust, Zwingli evidenced his commitment to communal values and to communal economic practices over individuals.[47] The next step of his argument makes those communal values more explicit:

> Whoever desires to defraud them is not a Christian; for he does not want to remain faithful to his neighbor, which he has promised him [his neighbor], but desires his own selfish ends.[48]

The payment of debts, that is, rents, dues, and tithes, is a part of being "faithful to one's neighbor." Economic practices reflect social bonds, human relations. Refusal to pay tithes and rents is not simply theft; it is the rejection of a deeper bond between a man and his "neighbor." The language recalls Matthew 22:39 – "You shall love your neighbor as yourself" – for in not remaining true to his neighbor, a man is not a Christian.[49] The motivation, Zwingli suggested, for that rejection

---

[44] "Die dritten, die das euangelium allermeist verhasst machend, sind, die darinn allein suochend, ob sy fundind, das sy gheinem nüts umb das syn geben muesstind, weder zinss, zehenden noch andre schuld bezahlen." *Wer Ursach gebe zu Aufruhr*, p. 387.

[45] Ibid., p. 387ff. See *Von göttlicher und menschlicher Gerechtigkeit*, pp. 500, 503, 508–22, in which Zwingli applied Romans 13:1–7 to the question of the *zins* and tithes.

[46] *Wer Ursach gebe zu Aufruhr*, pp. 387–8.

[47] On Summenhart's view of tithes as an obligation of love, see Oberman, *Werden und Wertung*.

[48] "Welcher nun die betriegen wil, ist nit ein Christ: denn er wil sinem nächsten trüw nit halten, die er aber im verheissen hat, umb sines eygnen nutzes willen." *Wer Ursach gebe zu Aufruhr*, p. 388.

[49] My own biblical quotations are drawn from *The New Oxford Annotated Bible*, Revised Standard Edition. Those which appear first in one of Zwingli's texts, I have translated from the German or Latin.

is *Eigennutz,* or self-interest. A notion of self-interest is central to Zwingli's thought;[50] in applying it to the issue of tithes, Zwingli brought the controversial practice into the very center of his theology. The payment of tithes was to play an important role in the economy of the Christian community. It was also symbolic of much more.

Zwingli then called forth traditional arguments for the collection of tithes, in order to justify them on the basis of their original function.[51] In addressing the rebellious peasants and the Anabaptists, he drew first upon canon law.

> From both ordinances of the elders [*der Alten*], everyone can see that each congregation gave tithes in order to support its poor people with it.[52]

Zwingli supported the collection of tithes for two uses: the maintenance of a preacher and the care of the poor.[53] These uses, he argued, had been designated in the Old Testament:

> For if the children of Israel were commanded to allow no poor or beggars among them, how much less should Christians allow their brothers, who with the blood of Christ are born unto them as members, to experience the perceptible filth of poverty? Therefore, let it be clearly understood, that each Christian community has collected tithes for the care of its poor.[54]

These uses would have appealed to the peasants of 1525, who placed first among their demands support for a preacher,[55] and the Anabaptists, whose position on property placed great emphasis on the care of the poor.[56]

---

[50] See below.

[51] On the earliest explanation of the purpose of tithes, see Boyd, chap. 2.

[52] "Ussz den beyden ordnungen der alten mag mencklich ermessen, das ein yede kilchhöre die zehenden ggeben hatt, das man ire armen lüt damit erhalten möchte." *Wer Ursach gebe zu Aufruhr,* p. 393.

[53] "Denn das Wort des Predigers ist den Armen an Seele und Leben zugewandt. Zwinglis Amt in Zürich war Heilsverkündigung und Reinigung durch das Wort Gottes. Die gewiss gewichtigen Beziehungen Zwinglis mit dem Rat decken dafür seinen Rücken, das Gesicht des Predigers ist der Kilchhöri zugewandt." Rublack, "Zwingli und Zurich," p. 3.

[54] "Dann ist den kindern Israels gebotten, das sy gheine armen oder bätler under inen söltind sin lassen, wie vil weniger söllend die Christen iren bruederen, die inen mit dem bluot Christi anerborn sind zuo mitglydern, zuo bärlichen unradt der armuot nit kommen lassen? Darumb häll verstanden wirt, das die zehenden zuo erhaltung irer armen ein yede kilchhöre zämengetragen hatt," *Wer Ursach gebe zu Aufruhr,* p. 393.

[55] Blickle, p. 196.

[56] See Clasen, pp. 187–8.

Why did Zwingli choose to defend the particular practice of tithes and at such length? It has been commonly accepted that he supported the position of secular authority.[57] Yet, his defense of tithes shared key elements with the position of the peasants and the nascent Anabaptists. Like them, he placed tithes within a moral framework. Like them, he found abuse and misappropriation in contemporary practice. He did not accept their choice of response to the abuse of tithes – refusing to pay; he demanded instead that tithal wealth be returned to its original, historical purposes. Like the peasants and Anabaptists, Zwingli applied a moral standard to the collection of wealth, a standard anchored in the Gospel. Unlike them, he used that moral standard to justify a community's collection of tithes, demanding at the same time that the community meet that moral standard.

Zwingli supported tithes for another reason as well. Although he discussed the care of the poor at some length in this work, he never mentioned almsgiving. Granted that the two practices are different in kind, they share a common function: the relief of the poor. It seems a strange silence. One difference between the two practices is particularly telling, however. Almsgiving, one of the Seven Works of Mercy, usually involved a direct exchange between a benefactor and a beggar; it was personal and individual. It established a specific relationship between the donor and the recipient, the poor man, one that reflected primarily upon the donor and placed the poor person in his debt, his power. Tithes, on the other hand, were not considered a "Good Work"; they held no special sanction. Tithes were a debt owed to human institutions, both ecclesiastical and secular. In their earliest form, tithes were meant to help support the church and the poor. They were an indirect and impersonal method of poor relief, placing a communal agency, the religious houses or the lay and religious lords, between the donor and the poor.[58] The preceding passage from *Who is the Source of Sedition* speaks

---

[57] Dieter Demandt, "Zur Wirtschaftsethik Zwinglis," in *Beiträge zur Wirtschafts– und Sozialgeschichte des Mittelalters*, ed. Knut Schulz (Cologne, 1976), pp. 306–21.

[58] In many ways, Zwingli's definition of tithes parallels the token coinage of late medieval poor relief: "the evidence surrounding the appearance of charity tokens suggests the background of lay society in the form of religious confraternities, municipal governments, and royal administration.... In general, this transformation may be called, to borrow a term from Strayer, the laicization of poor relief. It was also, as the use of charity tokens reveals, a simplification and a rationalization of the process of giving assistance to the needy." William J. Courtenay, "Token Coinage and the Administration of Poor Relief During the Late Middle Ages," *Journal of Interdisciplinary History* 3 (1972–3): 284–5.

of such a relationship between the community and its poor, and between the donor and the community. It speaks of "brothers" and "members" in "the blood of Christ," and of the "collection of tithes" for the relief of the poor: of communal relations and communal support. Zwingli sought to give institutional form to ties not between gift-giver and receiver, but between brothers.

The passage is also important in what it says about the poor. The condition of poverty is described in emphatically physical terms: One can see, touch, and smell it. Zwingli attributes to poverty no distinctive spiritual state, to the poor, no sanctity. Indeed, the poor are "brothers," "members" in the Christian community; they are a part of the same community as their wealthier brothers.[59] Equally important, in describing them as brothers and members, Zwingli denied that they were any poorer in spirit than any other member of the Christian community. Their poverty is material and external, and it could be alleviated through the payment of tithes.

Before turning to address the monks and nuns, bishops and priests, Zwingli made explicit the scriptural foundation for the relationship between the donor and the community and, by implication, between the community and its poor:

> Mark briefly therefore: God commands, you should love your neighbor as yourself. [Matthew 22:39] If you fulfill that, then you do not need many of God's commandments, namely: You should not kill, not steal, commit adultery, lie. For whoever loves his neighbor as himself, he does not lie to him; for he will also not suffer that one lies to him. Therefore we would not need many of God's commandments, if we keep the sum of all commandments Galatians 5 [:14]. We would not need the commandment in Romans 13 [:7]: "You should give to all men, what you owe them," if each man were to love his neighbor as himself.[60]

At the heart of Zwingli's challenge to the peasants and the Anabaptists was his commitment to the content of Matthew 22:39. For Zwingli, this

---

[59] It would seem that Zwingli was referring to the native poor in this passage, and possibly even deliberately excluding the itinerant poor, the beggars.

[60] "Merck kurtz also: Gott heysst: Du solt den nächsten als lieb haben als dich selbs. Wenn du das erfüllest, so darffst du ouch viler gotzgebotten nüts, nämlich: Du solt nit töden, nit stälen, eebrechen, liegen. Dann welcher den nächsten als lieb halt, als sich selbs, der lügt imm nit; denn er wil ouch nit lyden, das man imm liege. Also dörftind wir viler gotzgebotten nit, wenn wir die summ aller gebotten Galt. 5 hieltind. Wir dörfftind des gebottes Ro. 13: 'Ir söllend allen menschen geben, das ir inen schuldig sind' nit, wenn yeder den nächsten als lieb hielte als sich selbs," *Wer Ursach gebe zu Aufruhr*, pp. 401–2.

commandment had important ramifications for temporal goods. He did not argue for the communal ownership of goods; in the lines immediately following, he referred to his defense of private ownership in *On Divine and Human Justice.*[61] It is, he argued, the same error, to deny the ownership of property and to refuse to pay tithes; in either case one opposes God's judgment regarding the distribution of wealth. Like most of his contemporaries, Zwingli rejected any program for the eradication of poverty through the redistribution of wealth.[62] In juxtaposing Matthew 22:39 upon the nature of property ownership, Zwingli placed the issue of private property along with tithes in the context of Christian ethics and brought to both a moral dimension.

Zwingli's position on property ownership followed traditional lines: Property was ordained by God and had been distributed originally according to divine will.[63] The distribution and ownership of property were the result of man's fall from grace. Any attempt to redistribute property, either communally or otherwise, was in opposition to this divine disposition. What were the implications of this position? If the ownership of property was predisposed by God, a man owed whatever possessions he had to God; his property became a gift dependent upon God. For Zwingli, man was always first God's debtor.[64] Any discussion of property, its use or possession, must be framed in that context.

> We would not need the commandment in Romans 13: *You should give to all men, what you owe them,* if each man were to love his neighbor as himself.

Reiterating Romans 13:7, Zwingli linked the topics of ownership and brotherhood. This passage suggests the psychology of ownership that underlies all of Zwingli's thinking on property. Those who refuse to pay tithes, who refuse to give to all men what they owe them, have assumed their possession of goods is absolute, that is, that they have the full right

[61] The only study of Zwingli's attitude to private ownership is Gottfried Locher's brief treatment in *Der Eigentumsbegriff als Problem evangelischer Theologie* (Zurich, 1962), pp. 29–35. Locher does not distinguish private ownership of property from *Eigennutz,* but treats solely the question of ownership.
[62] Von Muralt has called his position on private property conservative, p. 296.
[63] Ibid., pp. 283–4.
[64] Naziazanus states that men are beggars before God in the sermon, *De amandis pau//peribus, Gregorii Naza-//zeni Episcopi Theologii//sermo,* translated and published by Oecolampad (Augsburg, April 1519), pp. Aiv & ff.; German translation, *Ein ser Christliche Sermon,* (Mainz, 1521) pp. Bii & ff., a position that Augustine, and later Francis, would echo.

to determine the use of their goods or wealth.[65] Their decisions about the use of their property are controlled by their own selfish concerns.[66] Love of neighbor, the ability to love another as much as oneself affects a man's attitude toward his property. It provides a counterforce to self-interest, weakening its hold. It enables a man to recognize himself as a debtor – to acknowledge that his ownership is contingent. It enables a man to recognize that his "neighbor's" need constitutes a fair and moral demand on his goods. Loving his neighbor frees a man sufficiently from self-interest to recognize that his property is subject to demands higher than his own, to uses determined by his community and by God.

The donor, the community, and the poor are linked in *Who is the Source of Sedition*. Zwingli's use of Matthew 22:39 provides the key. Zwingli designated the poor as brothers. The moral imperative of Matthew 22:39 applies equally to their case. As brothers, they should not experience poverty. Their condition, therefore, constitutes an authentic moral demand on the wealth of others. In recovering the original purposes of tithing, Zwingli defined a communal source of wealth specifically designated to answer that demand; the poor and the community were to be linked through the institution of tithes. Tithes were to be levied by the ecclesiastical or lay authorities in order to alleviate the condition of poverty.[67] As a means of caring for poor brothers, tithes became a fair and moral demand upon a portion of a man's goods. As a communal institution, they were situated between donors and the poor. As such, they became one medium through which a man could care for his poor brother, could share his wealth, without receiving any sense of personal reward or serving his own self-interest.

Striking throughout this section of *Who is the Source of Sedition* is the language with which Zwingli described the relations between men:

---

[65] "Ausführlich verweilt er dagegen bei den Worten des Paulus in Rom. 13:7 von der Steuerpflicht. Er lässt wieder sein Ideal ursprünglicher Freiheit und Gleichheit erkennen. Gott hat die ganze Erde den Menschen freigegeben; niemand hat von Haus aus ein Eigentumsrecht, und nach dem Gebot: 'Du sollst deinen Nächsten lieben als dich selbst,' wäre jeder verpflichtet, aus seinem Besitz dem, der Mangel leidet, zu geben." Paul Wernle, *Der evangelische Glaube nach den Hauptschriften der Reformatoren*, Vol. 2: *Zwingli* (Tubingen, 1919), p. 113.

[66] "Erst die eigennützige Gesinnung des Menschen hat das Eigentum geschaffen; es ist und bleibt für Zwingli das Zeichen dass wir Sünder sind. Hätten wir keine andere Sünde, so 'wäre doch das Eigentum eine grosse Sünde, um deretwillen uns Gott verdammen müsste, denn was er uns frei gibt, das machen wir eigen.'...Von Eigennutz ist nach Zwingli 'selbst der Bettler nicht sicher, denn er ist ein jeder Mensch eigennützig etlichen Weg' " Ibid.

[67] Zwingli also argued that tithes were meant to support preaching, which was a transformation of the traditional reason of helping to finance the Church.

"brothers," "neighbors," and "members." His argument is framed in terms that reflect a notion of community not unlike that invoked by the peasants in 1525, in terms that echo the language the "Swiss Brethren" used to describe themselves.[68] Although Zwingli's language of "brotherhood" ultimately differed from that of the revolutionaries of 1525, linked as it was to a notion of debt and supportive of the institution of tithes, that language nonetheless reinforces certain kinds of ties between men: horizontal ties.[69] Zwingli may well have been seeking to extend the notion of brother beyond the narrow circle of the Anabaptists' "brotherhood," and to reaffirm the peasants' and the Anabaptists' ties to Zurich: to draw the rebels back into his Christian community.[70] This section has important implications for the poor as well, for they, too, are linked to the Christian community by horizontal rather than vertical ties. In this section, Zwingli brought forth the egalitarian language of Matthew 22:39, suggesting that the form of the Christian community could be fraternal.

His language changed in the next section, addressed to the "true sources of sedition," indicating that his choice of terms was quite deliberate. In the first part he sought to demonstrate that the peasants' and the Anabaptists' rebellion against certain institutions, both ecclesiastical and political – and, by implication, their alienation from the community of Zurich – was based on a limited reading of Matthew 22:39. These rebels had restricted the number and depth of ties they formed with others and failed to recognize how deeply self-interest affected men's decisions. Zwingli framed his argument toward them in terms that acknowledged their intentions as well-meaning, if based on a misunderstanding of Scripture, terms that could bring them back

---

[68] One of Blickle's major themes is the choice of the peasants in 1525 to describe the social and political forms they sought to establish in terms of fraternal relations. See Blickle, pt. 2. See also the Twelve Articles of 1525. The Anabaptists referred to themselves variously, most often employing the language of fraternity. See Clasen, p. 12. The nascent Anabaptists in Zurich signed the letter to Müntzer as "your Christian brothers," and came to be known by contemporaries as the "Swiss Brethren." See William R. Estep, Jr., *Anabaptist Beginnings (1523–1533); A Source Book* (Nieuwkoop, 1976), pp. 31–7.

[69] On Zwingli's notion of "brotherhood," see my "Brothers and Neighbors: The Language of Community in Zwingli's Preaching," *Zwingliana* 17/5 (1988/1): 361–74.

[70] For a careful study of Zwingli's relationship with the countryside and the peasants, see Huber. Huber's description touches upon the personal as well as economic and political channels through which Zwingli worked to reach the lands surrounding Zurich. In another vein, Blickle sketches points at which Zwingli's thought approached the positions of the peasants in 1525 (pp. 158–61).

within the fold of his reformed Christian community. He was neither so generous nor so patient with the "true sources of sedition."

In turning to the ecclesiastical and, to a lesser extent, the secular authorities, Zwingli's tone became more critical, more strident, less conciliatory. He condemned those who had abused the human institutions that had been created for a moral purpose, whose self-interest so blinded them that they could no longer recognize the responsibility bound up with their authority.

> Where then is that saying of the monks, that also stands someplace in the Pope's new law: Monasteria monachorum sunt xenodochia pauperum, that is: The cloisters of the monks are the hospitals of the poor? They are the xenodochia militum, the hospitals of the warriors. Where do the poor find shelter?[71]

Zwingli's criticism of the ecclesiastical hierarchy belonged to a long tradition.[72] In the section addressed to the peasants and Anabaptists, he fully agreed with their claim that the Church had used tithal wealth for the enrichment of its own.[73] His second line of criticism reflected his sense of local ties, the preeminence he gave to local identities in his vision of the Christian community:

> Do you not see that all priests, whether they are in or without cowls, from the highest to the smallest, are sworn to the Papacy? Who has ever suffered such a thing in his realm, that his own are sworn to foreign lords to the disadvantage of his realm? For through such promises temporal goods are carried off to Rome in great piles.[74]

Early in his career, Zwingli had been a "papal partisan."[75] As he abandoned those sympathies, he accused the ecclesiastical authorities with increasing frequency of siphoning the wealth from the land and

---

[71] "Wo ist aber yetz das wort der münchen, das ouch in bapsts rechtenn neywen an eim ort stadt: Monasteria monachorum sunt xenodochia pauperum, das ist: Die klöster der münchen sind spitäl der armen? Es sind xenodochia militum, spitäl der kriegeren. Wo verherbergend sy di armenn?" *Wer Ursach gebe zu Aufruhr*, p. 422.

[72] See *Manifestations of Discontent*, ed. Gerald Strauss (Bloomington, Ind., 1971), chap. 2.

[73] See *Wer Ursach gebe zu Aufruhr*, pp. 394–7.

[74] "Sehend ir nit, das alle pfaffen, sy sygind in oder one kutten, von oben härab biss uff den kleinsten in das bapstuomb geschworen sind? Wär hat aber sölichs ye in sinem rych gelitten, das die sinem einem so frömbden veeren schwuerind zuo nachteyl sines rychs? Dann durch sölich schweeren sind die zytlichen guoter zuo grossen huffen gen Rom gefuert." Ibid., p. 439.

[75] The phrase is James M. Stayer's. See his "Zwingli Before Zürich: Humanist Reformer and Papal Partisan," *Archive for Reformation History* 72 (1981): 55–68.

stockpiling it in Rome.[76] The community's resources were to remain local, its wealth, applied to immediate rather than distant uses. The economy Zwingli envisioned for the Christian community was to be local as well as moral. It may be a particularly Swiss trait: In 1491, the Confederation had mandated that poor relief be conducted at the cantonal level.

The focus of Zwingli's attack on the ecclesiastical powers and secular authorities was their abuse of their authority, specifically, their neglect of its inherent responsibility:

> If you had been true fathers, you would have never allowed the usury [*zins*], that from twenty takes one, to be laid on the earth. Should you not have taken care that the ground, of which you call yourselves lords, would not be so deplorably pawned?... See however the situation of the poor common man. Among them one is turned out today, another tomorrow, and there is no compassion in you.[77]

For Zwingli, usury represented more than the sin of unjust profit.[78] Usury impoverished the countryside and the common man.[79] It was also a sign of a deeper wrong. Zwingli's accusations, "if you had been true fathers," and "there is no compassion in you," offer a clue. Zwingli's rhetoric has changed; the language of fraternal ties has been replaced with that of vertical lines of authority. The term, "fathers," which Zwingli uses often in this section, implies responsibility as well as authority, a responsibility for taking care of one's own.[80] The language of familial ties, reinforced by the last line, links the public authorities to their

---

[76] Von Muralt, p. 286, suggests that the papacy's fiscal demands on Zurich had already been reduced in the Middle Ages, that there were very few left, and that Zwingli was concerned with political rights.

[77] "Die zins, die von zwentzigen eins nemmend, die soltend ir uff das erdrych nie haben lassen leggen, wenn ir trüwe vätter wärind gewesen. Soltend nitt ir hie ynsehen gethon haben, dass der boden, dess herren ir üch schrybend, nit so jämerlich versetzt wurde?... Sehend, aber, wie es daby umb den armen gemeinen mann stand. Dero vertrybt man einen hütt, den anderen morn, und ist ghein erbermd in üch." *Wer Ursach gebe zu Aufruhr*, pp. 436–7. For a slightly different reading of this passage, see Rich, "Zwingli als sozialpolitischer Denker," p. 86.

[78] The classic study of the idea of usury is John T. Noonan, Jr., *The Scholastic Analysis of Usury* (Cambridge, Mass., 1957).

[79] Blickle has provided the most recent and provocative investigation of the social and economic identity of "the common man" and his role in the Peasants' War of 1525. Robert Lutz has challenged Blickle's identification in his work, *Wer war der Gemeine Mann?* (Vienna, 1979), though unsuccessfully, I believe.

[80] On the notion of "father" in the Reformation, see Gerald Strauss, *Luther's House of Learning* (Baltimore, Md., 1978); and also Steven Ozment, *When Fathers Ruled; Family Life in Reformation Europe* (Cambridge, Mass., 1983).

subjects. In this passage, Zwingli contrasted the imposition of interest with the responsibility of a true father. On one level, that responsibility involves economic fairness. It also works on a deeper level:

> Now then, we will show you the way, along which you will discover that you have not abandoned your own self-interest, but are immersed in it. For, however much you remove from papal property, that much will go to your people. The more that goes to your people, the richer you become, the more you are tyrants then and not fathers.[81]

The responsibility of authority does not rest in the simple issue of preserving the wealth of the community. Zwingli located responsibility not in the gestures of authority, but in what lay behind those gestures: in motivation. And, just as in the case of the peasants and the Anabaptists, he found that the lay lords' seizure of ecclesiastical properties was anchored in self-interest, *Eigennutz*. Zwingli agreed with taking property out of ecclesiastical control, but he differed as to the purposes that property should serve:

> Let no one out of the convents, for they provide honorable shelter. See to it, however, that they are made into hospitals for the poor. Such measures should be taken concerning them, that the goods serve the poor or the common needs.[82]

And later on:

> Let the monks, priests, or nuns die off in peace and accept no more in their place. So it will pass that there are no more religious, who command everyone, so that their charter and seal are held in freedom or safety. In this way then we will use the tithes according to their first designation, for the care of the teachers and the poor of each Christian community.[83]

Zwingli saw a norm for responsible action in the application of goods or wealth to the needs of the community, either its poor or its teachers.

---

[81] "Wolhyn, so wellend wir üch weg anzeygen, daran ir finden werdend, das üch an üwren eygnen nutz nüts abgon wirt, sunder uf. Dann so vil üch dess bapstuombs halb wirt enzogen, so vil wirt üwrem volck zuogon. Ye me üwrem volck zuogadt, ye rycher ir werdend, ir sygind dann tyrannen und nit vätter." *Wer Ursach gebe zu Aufruhr*, p. 448.

[82] "Uss den nonnenklöstern lassend niemant, sy habind denn erbere herbergen. Luogend aber, das sy zuo spitälen der armenn gemacht werdind. Ob denenn halte man mit sölcher ordnung, das die guoter den armenn oder gemeinen durfften dienend," Ibid., p. 450.

[83] "Man lasse die münch, pfaffen oder nonnen im fryden absterben, und nemme man gheine me an ir statt. So wirt es darzuo kommen, dass ghein geistlicher me sin wirdt, der yeman erfordre, das man in fryheyt oder schirm, brieff und sigel halte. Denn so brucht man die zehenden nach erstem ynsatz zuo enthaltung der lerenden und armen einer yeden kilchhöre," Ibid., p. 454.

It was not enough that wealth be turned away from its misuse by the ecclesiastical lords; it had to be used for the needs of others.

Again, Zwingli implied that the care of the poor and of preachers opposed self-interest. Conversely, in returning wealth accrued through the collection of tithes to its original purpose, Zwingli presented a moral justification for the appropriation of ecclesiastical property. His suggestions also have a pragmatic side: They offer a real source of wealth for the community to use in the care of its poor. It is a second source, after tithes, and one that would not be a financial burden to the community. And, according to Zwingli, the community was morally bound to use the wealth for that purpose.[84]

Two days before Zwingli began to write this work, the nuns of Fraumünster, a convent in the center of town, turned their seal and charter over to the Zurich town council.[85] During the time he was writing, the Franciscan, Dominican, and Augustinian houses were brought under the supervision of the Zurich town council.[86] Within this context, Zwingli's argument takes on added significance. The religious houses' goods had already been turned over to the civic authority. It would seem, then, that Zwingli was concerned with the use of those goods and with the motivation behind that use.

> You should be fathers; fathers do not seek profit at the expense of their children. It truly costs a great deal of labor and toil; but at the end, it brings such great fruits of brotherly love and peace that you will forget all toils.[87]

[84] There has been very little work on Zwingli's humanism, one side of which was his pragmatic involvement in civic charity. The approach to the elements of humanism in Zwingli's thought has been to connect him with Erasmus. See, for example, J. F. Gerhard Goeters, "Zwinglis Werdegang als Erasmianer," in *Reformation und Humanismus, Festschrift for Robert Stupperich* (Witten, 1969), pp. 255–71; Gottfried Locher, "Zwingli und Erasmus," *Zwingliana* 13 (1969–73), 37–61; and Joachim Rogge, *Zwingli und Erasmus* (Stuttgart, 1962). Stayer places Zwingli in the larger context of Swiss humanism, but still identifies him predominantly with Erasmus in "Zwingli Before Zurich." Kurt Maeder's excellent study of Swiss Humanism, *Die Via Media in der Schweizerischen Reformation*, Zürcher Beiträge zur Reformationsgeschichte vol. 2, (Zurich, 1970), unfortunately, does not treat Zwingli specifically, but does place him within the context that Maeder develops in his study.

[85] See Emil Egli, *Aktensammlung zur Geschichte der Zürcher Reformation* (Zurich, 1879; reprint Aalen, 1973) [EAk], nos. 595 and 598. According to Pfister, the Fraumünster, founded in 853, was one of the oldest religious houses in Zurich. A gift from King Louis the German, it was also one of the most noble houses. *Kirchengeschichte der Schweiz*, (Zurich: 1964), vol. 1, p. 92.

[86] EAk, nos. 599, 602–5.

[87] "Ir söllend vätter sin; vätter suochend nit vorteyl gegen iren kinden. Es kost waarlich vil arbeit unnd muoy; es bringt aber zuoletst wol so grosse frucht bruederlicher liebe und frydens, das ir aller muoy ergetzt werdend." *Wer Ursach gebe zu Aufruhr*, p. 459.

Three weeks after *Who is the Source of Sedition* was published, the Poor Law was enacted in Zurich.[88] In the work, Zwingli was addressing the secular powers, the *"Gwaltigen"*; the members of the Zurich town council, the legislators of poor relief, may well have belonged to his intended audience.

> In brief: where Christian hearts and the fear of God are, there will one perform all things honorably, piously, and correctly; for love can do all things and fails no one; for God is love. Where love is, there is God. Where God is, there one may not fail. What is begun with God no one may break. What is erected against him must break. Therefore one should see that the abuse of the tithes will be done away with. And if it is not done with the proper consideration and order, so in time it will happen with vandalism and disorder.[89]

It is appropriate to end a consideration of *Who is the Source of Sedition* with this passage, for nowhere else did Zwingli state more forcefully the foundation upon which the economic structures of the Christian community should be built. On the one hand, Zwingli maintained against the Anabaptists and peasants that tithes should be used for the care of the poor and the maintenance of preaching. On the other, he supported the secular powers' seizure of ecclesiastical property, on the condition that the wealth be applied to the needs of the poor and of the community. In both cases, he held that the highest moral use of wealth was the care of the poor and the relief of communal needs. In the case of the rebellious peasants and the Anabaptists, he argued that motivation in questions of temporal goods should be grounded in Matthew 22:39: "You should love your neighbor as yourself."[90] In the case of the ecclesiastical and lay powers, the motivation should be guided by the sense of responsibility felt by a father, a responsibility the fruit of which is "brotherly love."

Zwingli argued for a certain kind of link between a man and his

---

[88] EAk, no. 619. See Appendix B.

[89] "Kurtz: Wo christenliche hertzen und gotzforcht sind, da wirt man alle ding erberlich, frommklich unnd formklich ansehen; dann die liebe kan 's alles und välet nienen [cf. 1 Cor. 13.7f.]; denn gott ist die liebe [cf. 1 Joh. 4.8.16]. Wo die liebe ist, da ist gott [cf. 1 Joh. 4.16]. Wo gott ist, da mag man nit välen. Was mit gott wirt angehebt, wirt nieman mögen brechen [cf. Act. 5.38f.]. Was wider inn ufgericht wirt, muoss brechen. Darumb sol man sehen, das der missbruch der zehenden hingethon werd. Und tuot man das nit mit rechter betrachtung und ordnung, so beschicht es mit der zyt mit frävel und unordnung." *Wer Ursach gebe zu Aufruhr*, p. 458.

[90] In the end, what divided Zwingli and them was the question: Who is my neighbor?

neighbor and between a community and its poor. In this work he suggested that economic transactions reflected deeper motives. While wealth itself is neither good nor evil, its use is subject to the ethical standards of Matthew 22:39. Although the poor are not the subject of this work, they are its beneficiaries. He forged links between them and the Christian community, stating that their need constituted a proper goal for communal wealth and that they were to be included among all those who were the object of Christian love. Zwingli also implied that the converse is true: a community which used its wealth properly, which cared for its brothers, gave outward expression to its Christianity and evidence of God's presence within it. And: "Where God is, there one may not fail."

The true images of God

This we know well is a godly work. For from now on the goods which have been bestowed upon ornaments of the idols such as these, will be turned, if God wills, to the poor, who are a true image of God (*A Proposition Concerning Images and the Mass*, 1524).[91]

Zwingli returned in three more works to the metaphor first spoken in 1523: once in May 1524 and twice in the spring of 1525. While "A Proposition" was never published – Zwingli may have read it aloud, but he sought no wider audience – the two of 1525 received wide publication. The *Commentary on True and False Religion*, Zwingli's fullest statement of his theology, was published originally in two Latin editions in March, and a year later in German.[92] His *Reply to Valentin Compar*, addressed to the "Alt-Landschreiber" of the forest canton of Uri in defense of the reform in Zurich, was published on April 27, not in the clerical language of Latin, but in the language of town and canton, German.[93] In all three, Zwingli was concerned with the form of the new liturgy

---

[91] "Welchs wir wol wüssend ein götlich werck sin; denn hinfür die guoter, so an sölche zier der götzen gelegt, an die armen, die ein ware bildnus gottes sind, ob gott wil, verwendt werdend." "Vorschlag wegen der Bilder und der Messe," *CR*, vol. 90: *ZSW*, vol. 3, p. 130.

[92] See *CR*, vol. 90: *ZSW*, vol. 3, pp. 625–6. Finsler, *Zwingli Bibliographie*, nos. 45–6. Two other Zwingli texts are derived from *De vera et falsa religione commentarius:* "Von dem nachtmal Christi," and "Action oder Bruch des Nachtmals," (Finsler nos. 47 and 48).

[93] On Compar and the letter from Uri, see Walther Köhler's Introduction to *Eine Antwort, Valentin Compar gegeben*, p. 35.

and the function of images in worship.[94] In all three, he mapped out the nature of Christian culture. In all three, he placed the poor in the context of Christian culture.

Of the three, the *Reply to Compar* treats the subject of the poor most fully. The "Proposition," like *The Shepherd,* touches upon the subject only briefly, in the passage cited above. The *Commentary on True and False Religion,* on the other hand, is linked substantially as well as chronologically to the *Reply.* It preceded the *Reply* by one month in publication and provides the theological and ethical framework within which the arguments of the *Reply* are formulated. The two works are also linked visually: They share in their title page prints the motif of Christ among the poor. Indeed, the *Commentary on True and False Religion* has the same title page border, depicting Christ and his apostles beckoning poor folk and beggars, as *The Shepherd,* recalling visually the words of the earlier work – "the poor are the true images of God" – words that were echoed by the works of 1525. Insofar as the *Commentary on True and False Religion* amplifies and provides a context for the arguments posed in the *Reply,* we shall draw upon it in the following discussion.

The *Reply to Compar* was divided into four sections, each dealing with a facet of Christian culture: the Gospel; traditional interpretations of Scripture, including those of the church fathers; images; and purgatory.[95] Zwingli first touched upon a topic relevant to the poor in his treatment of the Gospel:

> For example: to give alms is undoubtedly a good work. Who gives them, however, without advantage? We all keep the best part for ourselves.... And no one gives gladly solely to honor God and for the good of his neighbor, but out of fear of the devil and of hell, or of God as a tyrant or in order to purchase time or eternity, or out of arrogant unspeakable honor, we give nothing.[96]

---

[94] Zwingli also addressed the issue of the mass, the Eucharist, in each of the works dealing with idolatry. Courtenay touches upon the *mensa Sancti Spiritus,* a table that was set up before the doors of the church to distribute food and other necessities to the poor, in "Token Coinage and the Administration of Poor Relief," (p. 285). There may well be a symbolic connection between the table of the Holy Spirit and the table from which the communion was administered in the Reformed Church. On the relationship between the "repas des pauvres" of the Old Testament and the "repas de charité" of the New, see Adalbert Hamman, *Vie liturgique et vie sociale* (Paris, 1968).

[95] Outlined on p. 48, *Eine Antwort, Valentin Compar gegeben.*

[96] "Byspil: Allmuosen geben ist ein aller ungezwyflestes guots werck. Welcher gibt es aber one vorteil? Wir behaltend uns all weg den besten teil.... Und gibt nieman frölich allein zuo gottes eer und guotem des nechsten, sunder uss vorcht des tüfels und der hellen, oder gottes als eines

It is now possible to understand Zwingli's silence on almsgiving in *Who is the Source of Sedition*. If tithes were paid in opposition to self-interest, almsgiving was motivated by forms of self-interest: fear, greed, the desire for immortality, honor. Indeed, Zwingli argued, almsgiving was never performed for the proper reasons: to honor God and for the good of one's neighbor. The gesture itself was good, but the motivation always self-serving and guided by false values.[97]

It was in the section on images and idolatry that Zwingli spoke of the poor directly and repeatedly:

> Third we lay luxury on them [the images] with silver and gold. . . . What we, however, should give to the needy images of God, to the poor man, we hang on the image of man; for the idols are images of man, but man is an image of God.[98]

The poor were connected to images at a number of levels in the *Reply*. First, Zwingli connected them in one of the traditional criticisms of church art: that art embodied wealth that could be used more ethically to care for the poor.[99] To contrast the opulence of churches with human misery belonged to an ancient line of attack. Bernard of Clairvaux, who was one of the most vehement opponents of ecclesiastical ornamentation, condemned the Clunaic church, which "clothes her stones in gold and leaves her sons naked; the rich man's eye is fed at the expense of the indigent."[100] Nor was this the first time Zwingli himself had expressed this criticism; as we have seen, he challenged church art in the face of

tyrannen, oder das zytlich oder ewig ze erkouffen, oder uss üppiger eer, das man nit könne reden, wir gebend nütz," Ibid., p. 65.

[97] On almsgiving and falsa motivation, see also *De vera et falsa religione commentarius*, CR vol. 90: ZSW vol. 3, pp. 678ff.

[98] "Zum dritten legend wir kosten an sy mit silber und gold. . . . Welchs aber wir den dürfftigen bilden gottes, den armen menschen, geben soltend, so henckend wir 's an des menschen bildnus; denn die götzen sind bildnussen des menschen, aber der mensch ist ein bildnus gottes." *Eine Antwort, Valentin Compar gegeben*, pp. 107–8.

[99] On iconoclastic theology, see Carlos Eire, *The War Against the Idols: The Reformation of Worship from Erasmus to Calvin* (Cambridge, 1985); Margarethe Stirm, *Die Bilderfrage in der Reformation* (Gütersloh, 1977); and Hans Freiherr von Campenhausen, "Die Bilderfrage in der Reformation," *Zeitschrift für Kirchengeschichte* 68 (1957): 96–128. Zwingli reiterated this theme on the same page: "Zum andren wirt hierinn aber gesündet, das an die götzen gelegt wirt, das man an die armen solt gehenckt haben." *Eine Antwort, Valentin Compar gegeben*, p. 108.

[100] "Fulget ecclesia in parietibus, et in pauperibus eget. Suos lapides induit auro, et suos filios nudos deserit. De sumptibus egenorum servitur oculis divitum. Inveniunt curiosi quo delectentur, et non inveniunt miseri quo sustententur." *Apologia ad Guillelmium, Opera omnia*, vol. 1, pt. 1, ed. John Mabillon (Paris, 1839), col. 1,243. The translation is G. G. Coulton's, from *A Medieval Garner*, ed. G. G. Coulton (London, 1910), p. 71.

human suffering during the Second Disputation in *The Shepherd.*[101] And it echoed Zwingli's argument in *Who is the Source of Sedition,* that one moral use of wealth in a Christian community is the care of the poor.

But the connection between the poor and images ran deeper for Zwingli. The poor were not merely the proper objects for the wealth formerly directed to church decoration. They were the "needy images of God"; human, each poor person was "an image of God." This metaphor was not new to Zwingli. Ambrose, Chrysostom, and Naziazanus had made the same connection, the last in a sermon Oecolampad was to edit and translate into Latin in 1519–21.[102] The Franciscan life played upon the paradox between outer destitution and inner sanctity. Yet Zwingli's formulation gave the metaphor a particular resonance; for the people of Zurich, it acquired substance and cultural depth. It refracted central ideas of his theology. And, as we shall see, it encapsulated his notion of Christian culture.

A passage from the *Commentary on True and False Religion* provides a first glimpse of the complex of associations embodied in the metaphor:

> Even if it were commanded nowhere in the Scriptures that so long as statues and images are cherished, they should be destroyed, love would be enough, which certainly admonishes the faithful mind to convert to the use of the needy what is bestowed on the cult of likenesses. For as soon as human reason says: "You will erect this statue in the honor of God or of a certain deity," faith certainly contradicts, saying whatever you wish to expend in the honor of the Lord ought to be converted to the use of the poor. For when Christ said to all his scornful disciples in response to the voice of Judas: "You will always have the poor with you, but me you will not have always, and you can do good to them," he turned all visible cults from himself to the poor.[103]

---

[101] Concerned with wider social and ethical issues, Zwingli's criticism of church art was broader than that expressed by Hätzer, who was present at the Second Disputation, and Carlstadt. Both Hätzer and Carlstadt called for the eradication of church art because man had been forbidden, by God in the Old Testament and by Christ in the New, to fashion images of God. See Ludwig Hätzer, *Ein urteil gottes unsers ee gemahels wie man sich mit allen gotzen und bildnussen halte sol* (Zurich: Christoph Froschauer, 1523), and Andreas Bodenstein von Karlstadt, *Von abtuhung der Bylder* (Wittenberg: Nicholas Schrylentz, 1522).

[102] *De amandis pau//peribus.*

[103] "Quodsi statuas et imagines nusquam scripturarum praeceptum esset, dummodo coluntur, demoliendas esse, satis esset charitas, quae indubie monet, quamlibet fidelem mentem in usum egentium convertere, quod in cultum simulacrorum insumitur. Ut primum enim dicit humana ratio: 'In honorem dei aut divi alicuius hanc statuam eriges,' contradicit nimirum fides, dictans in pauperum usum debere converti, quaecunque in domini velis honorem expendere. Cum enim Christus ad insultantis Iudae vocem discipulis omnibus diceret: 'Pauperes semper habetis

Zwingli asserts that caring for the needy honors God better than erecting statues and supports this assertion with a passage drawn from the Gospels. He has inverted the order of the original scriptural text, however.[104] Mark 14:7, which most closely approximates Zwingli's citation, reads: "For you always have the poor with you, and whenever you will, you can do good to them; but you will not always have me." Elsewhere, in Matthew 26:11 and John 12:8, Christ contrasts his own transience with the permanence of the poor's presence, but the line, "whenever you will, you can do good to them," is not included. These lines had been used traditionally to support the decoration of churches: The poor were a constant, but the unique and momentary existence of Christ was something to be cherished and honored. Zwingli deleted one clause, "whenever you will," and moved another, "you can do good to them," to the end, thereby inverting the meaning of the whole line. By deleting the one, he removed the contingency and voluntarism of the other. By moving the second clause, "you can do good to them," he shifted the emphasis from Christ's transience to the presence of the poor. More subtly, he has altered the nature of Christ's transience: No longer does Christ refer to the historical moment of His existence, but to the passing of His body, the physical and tangible Christ.[105] Zwingli's rendition suggests that Christ is no longer physically present, but the poor are. To them, not to statues, love and faith direct pious Christians to turn "what is bestowed on the cult of likenesses."

> [The images] had to be gilded or totally of silver or of gold or clothed in gold and gemstones, all of which one should have hung on the poor. Yes, all patrons of idols will have to give account to God, that they have let his own images go hungry, freeze, etc. and have so expensively adorned their own idols.[106]

In the *Reply to Valentin Compar,* Zwingli once again compared the poor to the images in the churches, giving the metaphor he had first

---

vobiscum, me autem non semper habebitis, et istis potestis benefacere,' omnem visibilem cultum a se in pauperes derivavit." *De vera et falsa religione commentarius,* p. 900.

[104] This observation is based on a comparison of Zwingli's lines in *De vera et falsa religione commentarius* with the Vulgate, *Biblia Sacra iuxta Vulgatam versionem* (Stuttgart, 1969, 1983) and with Zwingli's Swiss Bible, *Die heilige Schrift* (Stuttgart, 1980).

[105] On Zwingli's Christology, see Gottfried Locher, *Die Theologie Zwinglis im Lichte seiner Christologie* (Zurich, 1952); W.P. Stephens, *The Theology of Huldrych Zwingli* (Oxford, 1986), chap. 4.

[106] "Sy habend muessen vergüldet sin oder gar silbrin oder guldin oder mit gold und edelgstein bekleidt, das man alles solt den armen anghenckt haben. Ja, alle götzenbuwer werdend gott ouch rechnung muessen geben, das sy imm syne bilder habend lassen hungren, früren etc; und habend ire eignen götzen so tür gezieret." *Eine Antwort, Valentin Compar gegeben,* p. 146.

spoken in 1523 dimension and substance. He underlined the humanity of the poor. The allusion to Genesis 1:26–7 became more explicit. The contrast is no longer simply of material such as stone or wood to animate creatures, but of worldly wealth, silver and gold, to men who hunger and freeze. Men, not the stone or gilded idols, are the true images of God. Zwingli drew attention to the divine origin of the poor and reaffirmed the bond they shared with all men.

Earlier in the *Reply*, Zwingli had contrasted the poor to the "images of man." It seems strange that Zwingli chose to describe the poor this way, insofar as their material condition might be said to reflect the wretched spiritual condition of man.[107] Yet, in the definition of human nature that Zwingli presented in the *Commentary on True and False Religion*, it is possible to see why he never equated the material deprivation of the poor with the spiritual poverty of man:

> By nature, therefore, man is a lover of self, not by that nature, with which he had been furnished and provided by God, but by that fate, which God had given him, not content with his own house, he desired to become knowledgeable in good and evil, indeed to become equal with God. Since therefore man becomes accused of self-love, and condemned by this crime, it is manifest, that the death of sin, because it pertains to the mind, is that by which man loves himself continuously, pleases himself, trusts in himself, bears all things received to himself, thinks to see what is straight, what is crooked; and what he himself approves he believes ought to be approved by all, even his creator.[108]

Zwingli's definition of man, while at times adopting the dichotomy of flesh and spirit,[109] centers upon the psychological: Self-love defines human nature and is its essential flaw. Zwingli's understanding of human nature led him, then, to view material poverty (or well-being) as neither revealing nor concealing a man's inner self. Zwingli was far more con-

---

[107] "[Fishacre's analogy] stressed a principle of Augustinian theology – that man is a beggar in regard to the favors bestowed by God." Courtenay, "Token Coinage and the Administration of Poor Relief," p. 279.

[108] "Natura ergo est homo sui amans, non ea natura, qua institutus fuerat praeditusque a deo, sed qua sorte, quam deus dederat, non contentus domi suae voluit boni malique peritus, imo deo aequalis fieri. Amoris ergo suiipsius cum sit reus factus homo, eiusque criminis damnatus, manifestum fit, quod peccati mors, quod ad ingenium adtinet, ea sit, qua se homo perpetuo amat, sibi placet, se fidit, sibi omnia fert accepta, videre putat, quid rectum, quid curvum sit; ac quod ipsi probatur, omnibus probari debere opinatur, etiam creatori suo." *De vera et falsa religione commentarius*, p. 657.

[109] See for example, *De vera et falsa religione commentarius*, p. 709.

cerned with how a man came to poverty: the element of volition. Else-where in the *Commentary on True and False Religion*, Zwingli had attacked the religious vow of poverty precisely because it confused the material life with the inner life – the artificially poor, the monks and mendicants, presumed that the former, which a man could manipulate, affected the latter.[110] For Zwingli, the key distinction was not between rich and poor, but between voluntary and involuntary poverty. The one followed human will, the second, divine will.

Zwingli's definition of human nature has other implications for the poor as well: It bears on relations between men. Zwingli established a series of contrasts in the works considered in this chapter: between self-interest and the care of the poor, between the "images of man" and the "images of God." Each of these contrasts is founded in a deeper op-position, central to Zwingli's thought, between sin and the law. Sin, the essential flaw in human nature, was that same concern with the self, as Zwingli stated in the section on Adam from the *Commentary on True and False Religion*:

> This, then, is the bait, which he longed for, and by which he was captured: to be God, to know himself what is good, what is evil. Yet, where else could this appetite have originated, than love of self? For we all prefer that it be better for us than for others: *philautia* therefore, that is: love of self, was the cause, why Adam acquiesced to the evil counsel of his wife.[111]

Zwingli distinguished the origin of human sin with its Greek name, *philautia*.[112] *Philautia* promotes the self over all others, both brother and father, neighbor and God. It is the wish for "things to be better for us than for others." It generates the illusion of one's own sufficiency, here in the realm of ethics. It culminates in that self-interest, that focus on

---

[110] Ibid., p. 830. On the fifteenth-century Italian humanist rejection of Franciscan poverty, see Hans Baron, "Franciscan Poverty and Civic Wealth as Factors in the Rise of Humanist Thought," *Speculum* 13 (1938): 1–37. Philip Gavitt takes up Baron's argument in "Economy, Charity, and Community in Florence, 1350–1450," in *Aspects of Poverty in Early Modern Europe*, ed. Thomas Riis (Alphen aan den Rijn, 1981), especially p. 82.

[111] "Haec est ergo esca, quam adpetivit, quaque captus est: deum esse, ipsummet scire, quid bonum, quid malum. Veruntamen hic adpetitus unde originem habere potuit, quam ex amore sui? Omnes enim nobis malumus bene esse quam aliis: [philautia] ergo, id est: amor sui, causa fuit, cur malesuadae obtemperaret uxori Adam." *De vera et falsa religione commentarius*, p. 657.

[112] "Sed hic reclamat vetus homo, morbus, caro, Adam, peccatum; nam his fere nominibus vitium hoc [*philautia*] doctrina apostolorum adpellat." Ibid., p. 709.

the self, that excludes God and other.[113] It is the psychological stance most opposed to social ties and pious devotion.[114]

Unrestrained, this self-love would bring plunder, rape, murder, patricide, chaos – destroying all form of social life. To control this self-love, Zwingli argued, the Law was necessary, by which he meant not the laws of town councils, nor custom, but "the eternal will of God."[115] For Zwingli, that Law was stated in Matthew 7:12: "All things, therefore, which you wish men to do to you, you should do to them." He found it again in Romans 13:19, where Paul stated that all laws were gathered in one law: "Love your neighbor as yourself." Those laws that did not fall under this one had been made obsolete by Christ: "'For Christ is the end of the law' Romans 10[:4] and 'the end of the law is love' I Timothy 1[:5]."[116] Christ, as the fulfillment of the Law, and love became one and the same thing. True Christians, therefore, those who live in accord with the Law, were bound to do what love commanded.

For Zwingli, the Law, the basis of all ethics, was no more and no less than, "love your neighbor as yourself."[117] Love is the Law and fulfills it.[118] That love was manifested in the range of human relations. It served to confirm various mutual social obligations: those defined by law, such

---

[113] This is in comparison with Augustine's notion of self-love, for which my source is Oliver O'Donovan, *The Problem of Self-Love in St. Augustine* (New Haven, Conn., 1980). For a description of the broader tradition of thought concerning *caritas* and *amor sui*, I have relied upon the *Dictionnaire de Spiritualité*, ed. Charles Baumgartner (Paris, 1953), vol. 2, pt. 1, pp. 507–600.

[114] "[Die Selbstliebe] ist der bleibende Widerstand, der durch die Verderbnis des Sündenfalls die Natur im Menschen Gott entgegensetzt. Zwingli fasst das Liebegebot der Bergpredigt wieder in seinem ursprünglichen Sinne. Jede selbstsüchtige Regung – damit stellt Zwingli aufs entschiedeneste gegen die Lehre von der *concupiscentia* der Scholastik – ist Sünde and zerstört den Wert einer Handlung." Farner, p. 33.

[115] "Lex nihil aliud est, quam aeterna dei voluntas," *De vera et falsa religione commentarius*, p. 707. For the description of the Law that follows see pp. 707–8.

[116] " 'Omnia ergo, quaecunque vultis, ut faciant vobis homines, et vos facite illis," Ibid., p. 707. " 'Finis enim legis Christus' Rom. 10[.4] et 'finis legis charitas' 1 Tim. 1[.5]," p. 708.

[117] "Der Massstab des Sittlichen ist für Zwingli das Gesetz Christi, dessen Inhalt er in dem Gebot der Gottes– und Nächstenliebe findet. Da durch die Verderbnis seiner Natur dem Menschen die göttliche Vollkommenheit verloren gegangen ist, so ist es ihm nicht mehr möglich, das göttliche Gebot zu erfüllen. Daraus erhellt sich der Zusammenhang mit der Rechtfertigungsehre. Das Gesetz Christi ist dem Menschen von Gott gegeben worden und damit das sittliche Bewusstsein. Denn in Gesetz Christi hat Gott seinen Willen offenbart. Das Gesetz selbst ist der ewige Wille Gottes." Farner, pp. 35–6.

[118] "Fragt man nach dem Inhalt der göttlichen Gerechtigkeit als Forderung an den Einzelnen wie an die gesellschaftlichen Welt, so kann es letztlich nur eine Antwort geben, nämlich, 'Liebe.' " Rich, "Zwingli als socialpolitischer Denker," p. 73.

as subject and ruler;[119] those defined by custom, such as tithes; those defined by guild, by neighborhood, or by friendship. It strengthened the ties of kinship.[120] It brought to those ties a weight, a tenacity, and a greater dimension: Men were bound to one another not by convention, by words, nor by will, but through the imperative of the Law. Brotherly love was not an admonition for Zwingli, but a divine command. In *Who is the Source of Sedition*, Zwingli had used love of neighbor and brotherly love interchangeably; according to the Law, one's neighbor was one's brother. Christians were bound by a tie analogous to familial ties – a tie of love that overcame the self and enabled man to form ties to others, a tie that acknowledged and strengthened social and communal obligations.

In the texts considered in this chapter, Zwingli formulated each of his arguments in terms that reflect the essential opposition between sin and the Law. In *Who is the Source of Sedition*, self-interest opposed that love of neighbor that could not ignore the needs of the poor. In the works of the spring of 1525, worship of man-made idols opposed the active recognition of the needs of human images of God. In each of the works we have seen, Zwingli opposed love of self, self-interest, to the care of the poor. He not only found in the care of the poor one manifestation of love of neighbor, but presented that care as one of perhaps two or three ways to express love of neighbor. For Zwingli, the care of the poor represented a primary counterbalance to love of self. Why?

In order to resolve the opposition between sin and the Law, in order to explain, "how man is free from the Law," Zwingli shifted that opposition to the level of divine action. Man alone could not resolve that opposition; he was an instrument of God, not an agent. It was impossible, therefore, for man alone to love his neighbor, or indeed, to love God; man is defined by his self-love. Unaided, man could not look beyond his own self-interest.[121] God is the sole agent.[122] Man becomes free from the Law through grace alone.

---

[119] Michael Clanchy has studied the ways in which the language of love was used to validate medieval legal and contractual transactions in "Law and Love in the Middle Ages," in *Disputes and Settlements: Law and Human Relations in the West*, ed. John Bossy (Cambridge, 1983), pp. 47–67.

[120] John Bossy, "Blood and Baptism: Kinship, Community, and Christianity in Western Europe from the Fourteenth to the Seventeenth Centuries," in *Sanctity and Secularity: The Church and the World*, ed. D. Baker, Studies in Church History, 10 (Oxford, 1973), 129–43.

[121] *De vera et falsa religione commentarius*, pp. 675ff.

[122] On Zwingli's theocentrism, which he shared with other evangelicals, see Arthur Rich, *Die*

Thus are we made free: He who loves, does all things freely, even the most difficult. God therefore has sent into our hearts the fire, by which he lights love of him in place of love of ourselves; and he desires this fire to burn, Luke 12[:49]. And the Baptist promised this fire, as well as Christ himself going into heaven, Acts 1, which fire is love, and God is love. If this shall burn in us, we shall do all things no longer from compulsion, but freely and joyously. For love is the absolution of the Law. ... Now we are not under the Law, but under grace. And if under grace, the Law therefore cannot condemn.[123]

Zwingli placed love at the center of his theology: The sign of grace is the experience of God's love.[124] Here we see another layer of his notion of "brotherly love." It is the temporal, human manifestation of the experience of God's love and arises from that divine love. Zwingli used the word *charitas* in the Latin text – *"qui ignis charitas est, et deus charitas est"* – to describe the cycle of love between God and man, recalling Augustine's formulation of *caritas* from *agape* and *eros*.[125] God is love; the fire is love; love "admonishes the faithful heart to convert to the use of the needy what is bestowed on the cult of likenesses." Zwingli linked God, man, and the poor through *charitas,* the fire of God's love.[126] Although his formulation was simpler than Augustine's – love of self opposed love of God and neighbor – he returned to the elements originally encompassed by the terms Augustine had used: God's love, love of God, and love of neighbor. Zwingli returned to Augustine, also, in placing the divine "fire" at the center of his idea of *charitas:* The fire of God's love is the source for all those forms of human

---

Anfänge der Theologie Huldrych Zwinglis (Zurich, 1949), pp. 124–51; Stephens, chaps. 3 and 7.
[123] "Sic sumus liberati: Qui amat, libere omnia facit, etiam gravissima. Immisit ergo deus ignem in corda nostra, quo amorem sui pro amore nostri accenderet; et hunc ignem vult ardere, Luc. 12[.49]. Promiseratque hunc ignem et baptista et Christus ipse in coelum abiens, Act. 1[.5], qui ignis charitas est, et deus charitas est [1 Joh. 4.8]. Quae si in nobis ardeat, nihil iam coacte faciemus, sed libere iucundeque omnia. Absolutio enim legis est charitas [Röm. 13.10]. ... Iam non sumus sub lege, sed sub gratia. Quod si sub gratia, non potest ergo damnare lex." *De vera et falsa religione commentarius,* p. 710.
[124] "Vita vero Christiana, quid in universum est, quam charitas?" Ibid., p. 742.
[125] On the place of *caritas* in Augustine's thought, see *Dictionnaire de Spiritualité,* pp. 527ff. See also Anders Nygren, *Agape and Eros,* trans. Philip S. Watson (Chicago, 1982), especially 449–558. *Caritas* was also central to Bernard of Clairvaux's theology, but it was defined much more exclusively in terms of the relationship between man and God; see Bernard's letter to William of St. Thierry, which was published in 1495 by Angelus and Jacobus Britannicus, in Brescia.
[126] This is very similar to Erasmus's understanding of *caritas,* which held a central place in his political thought, Maeder, p. 33.

love that have as their object God or another, either pious devotion or brotherly love.

For Zwingli, the commandment to love God and one's neighbor was the centerpiece of any theological consideration and the basis for all social activity. Zwingli's theology and his social ethics were fused in his reading of Matthew 22:39.[127] Indeed, it bore upon political or civic relations as well,[128] as this passage from the section on the magistracy in the *Commentary on True and False Religion* states:

> Whoever is truly Christian will carry through everything according to [Christ's] character and will. ... If we shall love truly, we shall neglect nothing of theirs, which pertains to the health of our neighbor. If therefore you should add love for one's fellow citizen, it would diminish fraudulent zeal for private things. Since therefore the spirit of Christ has this thing which the state needs most, nothing more auspicious could befall the state than love; when however it carries this gospel with it, it follows that then the state becomes strong and holy in the end, if good minds should be united with good laws. No state, therefore, will be happier, than that in which true religion also dwells.[129]

Zwingli envisioned a true Christian as active, expressing his faith externally, through social and civic engagement.[130] Piety is experienced; it cannot be known through words or study.[131] The relation of faith to outward action is causal and immediate. Faith leads one to concern

---

[127] Many scholars have recognized a relationship between Zwingli's theology and his social ethics. Rother alone, however, has argued that the two are inseparable.

[128] I use "civic" here to refer to the political unit of what Largiader called the city-state. Anton Largiadér, "Die Anfänge des zürcherischen Stadtstaats," in *Festgabe Paul Schweizer* (Zurich, 1922), pp. 1–92.

[129] "Qui vero Christi sunt, iuxta illius ingenium ac voluntatem cuncta transigunt. Is nos amavit, ut se ipsum expenderet pro nobis. Faciemus ergo et nos idem, si eius spiritum habemus. Amabimus itaque omnes homines aeque ac nos ipsos. Si vero amabimus, iam nihil obmittemus eorum, quae ad proximi salutem pertinet. Si ergo civi amorem addas, iam concidet fraudulentum privatae rei studium. Cum itaque Christi spiritus hoc habeat, quo civitas maxime indiget, nihil poterit auspicacius civitati accidere quam amor; hunc autem euangelium qum secum adferat, constat civitatem tunc tandem firmam ac sanctam fieri, si bonis legibus bonae mentes adsocientur. Nulla ergo civitas beatior erit, quam in qua vera religio simul degit." *De vera et falsa religione commentarius*, p. 868.

[130] Rother illuminates an important distinction between Zwingli's view of man as God's instrument and Luther's of man as a vase, pp. 29ff. The one sees man as positive and active, the second, as passive. Zwingli held that man was called to God's work, "um darin die subjectiv-psychologische Bestätigung der Echtheit des Glaubens zu erfahren," p. 32.

[131] "Res enim est ac experimentum pietas, non sermo vel scientia." *De vera et falsa religione commentarius*, p. 705.

oneself with others in all the public forms of human association as well as the private: as neighbor, as townsman or villager, and as citizen. The experience of God's love is also manifested in good citizenship. The civic and the religious, the external and the internal, are linked in each pious Christian. The internal experience of God's love leads a Christian to form ties of community, both social and civic, and to care for the poor.[132]

For Zwingli, there was no visible distinction between the two forms of associative life: the church, "the whole people, the whole multitude gathered together," and the state.[133] The civic and the religious were linked collectively as well as personally.

> We discover that there are not, as these men say, a sacerdotal and a lay magistracy, but only one; for the power of the church, by which it keeps the shameless from communion, is not that of the magistracy [ruling elite], as the bishops have thus far used it; for it belongs to the whole church, not to those, who through tyranny have usurped for themselves the chief part of all things.[134]

Religious authority and civic authority were two forms of human authority; both were separate from sacred or absolute authority.[135] It was unnecessary, Zwingli argued, to have two forms of human authority; they both administered to the same Christian community. For Zwingli, the boundaries of the religious and the political or civic communities were one and the same.

Zwingli placed the Christian call to love one's neighbor firmly within

---

[132] Cf. the view of a fifteenth-century Florentine: "San Bernardino's discussion of usury was founded on a concept of Christian community, an ideal of a city held together by *caritas* and *dilectio fratris*. In this regard, his sense of hope and possibility bordered on the millenarian, with a consciousness of Augustine's distinction between the *civitas terrena*, ruled by avarice, and the *civitas Dei*, held together by charity; the former characterized by love turned inward, the latter by love turned outward. . . . and what held the two in close association was the notion, that the practice of charity not only held off collective damnation, but also courted the continued favor of God," Gavitt, p. 81.

[133] My understanding of this relationship differs strongly from that of Robert Walton, *Zwingli's Theocracy* (Toronto, 1967).

[134] "Invenimus autem, non ut isti dicunt, sacerdotalem et laicalem esse magistratum, sed unum tantum; nam ecclesiae potestas, qua impudentem a communicatione abstinet, magistratus non est, sicut hactenus usi sunt episcopi; nam totius ecclesiae est, non quorundam, qui per tyrannidem sibi rerum summam vendicarunt," *De vera et falsa religione commentarius*, p. 877.

[135] Zwingli presented this argument most fully in *Von göttlicher und menschlicher Gerechtigkeit*. See, for example, Rother, who offers the fullest and most thoughtful treatment, and Wernle, on the precise relationship of civic to religious authority, and of these kinds of authority to divine authority.

the context of the civic community for another reason as well. As his treatment of tithes intimated, he found in this community an effective human counterforce to self-love:[136]

> The state [*civitas*] demands that you care for the public weal, not the private; that dangers be shared in common, as well as fortunes, if practice demands it; that no one be sensible of himself; that no one be extolled; that no one stir up factions.[137]

The civic or political community placed nonpersonal demands on each of its members and offered nonpersonal constraints and protection. For Zwingli, the civic community was best able to supervise and regulate the many facets of its members' lives as those lives touched others, both publicly and privately: their finances, their behavior, their morals, and their religious practices. It was the local, immediate articulation of authority and public life.[138] The civic community could demand the payment of tithes and it could excommunicate – it could address issues not only of the economy of the Christian community, but of piety and ethics. It could reinforce the moral imperative of Matthew 22:39, give impetus and structure to the command to love one's neighbor as oneself.

And the poor were to serve a special function in that community, as a proper object of its resources and as the true images of God. Within the context of Zwingli's theology, they were to serve as one of the most effective counterbalances to human self-love. How, precisely, could they serve as counterpoints to sin? What did the poor represent to Zwingli?

The true images of God and the Christian community

Zwingli had contrasted the poor to the images of man. The "images of man" were those made by man and represented those persons – saints

---

[136] "Finally, Bernardino made explicit reference to the *Civitas Dei* of Augustine, and contrasted its citizens, who overcome self-love, who put selfishness behind them and subordinate it to the good of the community, to userers, whose failure to overcome economic narcissicism not only bars them from eternal blessedness, but endangers the spiritual health of the entire community." Gavitt, p. 111.

[137] "Requirit civitas, ut rem pub*licam* colas, non privatam; ut communia habeantur pericula, etiam fortunae, si usus postulet; ut nemo sibi sapiat; ut nemo extollatur; ut nemo factiones excitet," *De vera et falsa religione commentarius*, p. 867.

[138] The University of Michigan Library and the Beinecke Library at Yale University each possess a sixteenth-century edition of Marsilius of Padua's *Defensor pacis*, which they attribute to Zwingli as editor. Although Zwingli's view of the civic community is more hierarchical than Marsilius's, it draws upon a sense of collective will in its relation to each of its members and in the source of its legitimacy.

– and objects that he found meaningful in his pursuit of the sacred.[139] Designed and executed through human volition,[140] they served the purposes of human self-interest. They manifested self-love and gave form to self-worship. The "images of man" exacerbated the weaknesses inherent in human nature, not only in its psychology but also in its mode of perception:

> for man by his nature falls on the thing that is placed before his senses. Otherwise, why should it be so important whether a man has a representation in which he has honored Him? Thus the images and visible things increase more and more, becoming ever greater and greater with us, until at last man holds them to be themselves holy and begins to seek from them that which should be sought from God alone. For this reason has He forbidden images of God.[141]

According to Zwingli, human perception was anchored in the flesh. The sensible world was more accessible and thus, more attractive, to human nature. People came to seek the sacred in that world, therefore, rather than in the invisible and inaccessible realm of God.[142] Human perception consistently led men to see the divine in the physical, in the world of matter – to confuse the signifier, the image, and the signified, God.[143] The confusion of signifier and signified was one more manifestation of that self-love: Men substituted objects they had made themselves of substances they understood and could manipulate for that which was unintelligible, intangible, invisible, inaccessible, the true Creator.

Idolatry was not the practice of false religion, but the constant human and natural response to any visualization that seemed to enable men to locate and grasp the holy and divine. Men, moreover, attributed to their

---

[139] On the "images of man," see my "The Reform of the Images: New Visualizations of the Christian Community at Zürich," *Archive for Reformation History* 80 (1989): 115–20.

[140] *Eine Antwort, Valentin Compar gegeben*, pp. 107, 110, and 124.

[141] "dann der mensch vallt von natur an die ding, die imm in die empfindnussen gestellt werdend. Sust was solt daran gelegen sin, ob man glych ein bildnuss gehebt, darinn man inn vereret hette? So aber die bilder und sichtbaren ding by uns für und für zuonemend und ye grösser und grösser werdend, biss dass man zuoletst sy für heilig hatt und by inen anhebt suochen, das man allein by dem waren gott suochen sol, so hatt er die bildnussen gottes verbotten." *Eine Antwort, Valentin Compar gegeben*, p. 92.

[142] On Zwingli's refutation of the scholastic distinction between those externals and ceremonials that draw men away from God and other kinds of images, see *Eine Antwort, Valentin Compar gegeben*, pp. 92ff.

[143] Ibid., p. 94. On the terms, "signifier" and "signified," see G. W. Bromiley's Introduction to *Zwingli and Bullinger*, Library of Christian Classics, vol. 24 (Philadelphia, 1953), p. 36.

own images certain capabilities as well, capabilities that served their own interest:

> Thus God forbid the source of it all. Whoever honors the idols, before and after holds them in his heart as gods, that is, as fathers or helpers. For this reason they are idols. For who honors the stone ass in the fish market or the golden hen on the small tower? No one. For what reason? For the reason that man perceives divine help in no ass or hen.[144]

The "images of man" represented man's own visualization of the holy, made by his own hand, to serve him in the pursuit of his own purposes. They were artificial and man-centered. They were perhaps the fullest expression of human sinfulness, that human self-love that has as its object the self to the exclusion of God and other.

Evoking the text of Genesis 1:27 – "So God created man in his own image" – Zwingli reminded his audience that the Bible designated the true image of God: man. In none of the three texts of 1525 did Zwingli engage in exegesis of the lines from Genesis. He was not concerned with the location of God's image in man, whether it was to be found in the soul, in the mind, or in the heart, nor with the nature of divinity within man.[145] He was concerned with the nature of the image itself, what constituted an authentic image of God, and with the community's response to that image.

That image was, first of all, made by God. The poor shared with all men the human form of their creation, as Zwingli had reminded his audience. But Zwingli had designated not all men, but the poor, as the true images of God. Human, they were distinguished by a particular situation, poverty, a situation anchored in a material condition that had social and personal repercussions. The involuntary poor differed from other men in their material deprivation, in their dependency, in the

---

[144] "Also verbüt gott durch das nachvolgend das ursprünglich darumb, das gewüss ist, das welche den götzen eer antuond, vor und ee die imm hertzen für gott, das ist: vätter oder helffer, habind, dero die götzen sind. Denn wer eeret den steininen affen uff dem Fischmerckt oder den guldinen hanen uff dem kleinen türnlin? Wer brennt vor inen kertzen? Nieman. Uss was ursach? Darumb, das man sich zuo gheinem affen oder hanen hilff als zuo eim gott versicht." *Eine Antwort, Valentin Compar gegeben*, p. 106. Zwingli had developed this particular view as early as the First Disputation. See his *Auslegung der 67. Artikeln, CR* vol. 89: *ZSW* vol. 2, pp. 166–222, esp. pp. 217–19.

[145] On the multiple interpretations of Genesis 1:26–7 in patristic texts, see Ladner. On the exegetical tradition and Renaissance humanists' various readings of Genesis 1:26, see Charles Trinkaus, *In Our Image and Likeness*, 2 vols. (Chicago, 1970).

tenuousness of their lives, and in their powerlessness. They gave outward form to divine will in ways that most men did not.

Zwingli contrasted the poor to the "images of man." In challenging his readers and audience to turn from the images of man to the images of God, Zwingli was asking them to turn from their love of self toward that which was a reminder of God. Zwingli did not wish the human poor to become the new idols for men. He was very precise in the distinction between an idol and an image:

> Understand, though, dear Valentin, what we call an idol: an image of a helper or consolation, or that to which honor is done; images [*bilder*], however, we name likenesses of each thing that is visible here, but which is not made into any misleading hope or honored.[146]

The poor are the "likeness" of God, but they are not to be "made into any misleading hope or honored"; they are not to be worshiped like God. To honor the poor, to worship them, would be "abgöttery" for Zwingli, detracting from the sole authority of God.[147] But, then, it was very unlikely that the poor would be honored as the idols had been. If the poor might be recognized as a signifier of God, they could not be mistaken for the grandeur of the thing signified. Indeed, they manifested the absence of all divine attributes: power, splendor, majesty, control.

If the poor were not visualizations of God, then, how might they be "images of God," counterpoints to the "images of man"? Insofar as a man's work identified him with a certain guild, a man's property brought him membership in a village or in a town as a citizen, poverty would deny a man access to these forms of identification and rob him of his communal and social place, as well as his economic function. In this way, a poor man might be outside traditional forms of association.[148] In opposing the poor to self-interest, Zwingli acknowledged a view of the

---

[146] "Verstand aber eigenlich, lieber Valentin, das wir einen götzen heissen: ein bildnus eines helffers oder trosthuffens, oder dero eer wirt angeton; bilder nennend wir aber glychnussen eins yeden dings, das da sichtbar ist, aber zuo gheiner abfuerigen hoffnung nit gemacht, ouch nit vereret wirt." *Eine Antwort, Valentin Compar gegeben*, p. 96.

[147] "Haben sy nun ire hoffnungen in die creaturen, so sind sy abgötter, obglych dieselben creaturen nit abgöt sind; denn was mögend sy dess, das wir trost by inen suochen, den sy uns nit verheissen habend?" Ibid., p. 89.

[148] Richard Trexler has found evidence for late medieval and Renaissance Italy of "poor" who belonged to the wealthier strata of society and has argued that "poverty" was relative to social class. "Charity and the Defense of Urban Elites in the Italian Communes," in *The Rich, the Well Born, and the Powerful*, ed. Frederic Cople Jaher (Urbana: University of Illinois, 1973), pp. 64–109.

poor as that which one was not, as essentially other. The poor, not merely the "living images of God," but the "true images of God," made visible two characteristics of God that were central to Zwingli's theology: His will and His otherness.

In slightly more than a year, between the spring of 1524 and April of 1525, Zwingli published *The Shepherd, Who is the Source of Sedition,* and the *Reply to Valentin Compar,* which were linked by three separate title page prints depicting Christ with poor people, and the *Commentary on True and False Religion,* which shared with the first of the three its title page border. These works also shared with all of Zwingli's works published between 1522 and 1529 the text of Matthew 11:28 – "Come unto me all you who labor and are heavy laden and I will give you rest" – which was printed at the bottom of each title page. In the *Commentary on True and False Religion,* Zwingli himself told his readers how to interpret these words:

> Christ himself, that he might reveal himself totally to us, in Matthew 11[:28] cries thus: "Come to me all you who labor and are burdened, and I shall give you rest." What good God, is it to be generous and bountiful, if this is not? We all are swarming both with internal and with external evils, so that we are weighed down under them just as under some great bulk. The Son of God sees this calamity and calls all to himself. And in order that no one's conscience, mindful of his wickedness, should deter him, because he thinks himself less worthy to flock to him, he indicates clearly: "All, both those who labor, and those who are burdened"; for he had come to bring sinners back to salvation, and to the grace of God.[149]

The words of Matthew 11:28 were printed hundreds, perhaps even thousands of times, and they bore the message of God's benevolence and love.

In the texts of the works, Zwingli spoke of the poor. In the first and

---

[149] "Ille ipse Christus, ut se totum nobis exponeret Matt. 11[.28], sic clamat: 'Venite ad me omnes, qui laboratis et onerati estis, et ego requiem vobis dabo.' Quid bone deus, est liberalem ac largum esse, si hoc non est? Scatemus omnes tum internis tum externis malis, sic ut sub eis non aliter quam sub gravi aliqua mole deprimamur. Videt eam calamitatem dei filius ac omnes simul ad se vocat. Et ne quem sua mens sceleris sibi conscia deterreat, quo sibi minus ad eum concurrere licere putet, diserte loquitur: 'Omnes, et qui laboratis, et qui onerati estis'; ipse enim venerat peccatores salvos reddere, atque adeo gratis." *De vera et falsa religione commentarius,* p. 652.

last works published, he called the poor the "true images of God," and in the second, he linked the poor to the Christian community as its "brothers." Nowhere did he attack the poor, as lazy, as a burden. On the contrary, he referred to them in terms that underlined their humanity and reaffirmed their ties to God. They were linked as brothers to the Christian community and as "images" to God. The community was to strengthen those ties through love of neighbor, a love that had its origins in the experience of God's love and its object in God's "true image."

Perhaps Zwingli, in publishing texts that dealt with the relationship of the community to the poor, with title page prints portraying Christ calling the poor, wished his audience to draw a parallel between the community and God, a parallel based on his notion of Christian love. The Christian community, in reaching out to the poor, through Christian love, at once mirrored God's relation to man and reached out to that which mirrored God.

3

~~~~~~

Images of the poor

In 1524, the "living images of God" were given visual expression. This was, perhaps, the poor's first appearance in the visual culture of Zurich. We do not know, because all of the art in the churches – sculpture, altarpieces, stained glass windows, liturgical objects – was destroyed in 1524. Those descriptions we have of the art that existed in Zurich prior to 1524 do not include representations of poor folk or beggars.[1] Nor do the records speak of plastic or painted representations of those saints known for their concern for the poor, even though one of the oldest altars in the parish church of St. Peter's was dedicated to St. Martin.[2] Zurich's own saints, Felix, Regula, and Exuperantius, were identified by their martyrdom, not charity.[3] It seems that the poor were not a motif in the visual culture of Zurich, as they had been in Basel, where the cathedral presented to passersby the life-size figure of Saint Martin to the right of the main portal and the Works of Mercy framing the St. Gall portal on the north side, and to those who entered, figures of Pauper and Misericordia, carved into the capitals and reliefs decorating the chapels and nave.[4] The invocation to remember the poor, so explicit in Basel, had not been made visible in Zurich.

In Zurich, in the years 1524–6, the poor were depicted in the one form of visual art that not only survived the Reformation, but throve in

---

[1] See, for example, *Die Kunstdenkmäler des Kantons Zürich*, 8 vols., *Kunstdenkmäler der Schweiz* (Basel, 1938ff.); Joseph Ganter, *Kunstgeschichte der Schweiz*, 4 vols. (Frauenfeld, 1936–62); Paul Ganz, *Geschichte der Kunst in der Schweiz* (Basel, 1960); J. Rudolf Rahn, *Geschichte der bildenden Künste in der Schweiz* (Zurich, 1876); or W. Wartmann, *Gemälde und Skulpturen, 1430–1530* (Zurich, 1921), and *Tafelbilder des XV. und XVI. Jahrhunderts* (Zurich, 1922).
[2] K. Furrer, *Geschichte der Kirche und Gemeinde St. Peter Zürich* (Zurich, 1906), p. 19.
[3] Headless representations of them were scattered throughout the canton.
[4] On the Basler Münster, see, for example, *Basler Münster*, compiled by Dietmar Hund, text by Hanns U. Christen (Basel, 1971).

it: the printed image. This form, which preceded the Reformation – illustrated Bibles and devotional literature had been available in the vernacular since the 1490s – acquired a prominence in the visual culture of reformed communities.[5] Paintings and sculpture were removed from the churches in many centers of reform, diminishing the variety and number of forms in which religious culture was visually articulated. At the same time, printing presses were producing thousands of religious images in Bibles, pamphlets, and broadsides, multiplying and disseminating one particular form of Christianity's visual culture. Among the visual media of the Reformation, printed images predominated.

The ways in which printed images differed from the images in the churches were key to their efficacy as cultural media. Printed images could travel as the images in the churches could not. They could reach rural villagers whose churches were less visually rich, as well as urban parishioners who attended only their own local church. Portable, these images could enter shopkeepers' households, spinning rooms, and workshops, carrying representations of Christ or biblical narratives to the workplace and home. Mobile, these images would not be enshrined.

So, too, printed images were less costly to produce and purchase. Woodcuts involved little expense. Produced from a block of wood, quickly carved, and impressed on paper, a material in abundant supply, a woodcut could be printed as many as three to four thousand times.[6] Engravings involved slightly more expense initially; the image was engraved on a copper or metal alloy and required more care on the part of the engraver. Once the metal plate was prepared, however, the process was much the same.[7] Cheaply produced, printed images were affordable to new kinds of consumers: well-to-do peasants, shoemakers, weavers.

Perhaps the attribute that most distinguished printed images was their uniformity. Images in the churches might reach 4,000 pairs of eyes, if

---

[5] On the production and consumption of illustrated books in general, and the lay reception of illustrated Bibles, see Miriam Chrisman, *Lay Culture, Learned Culture* (New Haven, Conn., 1982).

[6] On woodcuts, see A. M. Hind, *Introduction to the History of Woodcut* (New York, 1963); Max Geisberg, *The German Single-Leaf Woodcut, 1500–1550*, revised and edited by Walter L. Strauss, 4 vols. (New York, 1974); and Campbell Dodgson, *Catalogue of Early German and Flemish Woodcuts in the British Museum*, 2 vols. (London, 1902, 1911). Antony Griffiths treats both woodcuts and engravings in *Prints and Printmaking; An Introduction to the History and Techniques* (New York, 1980).

[7] On engraving, the classic work is Max Lehrs, *Geschichte und kritischer Katalog des deutschen, niederländischen und französischen Kupferstichs im 15. Jahrhundert*, 10 vols. (Vienna, 1908–34). See also Griffiths.

those eyes entered the church – they were dependent on the mobility of their viewers, and that dependence created a certain kind of viewership, one that differed from locus to locus. A single printed image, on the other hand, could reach viewers in 4,000 places – viewers in different parishes, different localities – linking those locations by a single uniform image and forming thereby a very different kind of viewership.

Printed images were accessible in ways that church art could not be. Commissioned by a publisher, they were not the property of a private donor. Affordable to a greater range of consumers, they altered the demographics of private viewing: Artisans, peasants and laborers could look upon images of Christ in their homes or workshops. Mobile and inexpensive, printed images were able to reach precisely those viewers to whom they alone might speak: the semiliterate and illiterate, rural populations, those parts of urban populations who lived on the margins of town life – all who had little or no access to the culture of a community.

And printed images lacked that physical characteristic of church art that most offended iconoclasts: sumptuousness. Printed images lacked the blues, the crimsons, the gold. They did not embody wealth themselves, nor did they manifest the wealth of a donor or patron. They were not public statements of status or hierarchy, but mobile and transitory representations. Visible, they were not sensual: They would not be mistaken for that which they represented. Like the poor, these signifiers would not be confused with what was signified.

Most printed images in the Reformation appeared in tandem with printed texts.[8] Linked to words on a page, they shared certain characteristics with them. Like printed words, they could be reproduced thousands of times. Like them, these images were produced in black and white. And like words, they were "legible." Yet, these common characteristics should not obscure the images' independence from words. Printed images belonged to a different cultural language, one that often appeared with written language, but that drew upon its own corpus, of visual terms, for etymologies, analogies, associated meanings. Images printed with texts "illustrated" those texts not only by giving shape and form to words, but also by bringing to them analogies from a different tradition.

---

[8] According to S. H. Steinberg, the title page illustration was first added by printers, in the fifteenth century, *Five Hundred Years of Printing* (Harmonsworth, 1974), p. 22.

Printed images were as visually complex as their painted and plastic counterparts, their content, as allusive. If printed images lacked the sumptuousness of altarpieces and devotional objects, they nonetheless presented the same pivotal figures to the eyes of their viewers: Christ, the apostles, Old Testament prophets. If they no longer represented other figures, in particular the saints, they offered their viewers new images of equal complexity: the Godly Mill, the Vineyard, the Sheepfold, the Totenfresser.[9] In content, printed images frequently drew upon the same visual vocabulary as paintings and illuminations. In content, they presented to the eyes of their viewers images of many referents and allusions.

Nor should their size mislead us as to their importance. Printed images belonged to a visual culture in which detail was often significant, as in the landscapes and rooms of Flemish paintings,[10] and in which devotional images, the focus for pious contemplation, were palm-sized, in order to be portable.[11] Printed images appeared before eyes trained and accustomed to a different scale and a different distribution of meaning.

Printed images were the visual medium of the Reformation. Central themes of the reformers were given visual expression in woodcuts and engravings. Illustrated vernacular Bibles made the Gospel visible as well as audible to evangelical congregations.[12] Old Testament heroes, Moses and Abraham, David and Judith, acquired faces to accompany their voices; their stories had line and shape. Reformers' likenesses appeared in print: Luther, in particular, was represented in a number of striking images.[13] In Zurich, Christoph Froschauer published images of the new communion, showing the unadorned table, the common bread, and the community of participants (Figures 2 and 3). The simplicity of Zwingli's Eucharist was given form and definition. The reformed culture of evangelical Christianity was visualized in printed images. Woodcuts and engravings spread to thousands of eyes representations of its preachers, illustrations of its Bibles, and visualizations of its new liturgy.

[9] Some of these have been explored in Robert W. Scribner, *For the Sake of Simple Folk; Popular Propaganda for the German Reformation*, Cambridge Studies in Oral and Literate Culture, vol. 2 (Cambridge, 1981).

[10] Svetlana Alpers, *The Art of Describing; Dutch Art in the Seventeenth Century* (Chicago, 1983).

[11] A. Spamer, *Das kleine Andachtsbild vom 14.–20. Jahrhundert* (Munich, 1930).

[12] Illustrated Bibles existed before the Reformation, although they proliferated under its aegis.

[13] Scribner, chap. 2.

Figure 2 Zurich: Christoph Froschauer, 1525
Zentralbibliothek Zurich

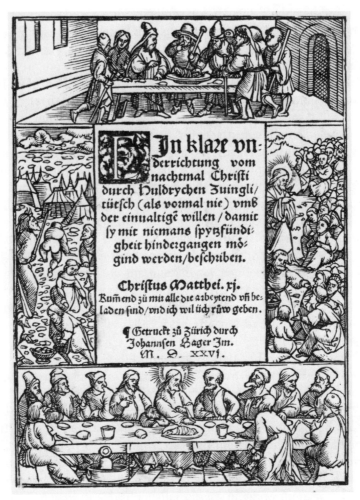

Figure 3: Zurich: Hans Hager, February 23, 1526
Zentralbibliothek Zurich

In Zurich, printed images appeared at a time when the visual culture of the town was undergoing a dramatic transformation. Reform called into question the nature of Christian culture, and in particular, its visual expression. The visual culture of Christianity was challenged, certain of its forms, destroyed or abandoned. Much of Zurich's religious culture had been visually silenced by 1524; printed images were one of the very few, if not the only, forms to survive. Printed images thus survived in a visual culture markedly different from that of five years earlier. Of the three prints we shall be considering, two appeared after the Zurich churches had been "cleansed" of their images. They appeared in a kind of visual silence: the walls of the churches had been painted white. At once under intense scrutiny and solitary, the visual language of the images, the terms they employed, was perhaps all the more striking to the eyes of sixteenth-century Zurich.

The poor were represented in three printed images that appeared on the title pages of a number of Zwingli's works. The images first appeared on three of the texts treated in the Chapter 1. The first to appear was an engraved border (Figure 4), which was published on the title page of *The Shepherd*, on March 26, 1524.[14] The second was a woodcut (Figure 5), first published on the title page of *Who is the Source of Sedition*, on December 28, 1524. The third, also a woodcut (Figure 6), was first published on April 27, 1525 on the title page of the *Reply to Valentin Compar.*

We have no words from their contemporaries to guide us as to the intended meaning of these prints: no record of their creators, no statement by their designers, no notes from their publishers. Scholars have been unable to uncover the identities of the designers and the woodcarvers of the two woodcuts. The style of the engraving suggests that Hans Holbein designed it, and the monogrammist C.V. engraved it.[15] But the verbal silence is pervasive for all three images: We do not even know to what extent the publishers, Christoph Froschauer and Hans Hager, participated in the selection of the design.

This silence is all the more intriguing because the three images are so striking. The plane of the picture in each is dominated by representations of Christ and beggars; their combined presence makes the images distinctive and important. The three images may well have startled their viewers as well with the disjunction between text and image: None of the three is a standard illustration of its respective title. The engraving appears on a work, *The Shepherd*, for which there was an established and popular tradition of representing Christ literally as a shepherd.[16]

---

[14] It was published again on the title page of Froschauer's 1525 edition of the New Testament and in March 1525, of Zwingli's *De vera et falsa religione commentarius.*
[15] *Zürcher Kunst nach der Reformation: Hans Asper und seine Zeit,* Exhibition Catalogue (Zurich, 1981), p. 144.
[16] Hans Sebald Beham published an image of Christ in a sheep shed, ca. 1524, which was copied

Figure 4: Zurich: Christoph Froschauer, March 26, 1524
Zentralbibliothek Zurich

Welche ursach gebind ze ufzûren / welches die waren

vfrûrer sygind / vnd wie man zû Cristlicher einigheit vnd fryden komen môge / durch Huld= rych Zuinglin zû Zürich.zc.

Lifz bis ans End vnd ermifz

nit allein wie ruch / funder wie waar es fye.

Christus Matth. xi.

Kument zû mir alle die arbeytend vnd beladen sind / vnd ich wil üch rûw geben.

Figure 5: Zurich: Christoph Froschauer, December 28, 1524
Zentralbibliothek Zurich

In Antwurt Huldrychen
Zuinglis Valentino Compar alten Landt
schrybern zu Vre ggeben über die, iiij. artickel. Die er jm vß sinen schlußreden angetastet hatt.

Vom Euangelio was es sye.

Von den lereren wie vil inen ze glouben sye.

Von den bilden vnnd wie an denen die
schirmer vnd stürmer mißlerend.

Vom Fägfhür/Das gheins sin mag.

Christus Mathei. xj.
Rumend zu mir alle die arbeytend vnd bladen
sind/vnd ich wil üch rüw geben.

Figure 6: Zurich: Hans Hager, April 27, 1525
Zentralbibliothek Zurich

Instead, a border containing allegorical elements and Christ calling poor folk to Him confronts the viewer. Woodcut I (see Figure 5) was published on the title page of a work, *Who is the Source of Sedition,* concerned with rebellion and popular reactions to economic and political injustices. Reformation prints had established a genre of images of rebellion,[17] yet this woodcut does not draw upon them, offering instead what would seem to be an image of reconciliation. Finally, the woodcut for the *Reply to Valentin Compar* neither is a portrait of Compar, nor does it seem to be an illustration of the text's central themes: the nature of the mass and Eucharist and the function of images.[18]

If we are to discover the message of the three title-page prints, then, we must learn how to "read" the images as their contemporaries did,[19] without aid of verbal statements of intention or design; we must become visually literate. The following is an exercise in that process. It seeks to distinguish the visual terms of the images through isolating them verbally – to analyze the prints' own language, the language of visual signs, through another, and in many ways, alien language, the verbal language of description.[20] That description enables us, however, to reconstruct, albeit artificially and schematically, the meaning of each image's text: to designate its particular vocabulary of visual terms; to delineate the syntax of the image, the relationships it depicts among the visual terms; and to trace analogies of figure and gesture. In all three, specific terms, the figures of Christ and the poor folk, dominate the plane of the picture. They are the focus of the following investigation. Their meaning, however, is mediated

by Master H. S. (now in Berlin, Kupferstichkabinett). For the history of the image of Christ as shepherd, see *Lexikon der christlichen Ikonographie,* ed. Engelbert Kirschbaum (Rome, 1968), vol. 2, pp. 289–99; Anton Legner, *Der gute Hirt* (Dusseldorf, 1959). The metaphor of the good shepherd was very important in Reformation propaganda. On the use of the image of the good shepherd in Reformation art, see Scribner, pp. 50–7.

[17] For examples of images of violence and resistance, see the many title page illustrations to the Twelve Articles and other literature arising in the Peasants' War, many of which appear in A. Laube, Max Steinmetz, and Günther Vogler, *Illustrierte Geschichte der deutschen frühbürgerlichen Revolution* (Berlin, 1974).

[18] Zwingli's texts, *Action oder Bruch des Nachtmals* (April 1525), and *Eine klare Unterrichtung vom Nachtmal Christi* (1526), have illustrations of the last supper and, in the case of the latter, of the dividing of the loaves and the rain of manna from heaven. (See Figures 2 and 3)

[19] On sixteenth-century "semiotics," see Scribner, p. 249.

[20] The problematic relation of verbal language to visual images has been the subject of much discussion among art historians recently. See Michael Baxandall, *Patterns of Intention* (New Haven, Conn., 1987); and Norman Bryson, *Word and Image* (Cambridge, 1981), especially chap. 1.

through a range of visual clues: other objects and figures in the plane of the prints that bring their own connotations to the images; the spatial arrangement of Christ and the poor folk, in relation both to other figures present in the images and to one another; their gestures, the language of the position of their bodies; each of which alludes to other traditions of visual representation.

Figure 4: The engraving

The engraving is organized in the format of a frame. It is possible to divide the frame structurally into four panels: upper, left, right, and lower. In the upper panel, a female figure, possibly a nymph, and a satyr crouch on either side of a fountain. The left panel contains instruments of war: a sheathed sword in front of a shield; a helmet; a suit of sixteenth-century armor; a long sword, running through the suit of armor; and, at the base, a crossbow and another shield. The helmet seems to be an imperial helmet and the long sword a noble's weapon. This panel might refer to the specifically Swiss issue of mercenary soldiers. The right panel contains musical instruments; a mandolin, a wind instrument, and a lute are the most prominent. All three panels contain elements found on the title pages of humanists' writings. The two side panels may well represent the instruments of war and of peace.

The lower panel does not consist of the allegorical forms found in the other three sides, but in what might be called a narrative presentation. As the movement seems to be from the right to the left, let us begin with the right corner, moving toward the left, and highlight those figures that are most prominent. The first figure we can distinguish is a man in a full-length tunic or robe, facing away from the viewer. He is carrying a tau, or Old Testament, cross.[21] Above this cross are other, identical crosses. Next to this man is a second full-length figure. This man, too, is wearing a long robe like the first, and faces forward, to the center of the panel. We can see, therefore, that his face is bearded, and that he wears a stocking cap, like those worn by artisans. A crutch runs the length of his body on the side of the viewer, and the second crutch is visible behind a beggar: he is a cripple. To the left of this figure we can distinguish two more full-length figures. The first of these figures, who

---

[21] George Ferguson, *Signs and Symbols in Christian Art* (Oxford, 1977), p. 165.

is also the most in the foreground, is a beggar; he is defined by his tattered clothes, his wrapped and crippled leg, and his pouch.[22] He seems to be moving: his leg and arm are raised in the gesture of a runner; even the muscle in his leg is defined. The leftmost figure on the right shares with the beggar a gesture implying motion, arm outstretched, leg forward, but is clad in clothes of no particular association. Like the beggar, he is bearded. At the center, in the background, is a city set against mountains. The central structure, a round, two-tiered tower, suggests that this might be a representation of Jerusalem.[23] The first figure we encounter on the left side is Christ. He faces the group on the right. His arms are outstretched, a gesture suggesting not motion, as with the two figures on the right, but with palms open, in a gesture of calling. The positioning of His body reinforces this impression, with the right leg extended and the weight of the body shifted back onto the left leg. The figure of Christ is also slightly larger than the others. Christ is separated from the rest of the group on the left by a space, which may reinforce His centrality in the image or may signify the holiness that distinguishes Him. Behind Christ, four figures who can be clearly distinguished are grouped together. Three of the four can be seen in full length. They face one another, not outward, not toward Christ, and seem to be speaking among themselves. Their long hair and robes suggest that they are apostles. We can see one face among them; he is clean-shaven, perhaps St. John.

Figure 5: Woodcut I

The first of the two woodcuts resembles the bottom panel of the engraving, both in the organization of figures, and in the kinds of people represented. What is perhaps most striking about this woodcut is the individuality of the faces and figures. The placement of the groups is exactly the reverse of that in the engraving. Let us proceed from the figures of the poor to Christ again, but this time we shall move from

---

[22] See Elisabeth Südeck, *Bettlerdarstellungen vom Ende des 15. Jahrhunderts bis zu Rembrandt* (Strasbourg, 1931), p. 10. Also, Theodor Hampe, *Fahrende Leute in der deutschen Vergangenheit*, Monographien zur deutschen Kulturgeschichte (Leipzig, 1902), pp. 82–8. The pilgrim's pouch looked very much like the beggar's; both were used to hold alms, and both were identifying features of their bearers.

[23] On the vision of the city of Jerusalem and the parallels drawn in Reformation art, see Philipp Schmidt, *Die Illustration der Lutherbibel* (Basel, 1962), p. 127.

left to right. In the foreground on the left is a cripple who appears to be dragging his legs. Dressed in rags to his waist and shirtless, he is also poor. His face is turned upward, to Christ. Behind him is a series of three figures. To the far left is a man with a long beard. Like the cripple in the engraving, he is dressed in a long gown, and his crutches are very much evident. He, too, looks at Christ and appears to move toward him. The second figure is also a cripple, with one leg on a brace, and poor. His clothes are tattered and he wears the beggar's pouch. The third of these figures is set slightly apart from the rest. Although barefoot, he does not seem to be destitute: his tunic is untorn. In the woodcut, he has reached Christ. He seems to be still in motion: his left leg is extended. He has drawn near, though, for he almost touches Christ with his extended hands, and Christ's right hand rests on his shoulder. A number of heads are behind these figures. We can distinguish four: three women and a man. At the center of the woodcut, in the background, is a city, this time set quite clearly in the mountains. Again, we find a round tower of two tiers, which is unlike any building in Zurich at that time. A gate tower serves as the entrance to this city, however, a tower very much like those found in medieval walled cities. There is a church, moreover, which resembles the fifteenth and six-teenth-century chapels, of which the Fraumünster in Zurich was one. Christ, who is the first figure in the group on the right, is separated from them by the placement of His head and by His halo. He also seems to be taller than the rest. He faces the group on the left, arms out-stretched. His knees are bent: His torso becomes a curve welcoming those before Him. Behind Christ's back we can distinguish two more full-length figures and two faces.[24] The two full-length figures are talking to one another; again, like the engraving, the one whose face we can see is beardless. They, too, are dressed in the simple robes of the apostles.[25]

The first two images contain elements that do not appear in the third: the group of figures behind Christ who are speaking together. There is

---

[24] The face closest to Christ on the right is very similar to portraits of Zwingli that we have, especially in the line of the forehead and the shading of the jaw.

[25] This is not to suggest that the entire group is apostles. Two heads which can be distinguished, are wearing hats of sixteenth-century design, the one above the two figures, possibly a cardinal's hat.

no place in Scripture where the three elements, Christ, poor people, and some of His disciples, are specifically brought together. One instance, however, offers suggestive parallels – Christ with the children.[26]

> And they were bringing children to him, that he might touch them; and the disciples rebuked them. But when Christ saw it he was indignant, and said to them, "Let the children come to me, do not hinder them; for to such belongs the kingdom of God. Truly, I say to you, whoever does not receive the kingdom of God like a child shall not enter it." And he took them in his arms and blessed them, laying his hands upon them (Mark 10:14–16).[27]

This parallel did exist in the visual tradition as well. A woodcut by Anton Woensam of Worms presents Christ blessing the children, who surround him (Figure 7).[28] To the extreme left in the picture is a beggar, who is also included in the blessing. The parallel is strengthened by Christ's gesture in the title page prints: He extends His hand in what appears to be a blessing.

Figure 6: Woodcut II

The third image differs from the other two in the arrangement of its visual terms and, as we shall see, in what it signifies. If movement is suggested in the first two prints – one figure approaching another – then the third is an image of stasis. Again, Christ stands at center, but He faces outward, looking neither at any figure within the picture, nor at us. His right hand is raised, perhaps in blessing, perhaps suggesting the wounds of the Passion.[29] The planes of Christ's figure – head, torso, legs – form an S curve, reminiscent of the Gothic formal rendition of a standing figure. It is a form, also, which contrasts with and brings attention to the cross Christ is holding. No longer the tau cross, this is

---

[26] I would like to thank Dr. Christianne Anderssen for suggesting this connection to me. For an excellent study of Lutheran treatment of this topos, see Christine O. Kibish, "Lucas Cranach's Christ Blessing the Children: A Problem of Lutheran Iconography," *Art Bulletin* 37 (1955): 196–203.

[27] Also Matthew 19:13–15 and Luke 18:15–17. My own biblical quotations are drawn from *The New Oxford Annotated Bible*, Revised Standard Edition.

[28] "Jesus Christ faisant approcher de lui les petits enfants," (112 × 139 mm), Graphische Sammlung, Albertina, Vienna. Reference: Adam von Bartsch, *The Illustrated Bartsch*, ed. Walter L. Strauss (New York, 1978ff.), vol. 13, p. 194.

[29] The copy of this woodcut in the Photographic Files of the Warburg Institute, London, is labeled "The Resurrection."

Figure 7: Anton Woensam von Worms, *Christ Lets the Little Children
Come to Him*
Graphische Sammlung, Albertina, Vienna

the cross of the Passion and the symbol of the Christian church.[30] The
cross divides the plane of the picture in this print. It is the largest of all
the crosses, rising above them. Christ has turned from the other figures
in the picture, turned His back to them; His figure no longer expresses
a direct relationship with them. He does not lead one group which meets
a second, but is encircled, enclosed, by figures.

Although two-thirds of the entire frame consist of figures with crosses,
only eight are distinguishable. These eight, however, have distinctive
features and individual faces. Because each figure's placement in relation

[30] Ferguson, pp. 164–5.

to Christ has symbolic value, let us divide the figures accordingly. To Christ's right (our left), are four figures who are in various stages of rising to stand with their crosses. At the lowest point of the spiral of figures, at Christ's feet, a man on his hands and knees grasps a cross, which lays on the ground between Christ's feet. He looks down, at the cross. The cross of the next man rises from his shoulder. This second man kneels. He wears the long robes of a cleric and a beard, perhaps of a hermit. He looks up, at Christ. Following the spiral, we arrive at a figure of a beggar, or perhaps poor cripple, for he has no pouch. His amputated leg can be seen below the transcept of the second man's cross. He is clothed in rags, and his hair and beard are thin. He stands, with his cross resting on his shoulder. He points with his free hand to Christ. Next to him stands the same sort of figure as we have seen in the other two prints: dressed in a simple tunic, with a short, clipped beard. Perhaps his face would have been recognized by Zurich viewers, perhaps he represents Blickle's "common man."[31] Perhaps, too, he represents St. Peter, an antipapal Peter, who has lost his singular authority and become just another member of the Christian community.[32] He neither touches nor moves toward Christ, but stands behind Him, looking at Him; he is static and passive.

A second spiral begins on Christ's left and our right. These people are better dressed than those on Christ's other side. At Christ's feet is another man on his hands and knees. We can see his clothing clearly: He wears the tunic, hose, and shoes of a successful artisan. His hands are on the transcept of a cross; he looks up at Christ, but not at His face. Again, we can follow a cross from this figure's shoulder to the next figure, another bearded man. He is dressed in robes and a cap such as can be found in portraits of Konrad Pellikan, Leo Jud, or Erasmus. He stands, bearing his cross over his shoulder. With his right hand he gestures with open palm, toward Christ. Finally, immediately to Christ's left stands a woman, whose collar and wimpel suggest that she is a

---

[31] There is a growing literature on the "common man" in sixteenth-century Europe. See Peter Blickle, *The Revolution of 1525*, trans. Thomas A. Brady, Jr. and H. C. Erik Midelfort (Baltimore, 1981), especially chap. 7; and Robert Lutz, *Wer war der gemeine Mann?* (Vienna, 1979).

[32] Such a representation of Peter would coincide with Zwingli's increasingly antipapal position. See James M. Stayer, "Zwingli before Zurich: Humanist Reformer and Papal Partisan," *Archive for Reformation History* 72 (1981): 55–68. Representations of this face appeared in the Zurich Bible of 1531. See, also, the representation of St. Peter on the title page to Thomas Stör, *Von dem Christlichen Weingarten* (Zwickau, 1524), which looks very much like the figure in the Zurich prints.

townswoman, and whose cross is barely visible over her right shoulder. She does not look at Christ, but toward the bearded man. Is he distracting her? Is he preaching the Gospel to her? Let us see what we can learn from the visual terms about these figures and their collective meaning.

The visual and scriptural traditions

These long descriptions enable us to separate the individual terms of visual language of the prints, to note particular allusions, to the controversy over mercenary service or to the Protestant view of Peter's relation to Christ, and to place the central figures within a matrix of both physical and hermeneutic associations. The figures at dramatic center in all three prints, Christ and poor and common folk, acquire dimension in relation to these other figures. Christ is represented as reaching out to one group among those depicted: not His disciples, not those designated with theologians' caps, but the crippled, the maimed, and the ragged. The meaning of that gesture, the nature of the relationship between Christ and the poor, is the subject of the following section.

I have stated that the three prints are distinctive, by which I mean that in their composition and content they do not directly correspond to a body of images, a genre of pictures; they are not immediately similar, "identical," to other representations. That distinctiveness makes them more significant as cultural statements; unfamiliar, they probably caught the eyes of their viewers all the more effectively. That distinctiveness also makes the work of the interpreter more difficult: if the whole belongs to no clear visual tradition for which there is an established verbal explanation,[33] then analysis must pursue the components, the words and syntax, of the images: figures, gestures, the relationships between figures. The following investigation rests upon the belief that those components function in ways similar to the elements of verbal language: analogous to nouns, figures remind their viewers of other contexts in which the same figures have appeared; analogous to verbs, gestures delineate specific relationships between figures.

Nor are the Zurich prints a new evangelical visualization of a specific text from Scripture. In no place does a verbal description exist for which

---

[33] Baxandall, Introduction.

the prints might be a visual representation. Christ and His apostles do not meet specifically with a group of poor or common folk, nor does Christ appear in the company of many people bearing crosses. Georg Finsler assumes that the prints are no more than a representation of the passage that Zwingli used as his motto, Matthew 11:28: "Come to me all you who labor and are burdened and I will give you rest."[34] This passage, however, appeared on all the title pages for Zwingli's works between 1522 and 1529, with a wide variety of images beyond the three under discussion here.[35] The passage from Matthew, moreover, makes no specific reference to beggars or poor folk, although it invokes a way of life very much like that of those marginal poor Maschke described.

If the larger grouping of figures, of Christ, some of His apostles, and the poor, belongs to neither a scriptural nor a visual tradition, it seems as though the central and smaller grouping of beggars or poor men and Christ might. In fact, beggars rarely appear in the New Testament, either as witnesses to Christ or as subjects in His parables, and only once is a beggar the focus of the narrative: the parable of Lazarus.[36] Even in this story, Abraham, not Christ, embraces Lazarus. And the visual representations of the parable followed the text; Christ is absent from the narrative center.

The implications of the story, however, do bear on the title-page prints. Lazarus's poverty is central to his salvation. Conversely, the rich man's wealth contributes most immediately to the loss of his soul. The story has as its basis the inequality of wealth in society, and as its theme, the contrast between material wealth and spiritual riches. Lazarus became a powerful image in the visual vocabulary of reformation prints. In a Lutheran broadsheet of 1556,[37] for example, Martin Luther is presented as Lazarus, signaled by the straw upon which he sits, by the dogs licking his wounds, and by his placement outside the feast of the rich man.[38] The rich man, as designated by his dress, is the Pope, and

---

[34] "Kummend zu mir alle die arbeytend und beladen sind und ich wil üch ruow geben." Georg Finsler, *Zwingli Bibliographie* (reprinted Nieuwkoop, 1968), nos. 25, 42, and 49.

[35] For instance, with Christ as the Man of Sorrows, first printed in 1522 with the text, "Von Erkeisen und Freiheit der Speisen," and with three different representations of the Eucharist in 1525–6.

[36] Luke 16:19–31.

[37] Reprinted in Ralph E. Shikes, *The Indignant Eye; The Artist as Social Critic* (Boston, 1976[1969]), p. 17.

[38] "And at [the rich man's] gate there lay a poor man called Lazarus, full of sores, who desired to be fed with what fell from the rich man's table; moreover, the dogs came and licked his sores." Luke 16:20–1.

the friends who attend the feast are various cardinals, clerics, monks, and nuns.[39] Following the analogy, the Pope, who manifests material wealth and leaves "Lazarus" to starve, is destined to hell; he is spiritually poor. Luther, conversely, receives Lazarus's attributes; though persecuted in the present life, he is destined for the arms of Abraham. Of the two, he is the one loved by Christ.

Visual representations of the parable of Lazarus centered upon the disjunction between material wealth and true piety. Although the three Zurich images are not express presentations of the parable of Lazarus, they are not entirely divorced from it. The figure of Lazarus, as the beggar who was saved, whose piety was authentic and justified, is the most striking representation of a beggar in the New Testament. In the three images, a beggar appears with Christ in a specific relationship and receives a certain importance from that relationship. Like Lazarus, he is about to be embraced; unlike Lazarus, it is Christ Himself, not Abraham, who is to embrace him. That disjunction was dramatized in 1529, when the people of Zurich had Lazarus before their eyes in a play, "A True History from the Holy Gospel of Luke, Chapter XVI, on the Rich Man and Poor Lazarus."[40]

Another image in which Christ appeared with poor people and beggars supports this connection between the three prints and the Lazarus story: Lucas Cranach the Elder's woodcut, from the *Passional Christi und Antichristi* (Figure 8).[41] It suggests another way in which poor folk and beggars might function in relation to Christ. Christ is encircled by cripples, poor and common people, as well as Peter and other apostles. Yet Christ, whose hands are formed in prayer, looks upward; He is not involved with those around Him. The woodcut opposite this one sharpens the intended meaning (Figure 9). The Pope observes a battle between armed knights; he "thinks it beneath his honor to humble himself."[42] The issue in the Cranach woodcuts is not the poor; it is the contrast between the power and ambition of the Pope, here "the An-

---

[39] See Ferguson, pp. 155–60.
[40] The play has been reprinted by Reclam under the title, *Das Zürcher Spiel vom reichen Mann und vom armen Lazarus* (Stuttgart, 1978), no. 8304. The date of production is based upon a comment in Stumpf's Chronicle (Afterword, p. 56). Stephen Wailes argues that the play is an attack on papal wealth and indifference toward the poor in "The Rich Man and Lazarus in Zwingli's Zürich," *Internationales Archiv für Sozialgeschichte der deutschen Literatur* 11 (1986): 21–50.
[41] Page Bi v. (96 × 118 mm).
[42] "Der Bapst meynt es sey seynen ehren tzu nahe das er sich demue-//tige/" p. Bii r.

tichrist," and the humble life that Christ preached. The poor in this woodcut are peripheral. In part, they serve to reflect the poverty of Christ; primarily, they function to reinforce His humility, His willingness to humble Himself. They serve as background, as the poor among whom He lived, rather than the objects of His attention.[43]

Scripture provided little basis for representing Christ together with poor folk, and no independent visual tradition developed. The Zurich prints, then, combine figures, Christ and beggars or poor people, who appeared together rarely. Each of those two kinds of figures, however, belongs to its own rich tradition of visual representation. Each brings attributes and associated meanings from those traditions to the Zurich images, tempering the meaning of the other figure in the plane of the picture. Let us begin with the beggar, whose meaning, of the two, is the easier to define; the visual tradition to which he belongs is neither so complex nor so controversial as the various representations of Christ. Once his meaning is delineated, it will be possible to define Christ's significance in the image.

The poor were represented most often in the figure of the beggar. It appeared frequently in plays, poems, *Fastnacht* processions, as well as in visual art.[44] Like the figure of the knight or the lady, the beggar became a figure drawn from daily experience, denoting a specific place within society. His was the bottom rung of the social ladder, and he came to represent the most unfortunate members of society. As such, he was presented as physically disabled, with hand outstretched in a gesture of begging, or clothed in rags and filth,[45] according to the particular function he served in a image.

Representations of the beggar appeared most often in the fifteenth and sixteenth centuries,[46] and in a number of different functions: as the

---

[43] Cranach's view of the place of the poor was reaffirmed in his illustrations to the Apocalypse: "Bei Dürer stampfen die Rosse der apokalyptischen Reiter über Kaiser, Handelsmann, Geistliche hinweg, bei Cranach nur über armes, gemeines Volk," Schmidt, p. 29.

[44] Otto Schmitt, *Reallexikon zur deutschen Kunstgeschichte* (Stuttgart, 1937ff), vol. 2, p. 444; Hampe, pp. 82ff.

[45] "Für die bildliche Darstellung des Bettlers ergeben sich drei Typen: 1. wird körperliches Siechtum, Krankheit und Verkrüppelung als typische Eigenschaft für den Bettler dargestellt, 2. wird das Moment der Anforderung an die Hilfe des Nächsten durch Bittgesten hervorgehoben, 3. wird die Armut und das Elend durch zerkrumpte, schlechte Gewänder und traurige erbärmliche Mienen geschildert. Der Bettler kann also entweder ein Kruppel sein oder ein Bittender oder ein armer, unglücklicher Mensch." Südeck, p. 2.

[46] For the emergence of the beggar as a well-defined social type in the late fifteenth and early sixteenth centuries, see Jean-Pierre Gutton, *La société et les pauvres en Europe XVIe – XVIIIe siècles*

Passional Christi und

Christus.

Christus aber wol yn der gotlichen form war/ dennoch hat er
sich des geewsert sich genydert vn geberdet wie ein knecht gleich
den andern menschen an zusehen vnd befunden ein mensch der
sich gedemütiget hatt/ vnnd ist gehorsam geweßen biß in den
todt. Philippenses. 2.

Figure 8: Lucas Cranach the Elder, *Passional Christi und Antichristi*
Wittenberg: Johann Grünenberg, 1521
The Beinecke Rare Book and Manuscript Library, Yale University

Antichristi.

Antichristus.

Der Bapst meynt es sey seynen ehren zu nahe das er sich demü-
tige/ dan der sich zu fast demütiget gedeyet yhm yn dem regi-
ment zuuorachtung. c. quando 86. dist.

Also sagt die glosa/ das ist waer bey den narren/ das ist so vill
man muß gestreng vbir die deutschen narren regiren/ so halten
sie veil von vns.   B ij

Figure 9: Lucas Cranach the Elder, *Passional Christi und Antichristi*
Wittenberg: Johann Grünenberg, 1521
The Beinecke Rare Book and Manuscript Library, Yale University

false beggar, an immoral and lazy rogue;[47] as the rustic, comic figure in plays; as the representative of a specific social group in series such as the Dance of Death;[48] as the attribute of certain saints and Saturn, the planet god;[49] as the objects of good works, especially the Seven Works of Mercy; as the personification of Christ's call to poverty;[50] and, allied with this Christian virtue, as we saw in the case of Lazarus, an embodiment of the economic and social inequality of this world. These are only the main functions of the beggar in fifteenth- and sixteenth-century culture; there are many others.[51]

The variety of roles represented visually by beggars suggests a complex perception of beggars among their contemporaries. The beggar was more than a social type or an object of mercy. The appearance and gesture of the beggar were evocative of the ideal of Christian poverty, interwoven with it historically in the persons of Waldensians, Franciscans, Spiritual Franciscans, and others. And yet, when this ideal was articulated in the figure of the beggar, with its wretched dress, its filthiness, its implied infectiousness, the viewer was confronted with an image, reminiscent of San Bernardino's toothlessness, at once repulsive and pious, an image of enormous tension. And this tension was reflected in the variety of ways that the beggar was presented and, during the later Middle Ages, in the changing representation of the beggar: If the beggar was depicted as a cripple in the fifteenth century, increasingly in the sixteenth, he was designated by a begging gesture and a pathetic condition.[52] This change suggests that a more complex reaction to the figure of the beggar was emerging. It was no longer a physical fact of disability that denoted a beggar, but something more amorphous, less tangible: a gesture, a demeanor, a condition.

This transition was mirrored in the *Liber vagatorum* (1510), the first pamphlet that dealt specifically with beggars.[53] The *Liber* described the life

---

(Paris, 1974); and Alexandre Vexliard, *Introduction à la sociologie du vagabondage* (Paris, 1956), especially the Introduction. Another work, Robert Jütte, *Abbild und soziale Wirklichkeit des Bettler– und Gaunertums zu Beginn der Neuzeit* (1988), was not yet available at the time of publication.

[47] See Catharina Lis and Hugo Soly, *Poverty and Capitalism in Pre-Industrial Europe* (Bristol, 1982[1979]), pp. 78ff., and Gutton, chap. 1.

[48] On this category and the next, see Schmitt, vol. 2, p. 444.

[49] On the connection between beggars and Saturn, see Raymond Klibansky, Erwin Panofsky, and Fritz Saxl, *Saturn and Melancholy* (London, 1964).

[50] See Matthew 19:16–30 and Mark 10:17–31.

[51] Schmitt, vol. 2, pp. 444ff.

[52] Südeck, p. 2.

[53] There have been many editions of this text, many with unknown publishers or places of pub-

Liber Vagatorum
Der Betler orden

Figure 10: *Liber vagatorum*, ?1510
The Beinecke Rare Book and Manuscript Library, Yale University

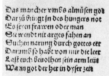

Figure 11: Barthel Beham, *The Twelve Vagrants*
Nuremberg: Hans Guldenmund, ca. 1524
Museen der Stadt Gotha, Schlossmuseum

and habits of various types of beggars, sometimes satirically, sometimes more expressly critically: "In conclusion: you should give these beggars nothing, ... among a thousand, not one will speak the truth."[54] Yet, the many title-page illustrations do not reflect the sceptical attitude of the text, but present beggars without visual comment, receiving alms,[55] or approaching a town (Figure 10).[56] The beggars, moreover, are presented as clearly crippled and poor. The various editions of the *Liber* reflected an ambivalence of response: The text that described various kinds of beggars as deceptive was often accompanied by images expressing the genuine poverty and disability of many such figures; the contrast on the page evidenced a tension between suspicion and compassion.

Around 1524, the Nuremberg artist, Barthel Betham, published a more sophisticated view of beggars in his broadsheet, "The Twelve Vagrants" (Figure 11).[57] He did not present one type of beggar, but twelve. Each told his or her own story about how he or she had come to beg: an unsuccessful alchemist; the old man who had never learned a trade; the servant girl to whom the priests and laymen "did what they wanted"; the man who lost his inheritance; the philanderer; the lazy maid, who could not control her tongue; the gambler; the woman who did not care for her honor; the spendthrift; the man who wanted always to fight; the drunkard; and the final beggar:

> If I have begged, it were not a sin
> I inherited it long ago
> Therefore it is not so great a burden for me
> as if I had been rich once.[58]

This man is the only one who is poor by birth, through no fault of his own. His lines are particularly poignant because they offer two important insights: some people are born to the beggar's life, born genuinely

---

lication. The full text has been reprinted by Friedrich Kluge in *Rotwelsch; Quellen und Wortschatz der Gaunersprache* (Strasbourg, 1901), pp. 35–55.

54 "Conclusio, disen betlern soltu nichts gebenn dann sie gond mit voppen und verben umb, under tauseten sagt einer nit war," (Von den Lossnern), Kluge, p. 39.

55 This image appeared with the first edition of the *Liber vagatorum* in 1510.

56 The Beinecke Library at Yale University dates the original of which Figure 10 is a reproduction, as ?1510. Title page illustrations to the *Liber* early on, therefore, suggested parallels between families of beggars and the Holy Family, a particularly sympathetic rendering of beggars.

57 "Die zwolf Vaganten," printed by Hans Guldenmund at Nuremberg. Source: Geisberg (1974), vol. 1, p. 138.

58 "Ob ich schon betel das syndt nit were/ Ich habs ererbt von alter her/ Darumb ist es mir nit so schwer/ Als ob ich reich gewesen wer," ibid.

destitute; the others, who have come to beg later in life, do so because they have lost something – wealth, purity, innocence. Five are beggars because of moral failure: the philanderer (or rake), the gambler, the spendthrift (or wastrel), the brawler, and the drunkard (or glutton). Three are poor because they chose foolishly: the alchemist, the old student, and the man who lost his inheritance. Finally, the last three are poor because of other moral flaws that occur solely among women: the servant girl who allowed herself to be led astray; the lazy maid; and the woman who was unconcerned with her own honor. Each of these three have breached important social standards of female behavior.

Eleven of the twelve became beggars not through a conscious choice, but because of their dispositions, their natures. By suggesting a number of causes for poverty, implying that the poor are sometimes victims to both internal and external forces, and bringing a certain ambivalence to their situation, Betham challenged that view that held beggars responsible for their own poverty. In his concluding lines at the bottom of the sheet, Betham offered another clue as to his intended meaning: "If the Lord God at this time was born poor into the world, then not every man can have money."[59] The reasons for poverty are many. Many people do not will poverty, they fall into it. The presence of poverty, however, is a part of the divine order: "not every man can have money."

These beggars are very different from the figures presented in the *Liber vagatorum* or in Cranach's woodcut. Each is distinctive, each has a personal story and an individual weakness. The broadsheet's message is in verse, a format more readily memorized than prose. Its form, as broadsheet, and its verbal format, in verse, would have enabled it to reach less literate audiences with its message, audiences who may have recognized neighbors among the twelve beggars. And the number of beggars corresponds to the number of Christ's apostles.[60]

Another visual tradition presented beggars as victims of circumstance as well: representations of the planet Saturn and his "children." This tradition would have been familiar to Beham. His close friend and fellow Nuremberger, Georg Pencz, designed a series of seven representations of the "planets and their children," including one of Saturn, which he

---

[59] "Wann got der her in dyser zeit/ Ward arm geborn in die welt/ Ain yeder kan nit haben gelt," ibid.

[60] As Herbert Zschelletzschky notes in *Die "drei gottlosen Maler" von Nürnberg* (Leipzig, 1975), p. 306.

published in 1531. Each of these woodcuts, approximately 208mm by 300mm, showed the ruling planet, "enthroned in the heavenly sphere – a reflex of the feudal system – removed from the earthly realm and concerned only with his own affairs, solitary and reclusive in his high carriage as it rolls over the human children."[61]

The carriage of "Saturnus" is drawn by dragonlike lizards (Figure 12).[62] The planet-god, in accordance with legend, is eating one of his children.[63] The children below him on the print, that is, those who are born under his influence, are engaged in those activities or way of life to which their natal star has given them inclination: a peasant plowing his field; a miller grinding grain; a man imprisoned; another criminal in the stocks; next to him, a mathematician; a group of cripples and poor folk receiving alms and food at the church door; and a butcher. Of all the children of the planets, according to late medieval thought, those born under Saturn are the most wretched of men, impoverished and de-spised.[64] According to this view, the temperament, disposition, talents, even outward appearance of men are deeply influenced by the planet under which they were born.

Pencz gave form to an astrological determinism that parallels Beham's view in one important way: many, if not all poor do not choose their way of life, but come to it through birth, through outside influences, internal destinies. Beham, his brother Sebald, and Pencz had all been deeply impressed by the ideas of Thomas Müntzer:[65] their views of the poor reflect that link. Their views were not held widely among the urban elite of Nuremberg and were considered heretical by some; they were brought to trial as "godless painters" in 1525. Yet, their perceptions of beggars, especially as they were articulated in "The Twelve Vagrants," were widely publicized. They may well have found resonance among

---

[61] "Denn in himmlischer Sphäre thront – ein Reflex des Feudalsystems – der regierende Plane-tengott, dem irdischen Bereich entrückt und nur mit seinen eigenen Angelegenheiten beschäftigt, einsam und volksfremd auf seinem hoch über den Menschenkindern dahinrollenden Wagen," ibid., p. 135.

[62] Publisher unknown, 1531. G. 990, Kupferstichkabinett SMPK, Berlin. Pencz also designed an engraving of Saturn, as a solitary figure, in 1528/9. For the authorship controversy and history of the woodcut, see Zschelletzschky, pp. 134ff.

[63] For a detailed history of the development of this image, see Klibansky, et al., pp. 127–214.

[64] Ibid., p. 191. This view serves as the starting point for Rudolph and Margot Wittkower's study of artists' self-perceptions, *Born Under Saturn: The Character and Conduct of Artists* (New York, 1969).

[65] This is the subject of Zschelletzschky's book.

Figure 12: Georg Pencz, *Saturnus*, 1531
No. G.990, Kupferstichkabinett SMPK, Berlin

the three painters' contemporaries, perhaps even in the printed images of Zurich.

The figure of the beggar provides a link, perhaps tenuous, between the three Zurich prints and the traditions embodied in the images of the three Nuremberg artists. Klibansky, Panofsky, and Saxl's study of the image of Saturn suggests another subtler link between the images. The design for the planets' influence on those born beneath it was derived from the one other visual tradition that made explicit the "influence" of a heavenly power on earthly lives: "the design of Christ's Ascension into heaven (or, to be more exact, the risen Christ addressing those left on earth), of Judgement Day, and above all, of Pentecost and similar mysteries."[66]

Although Christ and Saturn were not directly linked in Zurich,[67] the perception of "influence" articulated in the other two visual traditions does have resonance in the title page prints from Zurich. While the three images make no clear statement as to whether the beggars had any control over their material condition, a comparison with the images from Nuremberg highlights a statement in the prints that might otherwise remain silent, a statement which is not expressed dramatically, as in the woodcuts by Beham and Pencz, but tacitly. Again, let us recall Christ's gesture of calling in two of the prints, His attitude in the third. Could these beggars and poor people, whom Christ calls to join Him, be the "false beggars" described in the *Liber vagatorum?* Does not Christ, as God, know who is false, who is true?

In both sets of images, the condition of poverty is presented as a way of life, not that one should choose, but which may be one's lot. These images are not presenting the virtue of Christian poverty as an ideal to be sought in life; artisans and peasants who are not poor are among those reaching for Christ. The images present, instead, the fact of poverty in human life; they depict it in all its wretched detail. Whereas the title page illustrations no more than imply, the Beham and Pencz woodcuts state clearly that such poverty is involuntary. Indeed, their poverty must be involuntary, if they are to number among Zwingli's true poor.

Comparisons with other images of beggars brings greater definition to the Zurich prints, clarifying their meaning. The attitude, the gestures

---

[66] Klibansky, et al., p. 205.
[67] I found no evidence of any images of Saturn in Ganter, Ganz, Rahn, or Wartmann, *Gemälde und Skulpturen* and *Tafelbilder* (see note 1 for full references).

and stance, of the beggars in the three title-page prints is perhaps most striking. Unlike beggars in other images, these beggars are active, rather than passive. In the engraving and the first woodcut (Figures 4 and 5), they move toward someone, Christ, rather than merely receiving whatever another may bestow upon them. In the second woodcut (Figure 6), they surround Christ in various stages of rising and look toward Him. In all three, the poor and common folk seek Christ, who offers not alms, but Himself.

Christ is both visually and symbolically at center in the Zurich images. The Zurich images present their viewers with a heavenly influence, one who, like Saturn or the Renaissance figure, Fortuna, shapes the course of men's lives. This influence, however, is not capricious, like Fortuna,[68] or destructive, like Saturn. Divine providence is the teleological force at play in the Zurich title-page prints – Christ is present and efficacious in the world. The Christ that the images depict, moreover, standing among figures who are visibly "victims" of some external force, contrasts significantly with representations of other forms of "influence."[69] He is an image not only of divine omnipotence, but also of divine mercy.

Christ's gesture toward the poor and beggars places Him in a specific relationship toward them. In contrast to Saturn, who rides above his children, or Fortuna, which acts upon human life in capricious ways, Christ is among men – He faces them and welcomes them. That position differs from traditional representations of Christ; He is neither above men nor separate from them.[70] His gesture, particularly in the engraving and the first woodcut, evokes another visual tradition in which beggars can be found, however, that of certain saints' lives, and draws upon the meaning associated with the gestures of saints.

St. Martin of Tours, the soldier who shared his cloak with a beggar, was among the most popular of the saints connected with the poor; representations of him appeared throughout German-speaking Switzerland (Figure 13).[71] In Zug, the Zurich artist, Hans Leu the Younger,

---

[68] For a northern contemporary representation, see Beham's "Fortuna," reproduced in Geisberg, vol. 1, p. 220. For the history of the personification and allegorical representation of Fortune, see Raimond van Marle, *Iconographie de l'Art profane au Moyen Age et à la Renaissance*, Vol. II: *Allégories et Symboles* (La Haye, 1932), pp. 178–89.

[69] A late fifteenth-century Florentine engraving of Saturn's children, for example, seems to have been copied and widely distributed. A drawing after this engraving exists in Tübingen, at the University Library, Cod.M.d.2' fol. 267r.

[70] *Lexikon der christlichen Ikonographie.*

[71] See Louis Reau, *Iconographie de l'Art chrétien* (Paris, 1958), vol. 3, pt. 2, pp. 900–17.

Figure 13: Martin Schongauer, *St. Martin Dividing his Cloak*
engraving, 15.4 × 10.6 cm
Mr. and Mrs. Potter Palmer Collection, 1965.889
© 1989 The Art Institute of Chicago. All Rights Reserved

painted an altar wing depicting Saints Martin and Onophrius on either side of a beggar.[72] Within the canton of Zurich, St. Martin was represented in a fourteenth-century wall painting on the north transcept of the cloister at Kappel, and in a stained glass window of 1506 in the parish church of Maschwanden.[73] In these, like the statue in Basel, St. Martin appeared as a soldier, of particular significance for the Swiss,[74] mounted on a horse, designating a particular class of soldier, in the process of cutting his cloak in half for the beggar beside him.[75] The history of the statue in Basel intimates the significance of the saint in each town's religious culture; during the Reformation in the town, the beggar Martin leaned toward was removed and replaced by a tree stump.[76] Perhaps in Zurich as well, images of St. Martin stood over the altar dedicated to him in St. Peter's Church; perhaps they have been silenced even more completely than the statue in Basel.

The gesture that identifies St. Martin, of splitting his cloak with a beggar, does not correspond directly with that of Christ in the three printed images from Zurich. Yet that which the gesture signified – the relationship between the saint and the beggar – was analogous. Like the Christ of the images, St. Martin's attention is directed toward the beggar. Like Christ, he reaches out to the beggar, offering aid. The aid he offers, however, is material, while Christ's is a great deal more.

Only one saint of Swiss origins seems to have been connected with the poor, the second-century hermit, St. Beatus.[77] Although his sanctity seems to have derived originally from an eremitic life, by the sixteenth century, he had become associated with extraordinary gifts of alms.[78] Fewer representations of Beatus are extant in northern Switzerland than of St. Martin, perhaps because the hermit saint was less popular as a

---

[72] ca.1510. The altar wing and its companion are now in the Schweizerisches Landesmuseum, Zurich, nos. AG31/32.

[73] *Die Kunstdenkmäler des Kantons Zürich*, Vol. 1: *Die Bezirke Affoltern und Andelfingen*, by Hermann Fietz (Basel, 1938), pp. 67 and 117, respectively.

[74] By the sixteenth century, the Swiss were famous for their military skill, serving as mercenary soldiers to the King of France and the Pope.

[75] St. Martin was not always represented mounted; just as frequently, he was represented standing. See, for example, Figure 13, the engraving by Martin Schongauer (d. 1491), (15.4 × 10.6 cm). Reference: Bartsch, vol. 8, p. 265.

[76] *Basler Münster*, p. 26.

[77] On the life of St. Beatus and his namesake from Vendome, *Butler's Lives of the Saints*, edited, revised, and supplemented by Herbert Thurston, S.J. and Donald Attwater, vol. 2: April, May, June (New York, 1956), p. 259.

[78] For depictions of St. Beatus, see Reau, vol. 3, pt. 1, p. 190.

⁋ Zu dem Ersten ⦂ wie
sant Bat vß teildt syn zytlich gůt den armen lü
ten/vnd den kilchen.

Figure 14: Urs Graf, *St. Beatus Distributing Alms*
from *The Life of St. Beatus*, Basel, 1511
Oeffentliche Kunstsammlung Basel, Kupferstichkabinett

public figure than the warrior saint. In Zurich, he was depicted not in a public space, but in the house, "Zum Königsstuhl," in a fifteenth-century wall painting.[79] It is another image, however, one printed in Basel, that most closely approximates the Zurich woodcuts in gesture and detail. Urs Graf depicted his life in a series of woodcuts, one of which presents the saint distributing alms (Figure 14).[80] Here, the saint's gesture approaches that of Christ in the Zurich title-page prints: Striding forward from the right side of the image, the saint reaches out toward a beggar, in order to drop alms in the beggar's plate. The saint wears the long robe of the prosperous burgher, at once distinctive from the robes of the Zurich Christ in its contemporary detail and evocative of them in its length and line. And the beggar who stands before him looks very much like those in the Zurich prints: bearded, bareheaded and barefoot, crippled, on crutches, dressed in the tattered short tunic of the peasant or artisan.

Among the saints connected with the poor, two strikingly approximated Christ in gesture and demeanor: St. Francis and Saint Elizabeth of Thuringia or Hungary.[81] St. Francis was represented rarely in the art of northern Europe, or, perhaps more accurately, representations of him have not survived in northern Europe, despite the success of his order in establishing houses. The life of St. Elizabeth, on the other hand, was the subject of numerous images.[82] Her life, moreover, mirrored Francis's in its imitation of certain moments in Christ's life and in its embeddedness in the lives of the poor.[83] Not only did she practice

---

[79] Landesmuseum, no. LM20991: St. Beatus appears on the upper frieze, along with the visit of the three magi; on the lower frieze are represented Saints Felix, Regula, Exuperantius, Jacobus, Jodocus, Fridolin, Onophrius, Oswald, Barbara, Katherine, and Dorothea, as well as the Virgin and Mary Magdelene.

[80] Urs Graf (d. 1527/28), "Der hl. Beatus teilt Almosen aus," number 1 in the series, "Das Leben des heiligen bychtigers und einsidlers sant Batten," Basel, 1511, Oeffentliche Kunstsammlung Basel, Kupferstichkabinett.

[81] On the life of St. Elizabeth, see André Vauchez, "Charité et pauvreté chez Sainte Elisabeth de Thuringe d'après les actes du procès de canonisation," in *Études sur l'Histoire de la Pauvreté*, ed. Michel Mollat (Paris: Sorbonne, 1974), vol. 1, pp. 163–73. Caroline Bynum has explored the life of Elizabeth, in particular relation to fasting and feeding the poor, in *Holy Feast and Holy Fast* (Berkeley, 1987).

[82] On representations of the life of Elizabeth, see Friedrich Schmoll, *Zur Ikonographie der heiligen Elisabeth* (Giessen, 1914).

[83] Elizabeth became a Franciscan tertiary on the death of her husband. Even before the death of her husband, she sought to emulate the poor: "Avant son veuvage déjà, on la voit rendre visite aux pauvres et en particulier aux femmes enceintes, entrant dans leurs maisons et cherchant à participer matériellement et spirituellement à leurs peines," Vauchez, p. 166.

traditional forms of charity – almsgiving, founding and supporting hospitals – but she also sought a personal and direct involvement with the poor. Each Maundy Thursday she washed the feet of all the beggars in her region,[84] recalling the moment during the Last Supper, when Christ washed the feet of His apostles:

"If I, then, your Lord and Teacher, have washed your feet, you also ought to wash one other's feet. For I have given you an example, that you also should do as I have done to you. Truly, truly, I say to you, a servant is not greater than his master; nor is he who is sent greater than he who sent him." (John 13:14–17)

Hans Holbein the Younger, the possible artist of the Zurich engraved border and a leading graphic artist in Basel, knew the life of St. Elizabeth.[85] Although he chose to depict a different moment in her life, as she stands before a beggar, he may well have been familiar with the story of her Maundy Thursday ritual.[86] The implications of that ritual are made visible in the right wing of the altarpiece in the Hospital of the Holy Spirit in Reval, painted in 1483.[87] In the altarpiece, Elizabeth washes not the feet of the beggar, but those of Christ, who appears in the rags of a beggar. She imitates Christ in her gesture, capturing the complex nature of Christian humility; her act "cleanses" those whom she touches, both in washing their feet and in touching them with her humility. As the painting suggests, that gesture reflects upon her as well; in a way, she, too, is "cleansed," by her contact with the beggar *qua* Christ.

Gestures are perhaps the most elusive elements of visual language. They give expression to fluid relations of station and influence, reflecting patterns of behavior delineated and defined by social and political norms. As performance, gestures are ephemeral. As image, they acquire a constancy, becoming imitable, as we have seen in the lives of both St. Francis and St. Elizabeth, and normative, defining relationships between per-

---

[84] Ibid., p. 165. Schmoll notes that this gesture was recorded in the original cycle of images depicting the Saint's life, p. 3.

[85] In 1516, Hans Holbein the Elder had painted St. Elizabeth on the right wing of an altar to St. Sebastian, now in the Alte Pinothek, Munich. *Lexikon der christlichen Ikonographie,* vol. 6, pp. 135–6.

[86] A sketch, now in the Basel Kunstmuseum (catalogue no. 1662.147).

[87] *Lexikon der christlichen Ikonographie,* vol. 6, pp. 137–8. This panel was probably painted by Bernt Notke.

sons. The gestures of all three saints make visible a specific relationship between those saints and the poor who stand before them.

St. Elizabeth, in particular, came to epitomize the ideal relation of the pious Christian to the destitute, so much so that her figure superceded the allegorical figure of "Caritas" in German-speaking lands.[88] It was a significant visual shift: "Caritas" was represented as a female figure, usually in classical robes, but unlike St. Elizabeth, she was accompanied by children or a horn of plenty.[89] The allegorical figure did not touch the poor; it was abstracted from the social problem of poverty and the physical presence of poor people. St. Elizabeth, on the other hand, did touch the poor; herself expressly human, she fed them alms, cared for them in hospitals, and "cleansed" them. She brought to that contact another dimension, one that the allegorical figure could not express: Her posture and her gestures toward those who were economically and socially powerless manifested Christian humility. Unlike the allegorical figure of "Caritas," St. Elizabeth combined acts of charity with gestures of humility, wherein lay her sanctity. More than an allegorical figure, Elizabeth could represent in her gestures the complex nature of Christian brotherly love: at once self-cleansing and self-negating, at once magnanimous and subservient.[90]

Images of Elizabeth give expression to a notion of Christian brotherly love, or *caritas*, different from that articulated by another visual tradition, one which Christ's presence in the Reval altar wing invokes obliquely: the Seven Works of Mercy.[91] That tradition drew directly upon a biblical text:

> Then the righteous will answer him, "Lord, when did we see thee hungry and feed thee, or thirsty and give thee drink? And when did we see thee a stranger and welcome thee, or naked and clothe thee? And when did we see thee sick or in prison and visit thee?" And the King will answer them, "Truly, I say to you, as you did it to one of the least of these my brethren, you did it to me." (Matthew 25:37–40)

[88] Schmitt, vol. 3, p. 350.

[89] Ibid., pp. 343–56. See also the study of this figure in French and Italian art, by R. Freyhan, "The Evolution of the Caritas Figure in the Thirteenth and Fourteenth Centuries," *Journal of the Warburg and Courtauld Institutes* 11 (1948): 68–86.

[90] For this specific connection, see Schmitt, vol. 3, p. 350. My primary source for the discussion of Christian love is the *Dictionnaire de Spiritualité*, ed. Charles Baumgartner (Paris, 1953), vol. 2, pt. 1, pp. 507–600.

[91] The Seven Works of Mercy are: to give food to the hungry; to give drink to the thirsty; to give shelter to strangers; to clothe the naked; to visit the sick and imprisoned; and to bury the dead.

The visual representation of the Seven Works of Mercy, for which there are examples as early as the twelfth century,[92] did not become widely popular until the seventeenth century.[93] By the end of the fifteenth century, there are enough representations extant to compare and to discover that they share certain elements. Although the form of the beggar would seem to embody best four of the seven conditions for works of mercy – hungry, thirsty, homeless, and poorly clothed – it was not the standard form for the recipient of these works of mercy in visual representations. In the majority of representations, the recipient is non-descript; he need only represent all those who are in need of food, drink, shelter, clothing, or care.[94] Georg Pencz's seven rondel engravings, printed in 1534, represent the alternative visualization of the text; in each of the seven, Christ is the recipient. The equation of Christ with the recipient in the Pencz engravings reinforces the focus of the text; not the objects of the acts of mercy, but the act itself is of importance.

The Seven Works of Mercy did not encompass the same complexity as the gestures of St. Elizabeth. Although originally presented as acts expressive of Christian brotherly love, they lacked the psychological dimension, becoming superficial and mechanical, becoming those works that Luther and Zwingli found lacking in faith. The works of mercy did not have as their foundation that Christian humility that linked the saints to the objects of their attention. The gestures of Elizabeth, Beatus, and Martin may share with representations of the Seven Works of Mercy acts of feeding, clothing, providing shelter, but they also delineate be-tween the saint and the poor a relationship that binds them together, a relationship of Christian brotherly love. In this way, those gestures reflect that definition of Christian love given by Augustine – "*Caritas* is that movement of the soul toward delight in God and in one's neighbor that originates in God himself" – and recalled by Zwingli.[95] And here we approach the meaning of the Zurich title-page prints and their con-nection to Zwingli's words.

One more image, the title-page border to Luther's Twenty-seventh

---

[92] For example, British Museum Egerton MS, 1139, photographic copy in the Files of the Warburg Institute.

[93] Judging by the number of representations extant.

[94] This fact may tell us a great deal about fifteenth-century and sixteenth-century definitions of the poor; their definitions may have been far broader than ours.

[95] "Caritas est motus animi ad fruendum Deo propter ipsum et proximo propter Deo," *Dictionnaire de Spiritualité*, vol. 2, pt. 1, p. 572.

Sermon, published by Johann Schott of Strasbourg in 1523, provides the last clue as to the meaning of the three title-page prints.[96] Like the Holbein, it is a title-page border. Only the lower panel pertains to the discussion here. Its composition has certain similarities to the Holbein engraving: Christ is at center, addressing a group to His left, one of which is portrayed in excited movement toward Christ. Behind Christ, however, are not His apostles, but sheep and a hen with her chicks. There is no city in the background. The man in motion is clad like an artisan or a peasant; he is not specifically described, but he is clearly not poor. The man immediately behind him has what appears to be a tail extruding from his robe. Perhaps he signifies the wolf among the sheep, perhaps the devil.

Finally, below the border is printed the passage from Matthew 11:28, but it is Luther's translation: "Kumment all zu mir die ir muselig und beladen seind/ ich wil euch erquicken," (Come all to me, you who are tired in your soul and burdened, and I will refresh you).[97] This translation differs from Zwingli's in two places: it is addressed to those who are exhausted, rather than those who labor, and Christ promises to refresh, rather than give rest. The meaning of the passage shifts: Christ no longer addresses men who labor, but men who are tired, possibly spiritually tired, and He offers them not rest from their labors, but to refresh them, perhaps enabling them to continue. It is all the more striking that Zwingli's translation accompanies images in which there are men who are probably not working: beggars and poor. The two title-page borders present two images of Christ. In the Holbein, the nature of His appeal is active, direct, and He is calling people from all walks of life to join Him and His apostles. The border for the Luther text presents a Christ who stands, whose left hand is held in the folds of His robe, who is sought by a man wearing shoes and untattered clothing. The latter is the Good Shepherd; the former is much more. It is that difference that concerns us now.

Although the three Zurich title-page prints evoke in gesture and in arrangement of figures traditional representations of certain saints, they do not fully belong to any tradition of visual representations of *caritas*, whether saints' lives or the allegorical figure of "Caritas." Nor, on the

[96] Sonderforschungsbereich Z1: Flugschriften des frühen 16. Jahrhunderts, Tübingen, pamphlet no. 4148.
[97] I am grateful to Professor Dr. Heiko A. Oberman, who first pointed out this difference to me.

other hand, do the Zurich prints belong to any other visual tradition. Could it be that the designers of the title-page prints had abandoned "a typology which had become too crude," in order to formulate a new image of *caritas?*[98] It seems quite possible that the designers of Christian images were affected by that same biblical "literalism" as the textual scholars, a literalism that produced figures more historically accurate in their dress and more closely bound to the text in their meaning.[99]

Just as Saturn was unacceptable to Christian reformers such as Erasmus and Zwingli as an explanation for certain people's wretched condition, so, too, the allegorical figure of "Caritas" and the human forms of saints were inadequate to represent all that the notion of *caritas* or Christian brotherly love had come to signify for Zwingli and others. The allegorical figure of "Caritas" might still be associated with that text she had originally visualized through the presence of a lamb or chalice in the picture,[100] but that association had become attenuated: By the sixteenth century in German-speaking Europe, "Caritas's" attributes had come to symbolize no more than charity, human kindness, rather than the fullness of Christian love.[101] This shift is evident in an image of "Caritas" by the Lutheran artist, Lucas Cranach the Younger.[102] It presents a female figure surrounded by many children, not ragged beggars. This "Caritas" presents an image of maternal love,[103] of love extended not to strangers, but to one's own.

The figures of saints and of "Caritas" paled in comparison with the figure of Christ Himself. Here was the image of divine mercy and divine

---

[98] "We know that Dürer's engraving 'Melancholia' is a Saturn picture. It marks, however, a definite break with the realistic interpretation of earlier pictures which showed mathematicians and melancholics, both children of Saturn. Dürer chose a classical method – that of personification – to represent mathematics and melancholy together in one powerful picture," Fritz Saxl, "Macrocosm and Microcosm in Medieval Pictures," *Lectures* (London, 1957), vol. 1, p. 69.

[99] "Der exegetische Gehalt der Bibelillustration der Reformationszeit brachte ein Neues, das durch keine formale Vergleichung mit den alten Vorbildern erfasst werden kann, mögen auch noch so oft Züge dieser Vorbilder und Vorläufer verwendet worden sein. Für dieses Neue gibt es keinen Traditionsnachweis.

"Ein neuer Geist war eingezogen, erfasste die Inhalte des alten Bibelwortes neu und fand seinen Ausdruck auch im biblischen Bild," Schmidt, p. 30.

[100] The animal associated with "Caritas" is the lamb. See Schmitt, vol. 3, p. 348. Also, see van Marle, vol. 2, pp. 1–111, especially pp. 37–8, for a history of the development of this allegorical figure.

[101] According to van Marle, it was Giotto who introduced "Envy" as the vice opposing "Caritas"; earlier it had been "Avarice," thus implying that "Caritas" was a kind of generosity with material goods, a kind of charity, vol. 2, p. 66.

[102] See Schmitt, vol. 3, p. 353, for a description of this image.

[103] This is Schmitt's argument, ibid., pp. 351–2.

love that God Himself had presented to human eyes. Christ alone embodied at once the love of God and brotherly love:

> "This is my commandment, that you love one another as I have loved you. Greater love has no man than this, that a man lay down his life for his friends. You are my friends if you do what I command you. No longer do I call you servants, for the servant does not know what his master is doing; but I have called you friends, for all that I have heard from my Father I have made known to you." (John 15:12–15)[104]

In Zurich, new images of Christ, dressed in the robes of an apostle, dressed, according to the best contemporary biblical scholarship, in historically accurate costume, appeared on the title page and throughout the text of the German New Testament Froschauer published in 1525 and the Swiss German Bible he published in 1531.[105] Images of Christ close to those biblical images in their costume and in details of line in face and figure appeared on the title pages of many of Zwingli's works. Indeed, images of Christ outnumbered images of any other single figure among the printed images of Reformation Zurich.

Among those images of Christ were three that had no direct biblical text, three that depicted Christ among poor and common folk. Are the three Zurich prints new images of Christian *caritas?* The three do not present a single image of Christ, but two: His gesture and posture in the engraving and the first woodcut (Figures 4 and 5), differs markedly from those in woodcut II (Figure 6). In the engraving and in the first woodcut, His gesture is one of welcome toward the poor and common folk opposite Him and of movement toward them. He is depicted in movement, striding toward the poor and common folk as they move toward Him. In the second woodcut (Figure 6), His posture is stationary; He does not move toward the men and women, but is surrounded by them. What, then, is the meaning of Christ, of His posture and gesture, in the three prints?

In the first two prints (Figures 4 and 5), Christ is depicted as reaching toward the poor and common people who approach Him. His gesture is mirrored in theirs. Here is an evangelical Christ, the Christ who brought the message of God's love and called on men to replicate his gesture:

---

[104] This is the fullest single statement in the New Testament of the notion of Christian love. There are a number of texts dealing with some aspect of it, some of which appear in this chapter.

[105] See *Zürcher Kunst nach der Reformation*, pp. 150–2.

"Love one another just as I have loved you, you also must love one another. By this love you have for one another, everyone will know that you are my disciples." (John 13:34–35)

And the poor and common folk do indeed mirror Christ's gesture. Their expression, however, is directed not toward one another, but toward Christ Himself. The mimetic gestures of Christ and the beggars, that which distinguishes the Zurich prints from all visual traditions, also suggests that which distinguishes reformed notions of *caritas* from earlier formulations. In replacing figures of saints or of "Caritas" in the center of an image of Christian love with the figure of Christ, the designers of the images underlined the source of all Christian love:

"Beloved, let us love one another; for love is of God, and he who loves is born of God and knows God. He who does not love does not know God; for God is love." (I John 4:7–8)

In mirroring Christ's gesture, the poor and common folk at once point toward the source of their own gestures and make visible the presence of Christian love among them.

As the people of Zurich were looking upon these images they were hearing Zwingli's words, reminding them that true Christian love comes from God; a man is not capable of it if he has not received it from God. The sign of the gift of grace, Zwingli preached, was the presence of love; that presence defines the Christian community.[106] The engraving and the first woodcut placed before Zurichers' eyes the full implication of Zwingli's message. On one level, those images appealed to the poor, to peasants, to artisans, to laborers, to those on the threshold of poverty; and the words of Matthew 11:28 below the images affirmed that appeal. They presented an image of a loving and gentle Christ, a Christ who reached out to all men and women, no matter their status. On another level, those images spoke to the burgher, the merchant, the patrician, reminding him that grace alone did not define a Christian community – a Christian community mirrored Christ in its gestures. If Christ is present in a community, then He must be visible in its behavior and posture.

The first two images were published in 1524, the first woodcut at the end of December. The second woodcut (Figure 6) was printed on April

---

[106] See the *Dictionnaire de Spiritualité*, vol. 2, pt. 1, p. 595, for the relation of grace to love in the thought of Gabriel Biel, Pierre d'Ailly, and Jean Gerson.

27, 1525. Much occurred in the intervening four months. The Poor Law was passed on January 15. Equally as significant, the Twelve Articles had been formulated at the beginning of the Peasants' War, in late February or early March of 1525.[107] Traditional Zwingli scholarship has viewed this as the turning point in Zwingli's and the town council's political sympathies.[108] The second woodcut, therefore, should be more conservative in meaning. Yet, if the cross, which is so central to this woodcut, is given its full significance, the image's message is subtler and more complex.

Medieval representations of the virtues Christ manifested in the crucifixion often placed "Caritas" to the right of the crucified Christ.[109] In these representations, it is "Caritas" who executes the stab of the lance, capturing in that gesture the meaning of Christ's death as sacrifice and act of love. The allegorical figure "Ecclesia" often catches Christ's blood in a Eucharist chalice, reaffirming the church's special place as mediator between that sacrificial death and the beneficiaries of the sacrifice. In a fifteenth-century panel painting, now in Cologne, "Christ and Caritas in a Landscape," "Caritas" holds both the lance and the chalice; she is both the agent and the beneficiary of the sacrifice. She feeds on Christ's blood, just as she is the cause for His shedding it.

In the second Zurich woodcut (Figure 6), Christ stands among men and women, bearing the cross. Although the Zurich print does not make as graphically explicit the function and meaning of Christ's sacrifice as does the Cologne panel, it is analogous to the panel in its message. The symbol of Christ's sacrifice is no longer His blood, but the cross. In replacing Christ's blood with the cross, the designer of the second woodcut reflected a shift not only of sensibilities, but also in the interpretation of the crucifixion itself. For Luther and Zwingli, the meaning of the crucifixion became central to understanding the nature of the Eucharist and of man's relation to God.[110] As each interpreted the function of the Eucharist, each defined anew the symbolism of Christ's blood. For Zwingli, who defined the function of the Eucharist as a commemoration of fellowship – who denied that the Eucharist was a

---

[107] The dating here is Blickle's, p. 18.
[108] For example, Steven Ozment, *The Reformation in the Cities* (New Haven, Conn., 1975/1980), pp. 133–5.
[109] The following description and analysis is drawn from Schmitt, vol. 2, pp. 349–50.
[110] The most recent contribution to the literature on this aspect of Luther's thought is Alistair McGrath, *Luther's Theology of the Cross* (Oxford, 1985).

reenactment of a sacrifice complete with blood – the blood of Christ was no longer present in the ritual.[111] For Zwingli, not blood, but the cross most accurately symbolized the meaning of the crucifixion. And in the visual language of the Reformation throughout German-speaking Europe, it was the cross that became a central symbol, both of reformed theology in general and of its particular emphasis on the redemptive gesture of Christ.[112]

The Christ in the second woodcut is not a conventional representation of the crucified Christ; He does not have the attributes of the Passion or the Man of Sorrows, the crown of thorns or the wounds. He stands, His cross resting against His left side, His right hand raised in blessing, and His head encircled with a halo. The cross evokes the Christ who "loved us and gave himself up for us, a fragrant offering and a sacrifice to God." (Ephesians 5:1–2) This, too, is an image of God's love of man; the human form divinity assumed stands among men and women. But it presents a different face of that love: the cross, not a gesture, is its central symbol. This Christ "gave himself up" for others, made of Himself a sacrifice to God in payment for human sin. And this Christ stands – the sacrifice has been completed, His divinity confirmed in the Resurrection.

Like "Caritas" in the Cologne panel, the poor and common people are beside Christ. Like her, they take part in the sacrifice, although not in the same way: Carrying no lance or chalice, they visibly neither cause nor receive benefit from Christ's crucifixion. Their participation is of a different nature: Like Christ, they bear crosses.[113] Their gestures do not mirror Christ's as in the earlier two prints, but they do reflect it, contrasting with its completion their various stages of rising, of attainment. Only one figure among them has achieved full upright position, with his cross resting easily on his shoulder. Dressed in the tunic of an artisan or peasant, the "common man," he stands to the far left in the picture, pointing toward Christ. His gesture makes explicit the direction of the others' eyes: Christ and the cross.

All participate, albeit in widely varying degrees, in the sacrifice the cross symbolized. In this sense the woodcut is "conservative": it is an

---

[111] On Zwingli's interpretation of the Eucharist, see especially Stefan N. Bosshard, *Zwingli-Erasmus-Cajetan. Die Eucharistie als Zeichen der Einheit* (Wiesbaden, 1978).

[112] Scribner, p. 216.

[113] This is not a crucifix, which was the object of iconoclastic violence, but a simple cross.

image calling Christians to take up the cross, to bear a "sacrifice," which Zwingli had defined for the people of Zurich as the subjugation of self to the demands of others. Yet, the woodcut also promises more, for the cross also represents the link between the present and the resurrected life, the kingdom of God:[114] "And he said to all, 'If any man would come after me, let him deny himself and take up his cross daily and follow me.'" (Luke 9:23)

The third image completes the trilogy of images. It reminds the viewer that there are two faces to God's love: that described by John and that described by Paul – the embrace coexists with the sacrifice.[115] Christ stands among those who have begun to lift up their crosses. The second woodcut presents an image of the Christian community of the future: the community of the saved.

All three images depict a city. In the first two prints (Figures 4 & 5), the city has been placed in the center of the image; in the last (Figure 6), it has been moved to the periphery. In the first two, the city also contains a tiered round tower, which is missing in the third. Both the city's placement and the round tower suggest that it may well be a representation of Jerusalem. Such an allusion would suit a town like Zurich, which was seeking reform of its religious practices and a new definition of its collective religious life.

In the second woodcut, the city is no longer in the center of the frame, but removed to the horizon on the left side. This image went forth in the spring of 1525, after the Poor Law had been enacted, after the poor had been brought under the care of the town council. It appeared on a letter addressed to an official of a rural canton, a canton that had reacted strongly against the reforms in Zurich. It appeared when the peasants' and the Anabaptists' resistance was increasingly strong. It brought its vision of the Christian community to each of these groups, presenting an image not of the earthly Jerusalem, but of the community of the saved: Townsmen and women, peasants, and theologians surround the resurrected Christ. Its central sign was not a gesture of brotherly love, but the symbol of the cross in all its complexity. To the residents of

---

[114] On the cross as symbolizing redemption for Protestants, see William H. Halewood, "Rembrandt: Three Crosses," in *Six Subjects of Reformation Art: A Preface to Rembrandt* (Toronto, 1982), pp. 124–36.

[115] For the Johannine and Pauline formulations of *caritas dei*, see the *Dictionnaire de Spiritualité*, vol. 2, pt. 1, pp. 507ff., especially p. 512.

Zurich, the image presented the symbol of those duties that Christians take up in their faith: Among them may well have been the payment of tithes, that gesture of Christian love that Zwingli had preached. To outsiders, the image presented an image of the community of the saved, designated by its willingness to "take up the cross," to follow Christ in sacrificing oneself for others.

> without images we can neither think nor understand anything.
> (Martin Luther)[116]

Certain questions remain unanswered. In part this lies with the nature of all visual representations: Their terminology is less familiar to us, and less defined, than literature. In part, too, it belongs to the specific nature of title-page prints, neither emblem nor narrative. These three prints served to introduce Zwingli's texts. They presented images of a loving Christ, who cares for the poor and sacrificed Himself for the sake of humanity. They also function as images separate from the text; the text does not serve to define their meaning. To a certain extent, they remain independent participants in their own language, that of visual imagery.

Although their contemporaries probably possessed a much greater vocabulary for understanding them, I suspect that these prints would never have been fully defined. The elements of which they are composed, especially the images of Christ and the beggar, are too rich in associated meaning to be contained within a single line of interpretation. Like the idea of Christian love, they bring their variegated and rich association to each whole image, giving it added dimensions, layers of meaning. And like the idea of Christian love, the two figures of Christ and the beggar are intensely meaningful; they are symbols of exceptional power. For a culture rich in the vocabulary of visual images, a title-page print, through the presence of certain familiar visual elements, could touch inner wells of meaning, could extend its significance beyond its apparently simplistic design. In the unfamiliar combination of those elements, it could raise questions with a new force and present a vision that jarred accepted practice.

---

[116] "...sondern weil wir ja muessen gedancken und bilde fassen des, das uns inn worten fuergetragen wird, und nichts on bilde dencken noch verstehen koennen," WA 37, 63.

4

The poor in the language
of legislation

During the years 1520–5, in a series of statutes, mandates, and ordinances, the Zurich town councilors sought to define the poor and locate them in relation to the community of Zurich. In 1520, the town councilors were primarily concerned with separating the "truly poor" from the larger population and designating those who were both genuinely needy and deserving. In doing so, they defined different kinds of poor folk; they established categories of poor. At the same time, they sought to delineate the characteristics that separated those who were to receive relief from those who were not. By 1525, the town councilors had moved to the problem of administering to the poor, as they sought to delineate those civic institutions that were to care for the poor within a reformed Christian community.

This chapter is concerned with the perception of the poor articulated in the town council's legislation. It does not, indeed cannot, seek to determine who each of the poor were, to identify them and locate them socioeconomically; the sources do not provide this kind of information.[1] It is concerned, rather, with two interconnected questions: Did Zwingli's preaching and the printed images have an impact on practice, the actual care of the poor; and what does the language of legislation reveal about the perceptions of the poor and the values associated with the poor held

[1] Nicholas Smiar has explored the records of the Alms Office in great detail and found that those persons most often named in the records were not the recipients, but the officials, "Poor Law and Outdoor Poor Relief in Zürich, 1520–1529: A Case Study in Social Welfare History and Social Welfare Policy Implementation" (Ph.D. Diss., University of Illinois at Chicago, 1986), p. 166. For socioeconomic definitions of poverty, see Erich Maschke, "Die Unterschichten der mittelalterlichen Städte Deutschlands," in *Städte und Menschen,* Vierteljahrschrift für Sozial– und Wirtschaftsgeschichte, Bd. 68 (Wiesbaden, 1980), pp. 306–79; and Robert Jütte, *Obrigkeitliche Armenfürsorge in deutschen Reichstädten der frühen Neuzeit,* Kölner Historische Abhandlungen, Bd. 31 (Cologne, 1984), especially chap. 2.

by those who made the laws in Zurich? The two laws provide relatively clear and explicit statements of contemporary and collective definitions of what constituted true poverty, of the categories the legislators adopted to distinguish among poor people. They also articulate the much less concrete qualities that sixteenth-century burghers employed in evaluating the poor, in segregating those who were "worthy" of aid from those who were not. These poor laws present us with carefully crafted perceptions of the poor, which are colored and shaded by the application of collective values.

Many criteria and categories that appear in these statutes also appeared in canon law, some even earlier in the writings of the church fathers.[2] Primary among those continuities was the concern with begging.[3] We must be careful to distinguish, as canon lawyers and town councilors did, the act of begging from the persons of beggars. The behavior of begging was practiced by many different kinds of people, many of whom were temporarily impoverished, temporarily forced to beg. The more honorable of those poor are discussed below. Included among those who begged, however, was a kind of person whom both ecclesiastical and secular legislators distinguished from the other poor, a kind of person feared by town and church alike. Sometimes called the sturdy beggar, sometimes the false beggar, this person assumed the same pattern of behavior as those who had been made destitute through bad fortune. In a case brought before the Zurich town council during the 1520s: "Balthasar Furabint from the Würtemberger countryside, Stussi from Baden, and Berk from Biel all begged with Saint Valentine's illness [syphillis] yet they were not infected; for that reason they played false."[4]

---

[2] Brian Tierney, *Medieval Poor Law* (Berkeley, 1959).

[3] On medieval views of begging, see Tierney, and Michel Mollat, *Les Pauvres au Moyen Age* (Paris, 1978). On the similarity of Catholic and Protestant views of the beggar, as "fearful," "repulsive," "a rebel against God," and "an actual robber of Christ's own poor," see Brian Pullan, "Catholics and the Poor in Early Modern Europe," *Transactions of the Royal Historical Society*, 5th ser., 26 (1976): 15–34. On the problem of begging in fifteenth-century and sixteenth-century Central Europe, see Robert Jütte, "Poor Relief and Social Discipline in Sixteenth-Century Europe," *European Studies Review* 11 (1981): 25–52; Catharina Lis and Hugo Soly, *Poverty and Capitalism in Pre-Industrial Europe* (Bristol, 1982[1979]), especially pp. 79–92; *Aspects of Poverty in Early Modern Europe*, ed. Thomas A. Riis (Alphen aan den Rijn, 1981); Thomas Fischer, *Städtische Armut und Armenfürsorge im 15. und 16. Jht.*, Göttinger Beiträge zu Wirtschafts– und Sozialgeschichte, Bd. 4, (Göttingen, 1979).

[4] "Bathassar furabint uss dem Wurtembergischen land; stussi von Baden, Berk von Biell betlent all an Sannt Valentins kranckheit unnd breste Inen nudt darzu spilent sy flaschlich." Staatsarchiv Zürich (hereafter StAZ), A27, 4a: Nachgänge 1524–7. Three other cases for the years 1524–7, of beggars falsely claiming syphillis can be found in this same collection.

The sturdy beggar differed, because he or she adopted that pattern of behavior manipulatively, "falsely" through choice, to "play" the community for its charity.

These persons were outsiders, using the accepted forms of exchange between the dependent and his donor to their own advantage. Quite frequently these beggars were vagrants, a distinct, but often overlapping category of marginal people, that is, men, primarily (though there were some women), who had no ties to any community, who were not bound by mutual responsibilities and duties to a collectivity, but drifted.[5] Some among these vagrants simply stole – sacks of grain, small household items – from those who had offered them shelter, despite the guarantee of a *"pater meum."*[6] Others were criminals of some magnitude: each of the five vagrants prosecuted by the Zurich town council in the years 1524–30 admitted over twenty different thefts. One admitted some fifty-seven, and in one case, the vagrant admitted to having stolen at least one altar cloth each from the Fraumünster, one of the cloisters, and a nearby village church.[7]

Efforts to control begging represent the earliest legislation regarding the poor for both the Church and the towns. As early as 1343, the town council in Zurich banned begging within the town walls.[8] It was, however, a pattern of behavior that proved, well past the period of this study, impossible to eradicate. In 1491, 1504, and 1515, the council banned all foreign beggars.[9] In 1495, it forbade all begging, and in 1498, it outlawed gypsies.[10] By 1519, the town council of Zurich had established at least one overseer of beggars, or *Bettelvogt*.[11]

---

[5] Werner Danckert, *Unehrliche Leute* (Bern, 1963).

[6] "Uls hubensteink ist ein starcker knecht in einem grossen geshotlote har gat zuo den einfaltigen puren unnd Iren wibern zuo huss unnd haff zugt Inen ein korallis pater me unnd vom dess dann vber den seckel gand ist err geschwund vnnd stosst dar ein beims falsch pr me," StAZ: A27, 4a. There are two other cases in this collection of "false pater meums."

[7] In all of these cases, the vagrant simply listed his thefts, in a form of confession, without claiming need. StAZ: B VI, 248, *Ratsbuch: Liber natalis* 1524, fols. 172v–173v; StAZ: B VI, 251, *Ratsbuch: Liber natalis* 1527, fols. 46r–49v; StAZ: A27, 5, *Nachgänge* 1527–32, dated August 1528; StAZ: B VI, 251, *Liber natalis* 1529, fols. 94r–95r and *Liber baptistalis* 1530, fols. 158r–159v. There were relatively few vagrants in Zurich: according to the *Richtsbücher*, 3 were prosecuted in 1520; 5 in 1521; 0 in 1522; 1 in 1523; 2 in 1524; 1 in 1525; 1 each in 1527, 1529, and 1530; 0 in 1528; and 6 in 1531 (StAZ: B VI, 249ff.).

[8] Alice Denzler, "Geschichte des Armenwesens in Kanton Zürich im 16. und 17. Jahrhundert," *Zürcher volkswirtschaftliche Studien*, N.F., 7 (1920), p. 11.

[9] Ibid., pp. 6–13.

[10] Ibid., p. 12.

[11] Emil Egli, *Aktensammlung zur Geschichte der Zürcher Reformation in den Jahren 1519–1533* (Zurich, 1879; reprint, Aalen, 1973), (hereafter EAk), no. 43.

On August 22, 1519, the Zurich town council appointed two men to investigate "how one should now administer the poor sick folk."[12] This marks a shift in the town council's attention. It had begun to move from a concern with a pattern of behavior, begging, and the problem poor, false beggars and vagrants, who abused the hospitality of the community, to address the broader issue of poor relief: of caring for a group of poor, the members of which the council would delineate the following year. Five and a half years later, in 1525, the Zurich town council had formulated its complete program, encompassing both the criteria for the poor deserving of communal aid and the bureaucracy through which that aid would be administered.

The Alms Statute of 1520

On September 8, 1520, the council published its first major legislation concerning the poor. In its opening sentence, the Alms Statute recalled the familiar basis for charity: To give alms "out of right, good love, opinion, and mercy" was an exceptionally good work.[13] People would be more willing to give alms, it continued, if they could believe, and hope, that the alms were employed well, that is, that they were given to the needy and worthy, rather than to those who were not. With these opening words, the legislators established a foundation for the statute, placing within a context of communal civic life Zurich's first and most extensive effort to distinguish those poor deserving of care from those who were not.

The 1520 Statute next sketched brief portraits of two kinds of poor. The first were "those men and women, young and old, who squander or have squandered their belongings dissolutely, excessively, and presumptuously, be it on expensive, superfluous, or presumptuous clothing, which is not appropriate to them, or on costly, superfluous food and drink, of which they have no need, or on gambling or other brazen and unnecessary things." These people, who might not want to work, were to be left to suffer the misery of poverty. The legislators were to return to this first category, to describe the characteristics in greater detail, after they had portrayed the second kind of poor.

---

[12] "M. Rubli und M. Zeller söllent ordnen, wie man jetz die armen kranken lüt versehen sölle." EAk, no. 92.
[13] For the text of the Alms Statute of 1520, see Appendix A.

The second category of poor were those "many pious, honorable people, who are of good birth and who have not wastefully or presumptuously depleted or squandered their belongings, and [who] have truly sought in all manner all their lives, with God and honor, with their labor to employ their time honorably and to nourish themselves and their own." These people were poor not through wastefulness or extravagance, but through

> divine temptation, destiny and order, be it through fire, war, crop failure, drought, or through a variety of illnesses, either of themselves or of their families, or through far too many children of their own or of their poor friends, or that they have become so old and invalid, that they may well no longer nourish themselves, or through other unforeseen timely mishap and accident, which frequently are to hand [occur] among men.

The primary and crucial criterion the town council employed to distinguish the two categories of poor was the question of choice, whether a person's poverty was in some way voluntary. Wantoness, extravagance, wastefulness, an unwillingness to work – patterns of behavior certain persons chose – distinguished the unworthy poor. Divine forces, fate, natural disasters, or natural decline created the conditions within which the deserving poor were no longer able to support themselves. These people did not choose to beg; they were dependent against their will. For them, begging was shameful. As soon as they were able, moreover, such people ceased to rely upon others for aid and became once again independent.

This first characteristic of the deserving poor suggests a second: that their poverty could often be temporary, lasting only so long as those conditions remained that prevented them from supporting themselves. These poor seem not to have been the indigent, the homeless, but those who had had some resources, and a livelihood, which had been strained, depleted, perhaps entirely eliminated, by chance.

These involuntary poor, the legislators warned, moreover, could become polluted by begging:

> It is also often perceived of the same home poor people,[14] where they must publicly beg, that they themselves and other people with them

---

[14] I have chosen to remain close to the German with this term, "husarmen lüten," in order to retain its particularity: at times it seems to connote more generally people who do indeed remain

become variously vexed or fallen, as when young pretty women or maidens come to certain need and poverty.

Perhaps the condition of dependency, perhaps the gesture of supplication endangered the innocent, but begging was shameful and shaming to honorable folk.

The legislators then returned to the issue of charity, more specifically, to the problem of the proper application of charity. Both spiritual and secular persons, they claimed, thought it would be a good work, if the burgermeister and the town council could mandate a means both to inform potential donors who the seemly and pious home poor were and to ensure the orderly and correct distribution of gifts. In 1520, the town council placed itself as mediator between donors and their dependents, providing a mechanism through which the poor could be screened for worthiness and donations could be effectively administered. In 1520, the town council was primarily concerned with determining which poor were deserving of the donations and support offered by the community's members. In 1520, the town council provided its most extensive list of the criteria it would apply to weed out the unworthy poor. Let us turn to them.

There were fourteen characteristics or patterns of behavior that, singly or in combination, excluded certain poor from alms. The first screened out were (a) those who publicly demanded or begged alms in the streets, in the cloisters, in the church plazas or in other open places. Once again, the town council sought to eliminate begging, placing it first among those kinds of behavior that precluded the receipt of alms. The town council then listed thirteen other specific patterns of behavior that the community found unworthy of charity. These thirteen can be roughly divided into two general kinds of unworthiness: immoral behavior and impious behavior.

Seven concern immoral or "unseemly" behavior: (b) those who were procurers or had seduced and led people's children or wives [*gemachel*] to fall; (c) those of whom it was known that they had presumptuously, mischievously [*muottwilligklich*], or extravagantly wasted and expended their belongings, or who had not wanted to serve or work industriously,

---

at home in their poverty; at other times, it holds a more specific and legal meaning of those who are residents of the town, perhaps citizens, and whose poverty is very much temporary.

although it certainly would have been possible and seemly; (d) those who, without pressing or honest need, purchased costly food and drink – such as expensive fish, foul, and the like, and the best wines – who could have easily become accustomed to poorer food and drink; (e) those who sat in inns, wine shops, and pubs during public hours and spent their money; (f) those who wore velvet, silk, silver, gold, or other extravagant jewelry, clothes, or trinkets, which they could well put away [*enberen*] with honor and seemliness, on account of their station; (g) all those who behaved frivolously, presumptuously, or vexatiously, be it with bowls [*buolen*], gaming, or the like; (h) those who were married, but, for no good reason, would not live together. Thus, not only did procurement and gambling, more conventional forms of immoral behavior, preclude the receipt of alms. Extravagance, the bad management of one's household or resources, also made one unworthy to receive any help. Equally, "unseemly" behavior, dressing or conducting oneself inappropriate to one's "station" in the community, made one, for the town council, unworthy of charity. In some way, each of these criteria define some kind of impropriety, of "unseemliness" – of expenditure, of apparel, of consumption, of demeanor, of deportment. Certain among the poor were judged "unworthy," because their conduct did not accord with collective notions not only of moral behavior, but also of behavior appropriate to people of their "station." The last kind of behavior, (i) an unwillingness to abide by the vow (and practice) of marriage, provided a bridge, from forms of behavior that were unacceptable to the town's collective morality, to those that offended Christian piety.

The remaining six criteria of unworthiness range from lapses in Christian practice to forms of sin: (j) those who neither understood nor knew the Lord's Prayer, Our Father, and the angelic greeting, the Hail Mary, the creed and the Ten Commandments, yet were of an age and ability that they could have learned it; (k) those who did not diligently listen to the sermon, mass, and vespers on Sundays and feast days, yet had nothing that reasonably prevented them; (l) those who did not confess their sins to a priest at least once all year; (m) those who did not partake of the holy sacrament at Easter time, even if they postponed it on advice of their own priest; (n) those who were excommunicate and did not seek to release themselves from their state of sin [*versumlicheit*]; (o) and finally, those who regularly grossly and vexatiously cursed and swore, and blasphemed God and the saints, who conducted themselves unpeacefully and unfairly toward people, or who libelled and bore false witness, or gossiped [*verliegent und vertragent oder verschwätzent*] against one another, thereby frequently leading to great disfavor, envy, and hate, and to discord, exile, war and dispute, "which [was] a great shameful evil and the devil's own work, which Christian persons should in no case do."

Different patterns of behavior, habits, actions, designated some poor as unworthy, either in terms of collective notions of moral behavior, the first eight kinds of behavior listed, or in terms of the practice of Christian piety, the last six. These patterns ranged from the management of household resources, consumption, and the conduct of marriage, to religious practices, both individual, annual confession, and collective, the Eucharist. The range of behavior over which the town council sought to establish its supervision was thus extensive, addressing as it did questions of morality, propriety, and piety.

The 1520 Statute did not state explicitly that it held those patterns of behavior to be the expression of inward flaws of character, nor does its vocabulary connect it directly with scholastic debates about "habit" and "nature." Yet, the final example of behavior undeserving of gifts suggests that the town council's scrutiny of the poor reached beneath the surface, reached beyond questions of action to those of character. At the end of the list of forms of impious behavior, the town council placed those forms that destroy the peace of the community,[15] that destroy the concord among neighbors. Blasphemy, libel, gossip – words spoken against God and neighbor – corroded the bonds between man and God, man and his neighbor, and between the community and God. Among the poor, then, the legislators recognized some who could and might bring about "discord, exile, war and dispute," who could destroy the bonds of the community – who could destroy the charity of the community.[16]

The Statute then turned to those poor who deserved gifts of charity: those certain honorable [*erberen*] home poor "who are not tainted or burdened with the previously listed vices, causes, and hinderances, who

---

[15] On the importance of the norm of "peace" in civic communities in the early sixteenth century, see Hans-Christoph Rublack, "Political and Social Norms in Urban Communities in the Holy Roman Empire," in *Religion, Politics and Social Protest: Three Studies on Early Modern Germany*, ed. Kaspar von Greyerz (London, 1984), especially pp. 28ff.

[16] On this connotation of charity, see Adalbert Hamman, *Vie liturgique et vie sociale* (Paris, 1968), especially pt. 1.

131

would gladly nourish and maintain themselves with their own care and labor, if it were possible for them, and who are so honorable and modest [*Ersam unnd schamhafftig*], that they are ashamed to demand and collect alms from house to house"; those who were so ill or oppressed, that they were unable to support themselves, "as had been sufficiently addressed above." The characteristics that distinguished the deserving poor were fewer in number: a sense of honor and shame, a desire to support themselves, an unwillingness to beg. These were responsible Christians, "home poor" who behaved with propriety and with gratitude:

> Of certain people and of such honorable, familiar persons, one may well hope and trust that they pray truly and diligently to God in the divine offices and before and after every meal for all people, be they living or dead, from whom mercy, support [*stür*] and help has been made evident and realized for them, the same as they, through gratitude and through divine and natural order, rightly ought and are obligated to do.

The categories of deserving and undeserving poor were long established in 1520. In the twelfth century, the Decretist Gratian, citing Augustine, prohibited alms to be given to "followers of infamous professions," to those whose livelihoods were immoral.[17] In the fifteenth century, discussions of the poor were framed in terms of the false beggar and the deserving poor.[18] What is new in the Statute of 1520 is the detail of the description, the care of the town council's effort to catalogue the variety of patterns of behavior undeserving of communal aid. These criteria that were established in 1520 were the delineations and definitions adopted by the Poor Law of 1525.

Traditional forms of poor relief

The Alms Statute of 1520 did not propose new institutions for the care of the poor. It was formulated to work within the pattern of traditional structures of poor relief in Zurich that had been in place for a long time. In 1520, disparate and discrete forms of relief functioned independently of one another. Sometimes the kinds of poor administered by each overlapped; sometimes, however, certain kinds

---

[17] Brian Tierney, "The Decretists and the Deserving Poor," *Comparative Studies in Society and History* 1 (1958–9): 363–4.
[18] Lis and Soly, pp. 50–1.

of poor fell between the jurisdictions of the various forms of relief. During the next five years those structures came under increasingly critical scrutiny.

These structures were not all ecclesiastical. In Zurich, guilds offered the first level of protection against poverty: they gave aid to the widows and orphans of members, and loans to destitute members.[19] In addition, certain guilds had specific obligations of charity. The butchers' guild donated meat to the churches and directly to the poor; and the bakers' guild, bread to the hospice [*Spital*].[20] For the most part, however, the relief offered by guilds applied to a narrowly circumscribed portion of the population: those urban poor (or their families) who had been able at one point to purchase their place in the guild. And in the fifteenth century, the town council had twice to remind the guilds of their obligations to their poorer members.[21]

A second source to which the poor could turn for relief was the Hospital of the Holy Spirit, originally called the *Hospitale pauperum*.[22] Founded in the late twelfth century, the hospital lay within the town walls in the parish of the Grossmünster, the canons of which cared for the souls of the hospital's inhabitants. The hospital seems to have been a joint enterprise between the canons and the town; at least once, in 1520, the town council provided financial support for it;[23] and the staff of the hospital were lay brothers. Although the hospital was originally intended for the poor, those who held benefices could purchase a guaranteed place within it, which eventually eliminated almost entirely the number of beds available for the truly destitute sick.[24] Two other hos-

---

[19] As early as 1466, the wool weavers' guild ruled on widows' inheritances, with an eye toward both the guild's interest and the need to provide the woman with an income, StAZ: A77, 12: Verschiedene Handwerke, no. 1. On the charitable functions of guilds in general, see Susan Brigden, "Religion and Social Obligation in Early Sixteenth Century London," *Past and Present* 103 (1984): especially 96–9; and Barbara Hanawalt, "Keepers of the Lights: Late Medieval English Parish Guilds," *Journal of Medieval and Renaissance Studies* 14 (1984): 21–37. For a more general treatment, see Antony Black, *Guilds and Civil Society in European Political Thought from the Twelfth Century to the Present* (Ithaca, N.Y., 1984).

[20] StAZ: A77, 3: Metzgerzunft, no. 8, n.d.; StAZ: A77, 2: Weggenzunft, no. 8, dated before 1490 by archivist.

[21] StAZ: A73, 1: Allgemeines Zunftwesen, no. 4, dated 1498 by archivist; and A77, 3: Metzgerzunft, no. 4, dated 1455–60 by archivist.

[22] On the Hospital of the Holy Spirit, see Rudolf Pfister, *Kirchengeschichte der Schweiz*, vol. 1, (Zurich, 1964) p. 381.

[23] StAZ: C II, 18: Spital, no. 1067, dated 24 January 1520.

[24] In 1525, the town council settled a dispute between two men, one of whom wished to purchase a bed in the hospital by endowment, in order to ensure himself "against necessity," StAZ: B

pitals within the town walls and one outside them were designated for the "special sick," or lepers.[25] The latter was open to all lepers, but the two former could only take those patients who could provide for the treatment out of their own means.[26] Within the town walls the hospitals offered little shelter for the sick poor.

The poor could also receive aid from private individuals, in the form of either alms or endowments. Until 1525, alms could be distributed, from the doorstep of a home, in the market, in the street, before the churches, by any individual who wished to give to the poor.[27] In the later Middle Ages, endowments had become increasingly popular as a means of caring for the poor.[28] Interest from an endowment enabled religious houses, then later the civic government, to purchase bread or clothing for the poor. Endowments were often made in the form of masses for the dead, which required the recipient to distribute alms on the day of the donor's death or on the four ember days. Long before reform in Zurich, people increasingly entrusted this form of aid for the poor to the civil authority.

Little is known about another form of aid in Zurich: the confraternities.[29] In January 1525, the Zurich town council made an inventory of the possessions of the town's confraternities, intending to confiscate them.[30] The inventory is the only record of the confraternities' holdings and one of the very few records of their existence.[31] According to the inventory, there were at least ten, possibly eleven confraternities in Zurich involved in charity. What precisely

VI, 248: *Ratsbuch Natalis* 1525, fol. 231r. On the limited number of beds through purchases by benefice, see Denzler, pp. 9–10.

[25] Denzler, pp. 9–10.

[26] Pfister, p. 387.

[27] After 1525, private alms giving was strongly discouraged, but not prohibited by the town council. See below.

[28] On endowments for the poor, see Denzler, p. 8.

[29] There have been few studies of confraternities in Switzerland. Pfister notes one kind of confraternity, found in western Switzerland, which was established for the purpose of caring for the sick poor, p. 359. Pierre Duparc has explored this kind of confraternity in rural Savoy in his short article, "Confraternities of the Holy Spirit and Village Communities in the Middle Ages," in *Lordship and Community in Medieval Europe*, ed. Fredric L. Cheyette (Huntington, N.Y., 1975), 341–56. Apparently, there was no such confraternity in Zurich, at least not at the time of the town council's inventory of 1525.

[30] EAk, no. 620. Most of the early sixteenth-century civic records dealing with the poor have been reprinted in EAk. Most references to the town council's transactions, therefore, will be to this edition.

[31] See also EAk, nos. 667 (18 March 1525), 1394 (22 April 1528), and 1916 (31 December 1532).

they offered as relief to the poor, either their own or others, is not mentioned in the sources.[32]

Most often, the poor, both from the town and from the land, turned to the religious houses in Zurich for aid. Although neither as old nor as influential as the Fraumünster or the Grossmünster, the three mendicant houses in Zurich, the Dominicans, Franciscans, and Augustinians, were the primary sources for administering relief to all poor. Even these institutions could offer no more than a single allotment of bread or broth per person on a day-to-day basis, and overnight shelter for the itinerant poor. The numbers of itinerant poor seeking aid from Zurich's mendicant houses were probably increasing in the early sixteenth century; the rural religious houses, to which the rural poor historically had turned, were no longer offering relief.[33] In addition to private donations, the mendicant houses also received rents and tithes from their holdings in the canton, a portion of which was to be used for the care of the poor.[34]

That these mendicant houses were no longer meeting the needs of the canton's poor, that they were not applying the wealth they received to the care of the poor, was underlined in Zwingli's sermons and confirmed in the town council's ability to assume the management of their property unchallenged.[35] Six weeks prior to the Poor Law, on December 5 and 6, 1524, the town council would appoint one officer to manage the goods, property, and wealth of each of the mendicant houses in Zurich.[36] The friars could leave the cloister and take up a craft, support themselves, or remain within the cloister walls until they died.[37] Their wealth, however, was to be turned over to the care of the poor.

---

[32] Anton Largiadér notes them in his history of Zurich as "widmeten sich den Werken der Liebe und der Frömmigkeit," but offers no more specific description of their activities. Anton Largiadér, *Geschichte von Stadt und Landschaft Zürich* (Zurich, 1945), vol. 1, p. 294.

[33] "In den Gemeinden scheint die kirchliche Armenpflege am Ende des Mittelalters ganz aufgehört zu haben. Die Kirche teilte die ihr zu Verwaltung übergebenen Jahrzeiten und Stiftungen aus, aber aus ihren eigenen Mitteln leistete sie für die Armen nichts." Denzler, p. 8.

[34] See above, Chapter 2, for Zwingli's discussion of the role of rents and tithes in the care of the poor.

[35] On the history of the town council's relations with the religious houses, see Hans Morf, "Obrigkeit und Kirche in Zürich bis zu Beginn der Reformation," *Zwingliana* 13 (1969–73): 164–205; Emil Egli, "Die zürcherische Kirchenpolitik von Waldmann bis Zwingli," *Jahrbuch für Schweizerische Geschichte* 21 (1896): 1–35; and Paul Schweizer, "Die Behandlung der zürcherischen Klostergüter in der Reformationszeit," *Theologische Zeitschrift aus der Schweiz* (Zurich, 1885).

[36] EAk, no. 599.

[37] EAk, no. 598.

The town council and the poor to 1525

For two and one half years after the Statute of 1520, the council was silent on the issue of the poor. Having entered into the problem of poor relief, it did not venture any further. Its next involvement with the poor, moreover, was a return to the old problem of foreign beggars. In a mandate of January 1523, the council reiterated its ban of foreign beggars and its demand that resident beggars wear a sign by which they could be distinguished from foreigners.[38] The council did appoint two officers to oversee the beggars. Here, too, the council tentatively extended an administrative apparatus specific to the problem. It did not address the causes of begging, or attempt to allay the deeper problems of poverty, but sought to regulate and to monitor individual beggars.

During 1523, the poor became a more pressing issue in Zurich. The records of the town council speak not only of its own increased involvement with the poor, but also of the intensifying popular concern with the care of the poor. On three different occasions during the summer, officers and villagers from the canton brought grievances before the council that the poor were not receiving their due. On June 22, officials of the communes of Zollikon, Riesbach, Fallenden, Hirslanden, Unterstrass, and Wytikon lodged the complaint that the tithes given to the provost and canons of the Grossmünster were not being used as alms, as they should be, but for "unnecessary and frivolous things."[39] On July 9, two witnesses from Richterschwyl, Hans Bachmann and Welti Bosshart, testified, their priest had preached that tithes were alms given in order for the word of God to be spread.[40] In the third incident, recorded on August 4, Hans Klinger of Embrach argued that he paid only a portion of the tithe because the preacher had told his congregation, one should give alms to the poor, not more wealth to those whose chests were already full.[41] In each of these incidents, care of the poor was linked with tithes. By 1523, tithes had become a serious problem for the town council, as well as for the Church.[42] In addition to those three

---

[38] EAk, no. 322.
[39] EAk, no. 368.
[40] EAk, no. 379.
[41] EAk, no. 392.
[42] On rural resistance to tithes in the canton of Zurich, see Walter Claassen, "Schweizer Bauern-politik im Zeitalter Zwinglis," *Sozialgeschichtliche Forschungen*, vol. 4 (Berlin, 1899), chap. 9. On the place of tithes in the peasants' grievances in 1524–5, see Lawrence P. Buck, "Opposition

episodes, the council addressed nine cases in which either individuals or, more impressively, entire villages refused to pay tithes.[43] In each of the nine cases, the council supported the right of the churches to collect tithes and fined the miscreants.

The three incidents mentioned above are the only ones in which the council did not take action against the tithes' critics.[44] The reason for their exemption from punishment lies in the nature of their criticism. They did not complain, as did others, that the tithes had become larger in proportion to their possessions or wealth, or that they were a financial burden. Their criticism focused upon the use to which tithes had been applied, or rather, the misuse. If, as had been commonly held and Zwingli argued, the collection of tithes was justified by the purpose to which the wealth was to be applied – the care of the poor and the support of the local congregation's pastor – then the use of that wealth for "unnecessary and frivolous things" was morally wrong. The men who chose not to pay tithes, but to give alms instead, were doing no more than giving expression in their actions to the popular perception of the abuse of tithal monies. This line of criticism echoed Zwingli's and reflected the distinction he made between the tithes themselves, the original purpose of which was good,[45] and the current use of tithes, which had become an abuse of authority and neglect of charitable responsibility.[46] It was only in their choice of response to the abuse that these rural critics differed from Zwingli; and in the logic of their response he found a real challenge.

These critics were heard. The Grossmünster, one of the primary recipients of tithes in the town of Zurich and the object of much criticism on that account, was reformed jointly by the canons and the town council on September 29, 1523.[47] Among the practices reformed was the use

[43] to Tithes in the Peasants' Revolt: A Case Study of Nuremberg in 1524," *The Sixteenth Century Journal* 4 (1973): 11–22; and Henry J. Cohn, "Anticlericalism in the German Peasants' War 1525," *Past and Present* 83 (1979): especially 20–5.

[43] See EAk, nos. 351, 365, 370, 375–6, 391, 397, 452, and 477 for 1523; nos. 558, 568–9, and 577 for 1524.

[44] Like Zwingli, the town council endorsed the institution of the tithe, and his explanation of its function probably provided support for the town council's position. But the town council did not follow Zwingli's demand that the tithe be used solely for moral purposes: those tithes that rested in secular hands, and there were a number of them, went unchallenged and unexamined in the years of the Reformation.

[45] On the original purpose of tithes, see Catherine Boyd, *Tithes and Parishes in Medieval Italy* (Ithaca, N.Y., 1952), chap. 2.

[46] See preceding pages and Chapter 2, above.

[47] EAk, no. 426.

of monies from benefices, offices, rents, and tithes; they were to be used first to support preaching, both in Zurich and in the rural parish churches, and then, with whatever remained, to help the needy in hospitals and the poor at home. The town council, working with the provost and the canons of the Grossmünster, returned the tithes to the use for which they had been originally designed: the support of preaching and the care of the poor. The records speak eloquently of how well these measures met popular approval: there were no more refusals to pay tithes to the Grossmünster, but only to pay it to those churches that had not yet reformed their practices.

Another issue in which the town council became involved that had a bearing on the problem of poor relief was iconoclasm.[48] The autumn of 1523 witnessed increasingly violent attacks on images in rural churches and intensified invectives against church decoration within the walls of the town itself.[49] Within the two weeks preceding the reform of the Grossmünster, three cases involving destruction of church art in Zurich came before the town council.[50] The first iconoclast, Lorentz Meyger, who was an assistant at St. Peter's parish church, justified his destruction of an altar retable and various ornaments in terms of a Christian economy: "there were so many poor human beings who sat before the church and elsewhere, and who had nothing, but had to suffer great hunger and drudgery [*arbentzäligkeit*], who could be helped with such expensive ornaments; for, as one finds in Ambrose, such ornaments are the food of the poor."[51] Again, in the third incident, the iconoclasts, who brought down a large wooden cross just outside the town gate at Stadelhofen, stated that their intention had been to sell the wood in order to give the money to the poor.

The iconoclasts justified their acts in terms that echo the criticism of

---

[48] On iconoclasm in Zurich, see Charles Garside, Jr., *Zwingli and the Arts* (New Haven, Conn., 1966), especially chaps. 7–8; and my "Iconoclasts in Zurich," to be published by the Herzog August Bibliothek, Wolfenbüttel, in a volume on iconoclasm.

[49] See EAk, nos. 414, 415, 421–3, 440, 442, and 462 for 1523; 491–2, 497, 502, 511, 535, and 548 for 1524.

[50] For the narratives of these incidents, StAZ: A27, 4: *Kundschaften und Nachgänge*; StAZ E I, 1a: *Religionssachen*, nos. 1.63, 1.64, 1.43, 1.45, and 1.46; and StAZ: B VI, 249: *Ratsbuch 1523*, fol. 70r. Much of the narrative is reproduced in EAk, nos. 414 and 421. I have analyzed in detail these cases, with others, in "Iconoclasts in Zurich."

[51] "dann es wer so meings arms mensche das vor den kilchenn vnnd sunste allenthalb sässe vnnd wedr vmb noch an hette sondre grossen hunger vnnd arbentzäligkeit lid müsste mit wellichem kostlichen zierden den selben wol geholfen möcht. were dann man heiter finde in Ambrosio das solich gezierden ssyg ein spys der armen," StAZ: A27, 4: *Kundschaften und Nachgänge*.

tithes: the wealth invested in church art was better used to feed the poor. They did not request the redistribution of wealth, nor was their criticism of church art framed in terms of false worship. For the iconoclasts, to invest, to freeze, wealth in the art in the churches was wrong, when that selfsame wealth had an organic function, to feed the poor. For them, all ecclesiastical wealth, both income and invested wealth was embraced in a single Christian economy which should be guided first by principles of charity.

The town council responded to the iconoclasts. On 16 May 1524, seven months after these three incidents,[52] it assigned eight officers and three preachers to investigate what was to be done with the church decoration.[53] One month later, on June 15, this investigation produced a mandate.[54] In it, the council ordered the removal from the churches of all objects that might be worshipped. Each family was permitted to remove those objects which it or its ancestors had commissioned or donated. On 2 July, a committee that included the three preachers removed all that remained to public squares outside the churches and destroyed them. One provision of the mandate pertained specifically to the poor: "and the goods and riches, donated thus to such images, should be turned to the poor, needy people, who are the true image of God."[55] The town council had adopted the criticism of church decoration, as the misuse of wealth, that the people, and Zwingli, had voiced. It echoed Zwingli's words, reaffirming that the poor were to be the true images of God in the new Christian community. Those criticisms became the foundation of the town council's formal position on church decoration. In the argument that church decoration was the misuse of wealth better applied to the needs of the poor, the town council found a justification for its own involvement in the cleansing of the churches. It also found in it a new source for poor relief.

The town council also addressed other religious practices with an eye toward poor relief. On May 14, 1524, one month prior to the mandate

---

[52] The incidents in Zurich were followed by ones in Höngg, Altstetten, and Zollikon.

[53] EAk, no. 532.

[54] EAk, no. 546.

[55] "und die güeter und kosten, so an soliche bilder gelegt, söllent an die armen, dürftigen mentschen, die ein ware bildung Gottes sind, verwendt werden," ibid. The phrase, "a true image of God," probably came from Zwingli, who used it, as early as the Second Disputation, as the centerpiece of his discussion of the poor. (See Chapter 2) It was, however, a phrase used by other reformers as well.

on images, the town council turned to the annual pilgrimage on Pentecost Monday from Zurich to Einsiedeln.[56] It ordered that the pilgrimage cease, because it had become the occasion for "disruption, mischief, [and] improprieties." In its stead, the council asked that "every house should give one penny [*batzen*] for food and maintenance of the poor, and place it in the box of the Water Church for the hands of the poor, needy, resident poor."[57]

The final and perhaps most dramatic act of the town council before the Poor Law was the seizure of the mendicant houses in Zurich in December 1524. The Grossmünster had been reformed, as we have seen, in September of the preceding year. On November 30, 1524, the abbess of the Fraumünster, Katharina von Zimbern, turned her convent over to the town.[58] The provision for the convent, issued on December 5, was that the abbess and nuns would remain in the convent to the ends of their lives.[59] The council appointed two men to oversee the convent. In the same act the council announced to the men's houses: "the monks from the Augustinian and from the Dominican houses should, if they leave the order and learn a craft, give away the goods they brought with them, in order that the impecunious be helped through the property of the cloisters."[60] Although the numbers of mendicants had dwindled to a very few in each house, the town council's move against the mendicant houses had no precedent; the friars and hermits had not sought its intervention or reform. On the following day, December 6, the council appointed one supervisor for each of the three cloisters, each of whom were to make an inventory of moveable and landed property.[61] The council did not address here, as it had with the

---

[56] EAk, no. 527. See also *Johannes Stumpfs Schweizer- und Reformationschronik*, ed. E. Gagliardi, H. Müller, and F. Büsser, *Quellen zur Schweizer Geschichte*, section 1, vol. 5 (Basel, 1952), pt. 1, p. 197.

[57] "uf solicher fart mer ufruoren, muotwillens und ungeschicklichkeiten mit unschickung allerlei jungs volks vollbracht ... dass ein jeklich gehuset, zuo spis und ufenthalt der armen, solle geben 1 batzen und den selbs legen und tuon in den stock in der Wasserkilchen zuo den armen, notdurftigen huslüten handen," EAk, no. 527.

[58] EAk, no. 595. Stumpf noted that she also handed over her rights for minting coin, making possible the first coins issued by the civic government of Zurich (pp. 200–1). In two weeks, the nuns of Grimmenthurn were rehoused with the Dominican nuns at Oetenbach (pp. 250–1).

[59] EAk, no. 598.

[60] "Den Mönchen zu den Augustinern und zu den Predigern soll, wenn sie aus den Orden treten und ein Handwerk lernen, ihr zugebrachtes Gut hinausgeben, den unbemittelten aus des Klosters Gütern geholfen werden." EAk, no. 598. See also, Stumpf, pp. 250–1.

[61] EAk, no. 599.

Grossmünster, any reform of specific practices or behavior. It was concerned solely with the administration of the mendicant houses' property. On 24 December, the town council requested further that all those who owed debts or other rents to the three houses report to the caretakers on the following day, in order to determine to what extent the debts were correctly assessed.[62] The town council was thus assuming the administration of the three houses' various incomes as well as their property. It had also assumed the role of judge as to the fairness of the debts to the religious houses incurred by the urban and rural populace of Zurich. It sought both to administer all wealth of the religious houses and to protect its own populace.

The town council did not make explicit in these two entries to what end it intended to use the mendicants' wealth. It had, however, already linked the cloisters with its concern for the poor some seven months before it took over the mendicant houses, on May 3, 1524, when it assigned six men to present to the council "advice and orders concerning the cloisters and the poor."[63] As we have seen, the Church's, particularly the mendicants' misuse of wealth, both donated and received as tithes, that was intended for the care of the poor, was a major theme in fifteenth- and sixteenth-century anticlericalism and, specifically, in Zwingli's opposition to mendicancy. On January 4, 1525, the council returned again to the proper use of religious wealth. In an act addressing donations traditionally given to support religious houses, the council stated:

> that all those who have given, endowed and directed to the cloisters chasubles and other ornaments, and also memorial masses, vigils and the like, on account of God's will as well as their own and their ancestors' salvation, desist from their proposed plans and demands. Such gifts to God are best turned from my lords to the poor folk; otherwise nothing shall ever be given out.[64]

In taking over the management of the mendicant houses' property, the town council had assumed control over those institutions primarily

---

[62] EAk, no. 606.

[63] EAk, no. 522: "Ratschläge und Ordnungen betreffend die Klöster und die Armen."

[64] StAZ: B VI, 248: *Ratsbuch Natalis*, fol. 224r: "Es ist erkent dass alle die so in die clöster messgewender und ander ornaten dessglich Jarzit vigilien vnnd derglich ding vmd gottes ouch Ir vnd Irer vordren selenheyls willenn gebenn gestifft vnnd geordnet habint Irer vermeinte vordring vnnd ansprach abstan vnnd söllint sollich gotsgabenn von minen herren armen lute zumm beste verwent vnnd suonzt niemas nudt hinuss gegeben werdenn." Reproduced in EAk, no. 611.

responsible for the care of the poor. It is no coincidence that the takeover of their property preceded the issuance of the Poor Law by only two weeks. Not only religious practices, but also forms of religious life were to be judged in terms of the care of the poor.

The town council returned again and again to the use of religious wealth for the care of the poor: in its rulings on tithes, on church decoration, on the Einsiedeln pilgrimage, and on bequests. In Zurich, the concern with the care of the poor was bound up with the attack on traditional religious practices and the form of religious life. Many religious practices were criticized precisely because they drew resources or attention away from the care of the poor, from Christian charity. The care of the poor was becoming the public standard by which the forms and practice of religious life were judged Christian.

In the two weeks preceding the Poor Law, moreover, the town council became increasingly concerned with the care of the poor. On January 5, 1525, the day following its ruling on donors, the council assigned four of its leading members, J. Jörg Göldli, Hans Rudolf Lavater, Rudolf Stoll, and Ulrich Trinkler, to present advice on alms and the poor.[65] In the meantime, these four men were to feed the poor and turn away foreign beggars. On January 9, the council ordered another four men, M. Binder, Peter Meier, Hans Schneeberger, and Stephan Zeller, to "seek out the chasubles, albs, altar cloths, and other pieces that are discovered in the three cloisters, to exchange the precious stones and pearls for money and to distribute to the poor the chasubles and albs that cannot be sold, so that nothing will be lost or gobbled up by moths."[66] In its management of ecclesiastical wealth, the council was concerned that nothing be wasted, be "gobbled up by moths." The wealth taken over from the churches was to be conserved,[67] converted into currency, and that which could not be converted into coin was nonetheless to be made useful to the community as clothes for the poor. In Zurich, at least in January of 1525, certain poor were to be dramatically visible in the robes of the

---

[65] EAk, no. 612.

[66] EAk, no. 614: "'söllent ersuochen die messgwand, alben, altertücher and andere kleinot, so in den dryen klöster(n) erfunden sind,' die Edelsteine und Perlen zu Geld machen und nicht verkäufliche Messgewänder und Alben den Armen zutheilen, damit nichts verdorben und von Motten zerfressen werde."

[67] On the same day and those following these men produced a partial inventory, EAk, no. 616.

priests. In Zurich, the vestments of the churches became the vestments of the poor, at once manifesting the new Christian economy and signalling the transformation of religious life.

On the same day, January 9, the town council also issued instructions to the four Officers for the Poor, the four men whom it had assigned four days earlier.[68] The instructions were divided into three parts. First, they were to examine the earlier and current articles concerning alms and recommend the best course to the council. They were to send messengers into the wards of the town to inform the needy of the alms. They were to advise "how and what should be done in the countryside, so that each congregation cares for its own poor and does not send them to their neighbors and other folk."[69] Second, these four were given full authority, until further notice from the council, to order two or more priests to distribute alms daily in the Dominican cloister at the sound of the morning bells. Third, they were to consult with the Dominican nuns at Oetenbach, which lay next to the Dominican cloister in Zurich, whether it would be possible to offer care for the lepers, and to ensure that the convent had enough wine and bread for the sick. A nurse was to be procured from the hospital, or, if necessary, from elsewhere. It seems that the four Officers of the Poor were to be permanently in charge of the convent, for the council continued: If there was no room for the four officers at Oetenbach, they were to seek a place in the Sacrament house or elsewhere; the convent was always to give them food and drink. If the women wished to give alms in addition to this, it was to be permitted until further notice from the council.

The council had thus begun to formulate a broad program of care for the poor, beginning with the care of lepers. It had also placed four of its most important members in charge of deciding what would be the best form of relief and how to place care of the poor in local hands, how to prevent the poor from the canton's villages from relying always upon its largest urban center for relief. Each of these four men were major figures in the town. Two of the four, Lavater and Trinkler, were close personal friends of Zwingli.[70] Göldli, Stoll,

---

[68] EAk, no. 615.

[69] "'wie und was uf dem land ze tuond sye, damit jedes kilchspel sine armen lüt selbs erziehen und uf ire nachpuren und ander lüt (nit) schickent.'" EAk, no. 615.

[70] For the portraits that follow, see Walter Jacob, *Politische Führungsschicht und Reformation*, Zürcher

and Trinkler became Caretakers of the Poor when the Poor Law was passed, and remained in that post until August 1528. Göldli, who was from an old Junker family, belonged to the patrician Constaffler. By far the wealthiest of the four, possessing some 6,400 gulden in property, he was a rentier, a man whose wealth was drawn at least in part from the countryside. Of the four, his position toward Zwingli and his reforms was the least sympathetic; although he remained uncommitted, his brother was one of Zwingli's most vocal opponents. Lavater, who was a glazier and glass painter, belonged to the less powerful *Gerwe* guild.[71] Lavater eventually became Burgermeister, the first of his guild and his craft to do so in Zurich. He was also one of Zwingli's strongest supporters, and part of his political success may have arisen from his involvement in the reform. Stoll was a goldsmith, apparently a less affluent member of his craft, for he belonged to the *Zimmerleuten* guild, rather than the more powerful and wealthy *zur Meisen* guild. Of his relationship with the reform in Zurich, Walter Jacob writes: "On the other hand, his office as Caretaker for the alms as well as his official activity from 1524–5 on shows that he played a truly significant role in the implementation of the Reformation."[72] The last of the four men was also the closest personally to Zwingli; Zwingli's second son was named for him and carried by him to his baptism. Trinkler, like Stoll, was a goldsmith. He was also a woodcarver and a merchant and, unlike Stoll, did belong to the wealthy *zur Meisen* guild. He was very rich, possessing more than 5,000 gulden, so much so that it was sometimes believed that he belonged to the Junker class. Much of his wealth seems to have come from his art, his goldworking and woodcarving, rather than his commercial activities. That four men of such influence should be chosen to organize relief in Zurich speaks not only of their integrity in dealing with valuable property and income, but also of the importance that the reform of the care of the poor held for Zurich's leaders. That men who were not instrumental in the Reformation in Zurich

---

Beiträge zur Reformationsgeschichte, Bd. 1, (Zurich, 1970), pp. 167–70, 208–11, 267–9, and 273–6.

[71] His success in reformed Zurich tells us something about the place of his craft in the new Christian community: glass painting flourished in the 1520s and 1530s in Zurich.

[72] "Anderseits zeigen sein Pflegeramt für das Almosen sowie seine Verordnetentätigkeit ab 1524/25, dass er bei der Durchführung der Reformation eine recht bedeutende Rolle spielte," Jacob, p. 268.

were made Caretakers of the Poor may also suggest that poor relief
was not to mirror religious divisions.

The Poor Law of 1525

On January 15, 1525, the town council passed the Poor Law.[73] Drawing
on its experience with the problems of unworthy and deserving poor,
begging and itinerant poor, and the use of the mendicants' wealth, it
set forth standards and regulations for treating the poor.[74] With this law,
the Zurich town council broke new ground, for it brought all forms of
care for the poor – food, shelter, and hospitals for the sick – under a
single, local administration. In this respect, it was similar to the poor
laws of Strasbourg and Nuremberg.[75] Each of these poor laws represented a break with past practice. Care of the poor was no longer to be
managed by disparate and discrete agencies, most of which were ecclesiastical, but by a single civic agency.[76] The Zurich town council was
not simply to monitor the actions of religious houses, nor designate
specific houses for specific kinds of care. Officers of the council were
directly responsible for the care of the poor.

The Poor Law has been viewed almost exclusively from the vantage
point of what it says about larger themes of the Reformation, in particular, the reevaluation of labor and the opposition to mendicancy.[77] Yet
the Poor Law also represents the only description of the civic program
of poor relief in Reformation Zurich and the fullest statement of the
town council's intentions for the poor. It delineates some of the Zurich

---

[73] On the Poor Law, see Denzler; Walter Köhler, *Armenpflege und Wohltätigkeit in Zürich zur Zeit Zwinglis*, Neujahrsblatt der Hülfgesellschaft in Zürich, vol. 119 (Zurich, 1919); and S. Vögelin, *Geschichte des zürcherischen Armenwesens*, Neujahrsblatt der Hülfsgesellschaft in Zürich, vol. 38 (Zurich, 1838). The Poor Law of 1525 represented the fullest treatment of the problem of poverty facing Zurich – begging, how to care for the poor, and the resources for their care – until the middle of the century. In the 1550s, the Poor Law was revised in the face of increasing numbers of poor. See Hans Ulrich Bächtold, *Heinrich Bullinger vor dem Rat*, Zürcher Beiträge zur Reformationsgeschichte, vol. 12 (Bern, 1982), chap. 7.
[74] According to Denzler, the Poor Law of 1525 served as the foundation for all programs of relief in Zurich until the eighteenth century, p. 30.
[75] On the poor laws of these Reformation centers, see Otto Winckelmann, "Uber die ältesten Armenordnungen der Reformationszeit (1522–1525)," *Historische Vierteljahrschrift* 17 (1914–15): 187–228, 361–400; and "Die Armenordnungen von Nürnberg (1522), Kitzingen (1523), Regensburg (1523), und Ypern (1525)," *Archiv für Reformationsgeschichte [ARG]* 10 (1913): 242–80, and 11 (1914): 1–18.
[76] Whether centralization is a "Protestant" innovation has been much debated.
[77] This is especially true of Köhler. See also Denzler, especially pp. 21–4.

town council's goals and helps us to map its changing definition of itself and its emerging role within its people's collective life. It reaffirms the categories, first articulated in 1520, by which the poor were to be evaluated and located within the matrix of religious and social values of the community of Zurich. It is worthwhile, therefore, to examine the Poor Law's language and the institutions that it defines.

The Poor Law is divided into twenty-one articles.[78] The first six define the responsibilities of the Caretakers and organize the relief of the poor by function and place. Articles seven and eight describe those who should not receive alms. Article nine describes how each of the home poor are to be designated and marked. Articles ten and eleven deal with begging. Article twelve addresses private charity and article thirteen, schools for orphans and poor children. Article fourteen concerns foreign beggars. Article fifteen deals with lepers. Articles sixteen and seventeen address the role of the religious houses in the program of relief. Article eighteen concerns the poor in the countryside. Nineteen treats the right of the poor to inherit, and twenty deals specifically with pregnant poor women. The last article is a warning to those who would abuse or disrupt the care of the poor.

Some subjects are discussed in great detail; others, but sketchily; and on some subjects the town council was silent. The concerns of the town council in 1525 differed from those of 1520. In 1525, the first priority of the town council was to ensure food for the poor:

> (Soup and Bread at the Dominicans) First, in order to bring the poor folk off the streets, it is intended as a beginning, that every day a kettle of oatmeal, barley, or other broth is prepared at the Dominican kitchen, as following: broth and bread should be given in the morning, after the Dominican bells have been heard.

This food was to be prepared in a communally administered kitchen. The council also made three men, the priests H. Antoni Walder and H. Jörg Syz, and the overseer of beggars, Anderesen, specifically responsible for preparing the food and seeing that it was distributed to the poor. The chairman and four officers were to supervise the distribution. These five are named in article two:

---

[78] In his transcription, Egli divided the Poor Law into 21 articles, EAk, no. 619, which I follow. The full text of the Poor Law, StAZ: A61.1, can be found in Appendix B.

(Four Caretakers and scribe) And in order that these alms will be increased to the honor of God and for the consolation of the resident and foreign poor folk, and better and therefore more consistently and longer taken in and distributed again to the home poor or otherwise suffering people, four men from the Small and Great Councils are hereby appointed, namely M. Rudolf Stoll, J. Jörg Göldli, Ulrich Trinkler, and Hans Schneeberger, cloth merchant; moreover, H. Heinrich Brennwald, provost at Embrach, should be their chairman and scribe in this matter, move into the town, but not serve his prebend any less (on that account).

Three of the four officers appointed here, as we have seen, had been assigned to investigate the problem of poor relief. The fourth, Hans Schneeberger, a wealthy cloth merchant, had been a member of the committee appointed six days earlier to oversee the cloisters' wealth. He belonged to the same guild, the *zur Meisen,* as Trinkler. As in the case of Stoll, Jacob found in Schneeberger's service as Caretaker evidence of his connection to the Reformation in Zurich: He was sympathetic, but not actively supportive of reform.[79] This article created a central agency to administer relief to the poor. The four men were to work closely with the chairman, whose move to the town made him more readily accessible; and he, for his part, was to call frequent meetings with his staff. The program was unified, under four prominent citizens, men who were recognizable, and whose public faces, reputations, and careers were now linked with the care of the poor.

The next three articles address the security and integrity of the administration of poor relief. The first two delineate the mechanisms to protect the funds and accounts from tampering. Article three mandated that each Caretaker was to have his own key to the alms chest and stores; each key worked only in conjunction with the other keys, "so that no one may have access to the chest without the others." The fourth article required that one of the three people's priests be present whenever someone reviewed the accounts or the stores. In article four, the town council delineated one form of control on the actions of the Caretakers: the priest, who served as a witness to their propriety, was an external restraint. The conscience of each Caretaker was also to be bound by an oath:

---

[79] "Anderseits stand seine frühe Tätigkeit als Verordneter und vorab seine Wahl zum Almosen pfleger in enger Beziehung zur Reformation," Jacob, p. 245.

(Oath) The chairman and the Caretakers, as each will be appointed to these alms in time, should swear that the annual rents or other daily taxes, be they of money or of other possessions, are given as alms and given for that reason; that they will bring in and receive them, faithfully distribute them to such home poor folk, as belong to the three parishes and seven wards in our town, and to the foreign wandering beggars according to the ordinance as stated below; that in this matter they will acknowledge no danger, prejudice, presumption of persons, neighborhood, friendship, or similar concerns; and that they will present an account of their income and expenditures annually to a burgermeister and council, or as often as it is required of them, all faithfully and harmlessly.

By this oath, the office of Caretaker was insured as a civic office of moral integrity and force. Each Caretaker was to swear to perform his duty honestly and refrain from using the resources of the alms chest for his own purposes. He was also, and this is striking, to allow no prejudice of familiarity or hostility to influence or affect the distribution of alms. The distribution was to be impersonal and based upon principles determined by the town council alone.

The next article established the network of local supervisors through which the poor could be screened.

(Overseers in the wards) It is moreover resolved: Since there are seven wards within and outside of the town, which serve internally the cross together, as well as in other ways externally the cross, which belong thus in the three parishes and do not have their own parish church, that the chairman and the four caretakers (should) then choose from each ward an honest priest and assign to the same a pious layman.[80]

The town council anchored its program of relief in the pattern of association delineated by the wards or neighborhoods.[81] It was also bringing to that pattern a new dimension. In designating a priest as the official representative of the program of relief in each of the seven wards,[82] the town council gave to each ward that which was essential to a parish, a

---

[80] The priests and laymen for each of the seven wards were: a) auf Dorf: H. Heinrich Utinger, sexton, and Hans Kleger; b) zur Linden: H. Ulrich Tormann and Rudolf Rey; c) Neumarkt: M. Jakob Edlibach and Kaspar Nasal; d) Niederdorf: Peter Kistler and H. Heinrich Städeli zuo Lienhart; e) Münsterhof: H. Jos. Meyer and Jakob Ammann; f) Kornhaus: H. Hans Pfifer and Kuonrat Kramer; g) Rennweg: H. Hans Tormann and Stephan Zeller.

[81] This pattern of organization was not employed in Nuremberg, Kitzingen, or Regensburg. See Winckelmann.

[82] Cf. Ypres, Winckelmann, *ARG* 11 (1914): 14–15.

priest. In a way, the town council was redrawing the map of lay piety, from three parishes to seven neighborhoods. As the town council acknowledged, the ward, too, "served the cross"; although its boundaries had been drawn originally for purposes other than those of the parish, the ward, the neighborhood, too, could provide a location for the practice of Christian belief. The town council had designated a priest as its representative in each of the seven neighborhoods. The program of relief was to be visible and audible in the persons of the priest and his lay assistant:

> [The priest and layman] should go about in each ward weekly with the Overseer of beggars, discover and designate, whom the alms serve, who of these (same) are able and needy, likewise immediately thereafter, every month or so often as is necessary, ascertain, who are citizens, so that (insofar as there is no impediment such as follows hereafter) they can be marked for alms; also (to those), who are from the town, [from] the countryside and territory or otherwise not citizens, should be given alms for the present, until the congregations in the countryside can also supervise their own alms. Moreover, whoever are not citizens, nor from the town of Zurich, should be firmly turned away. With the help of the Overseer of beggars, one should inquire through the neighbors and discern the nature and form [*das waesen und gestalt*], as well as the background of those who mean to take alms

In incorporating the neighborhoods into its structure of poor relief, the town council enabled its officials to draw upon the kind of personal knowledge, of familiarity, possible only in a narrowly local context. The ability of the Caretakers to distribute relief according to the principles established by the town council rested on the simple fact that the deserving poor were *known*. If a person was not known directly to the Caretakers, they could enter the neighborhood and learn about both the person's financial condition and his or her "character"; they could uncover not only whether an alms recipient was economically needy, but also whether he or she was morally deserving.[83] In a town as small as Zurich, the ability to investigate each individual's affairs increased. It was a system at once centralized and localized, nonpersonal and familiar.

Article six also introduced criteria for the poor. In 1525, the first criterion was residency. Those who were not from the town – those

---

[83] "so that everything, as stated above, will be indicated to the chairman and the four Officers, by which they may that much better advise, how much and what one will give each."

who were unfamiliar – were not only excluded from alms; they were to be turned away.[84] It is not clear in this article if citizenship was a prerequisite for aid; familiarity, rather than citizenship, seems to be the crucial factor. The antipathy to foreign poor, however, and the desire that poor relief be administered by each congregation to its own poor, was clear. Poor relief in Zurich was to be local, circumscribed by boundaries of parish and neighborhood, of familiarity.

Article seven gave a list, abbreviated from that of 1520, of those who were not to be given alms. The entire paragraph, however, was framed differently. It addressed those "home poor and local people" who were undeserving, and it closed by restating that "whoever are not citizens, nor from the town of Zurich" were to be turned away. Relief was to be local, available for members of a physically defined and clearly conceived community.

The criteria for discriminating among the poor, given in such full detail in the Alms Statute of 1520, suggest the nature of that community.[85] The first criterion addressed extravagance of personal behavior: those who "squandered their own frivolously, for nothing, extravagantly, gambled away, wasted, that is, consumed, and have never wanted to work, but have frequented public houses, pubs, and all kinds of whores." Although extravagance was all the more reprehensible in those seeking aid, the language of the statement condemns it generally. The second criterion was dress; the same frugality required of people's actions was also required of their appearance. Again, this criterion was not specific to the poor. Three years later, on April 14, 1528, the town council issued a mandate on dress and morals for all of Zurich.[86] Dress and demeanor were to reflect the nature of that community the town council was seeking to define and effect.

That nature emerges more clearly in the next criterion: Prostitutes, pimps, and panderers were excluded from all relief. The town council excluded from aid all those whose professions were traditionally considered dishonorable or immoral. These three criteria, when viewed together, delineate a group of persons whose nature was expressed both

---

[84] Smiar has found 305 cases over five years, 1525–9, in which foreign poor, including refugee pastors, itinerant journeymen, and apprentices, were given particular kinds of relief, pp. 170–1.

[85] On the different notions and forms of community, see Susan Reynolds, *Kingdoms and Communities in Western Europe, 900–1300* (Oxford, 1984).

[86] EAk, no. 1385.

in appearance and in behavior. That appearance and behavior placed them outside the boundaries of the Christian community. The three criteria also suggest what was to constitute moral and reformed behavior, the behavior the town council would demand of those poor it labeled deserving.

Piety, too, defined the community the town council was pursuing. Excluded were those who "do not attend sermons with no reason to speak of, who will neither hear nor see the divine word and offices, who blaspheme, curse, swear." The notion of piety expressed in the Poor Law was articulated in terms of ties to God and to others. Also excluded, in the same category, were those who "quarrel, make war with people, hate, falsely accuse one another, create dissension and enmity" – those who create a division within a community through contentious behavior or false accusations.[87] Such actions eroded all ties of association. And upon those ties rested the ability of the officers of poor relief to determine who should receive aid.

The fifth criterion echoed values articulated earlier: Those "revellers" who "go to public places and pubs, play games and cards, and practice other such mischiefs and frivolities" were not eligible for alms. Yet the kind of person it described did not keep an "evil house," as in the first category; the nature defined by this pattern of behavior was frivolous, mischievous. This person, too, disrupted the community, but his actions were guided by folly, not malice.

The article concluded by reiterating exactly the position on residency given in article six, bracketing the other criteria and reaffirming the importance of place, of home, in determining the right to receive aid. In 1525, the poor were differentiated according to the standards, the same patterns of behavior, that the legislators had established in 1520, but those standards were applied more specifically: to the home poor alone. In 1525, the boundaries that excluded the unworthy poor began at place of residence and extended to the inner man. Those same boundaries encircled the deserving poor:

> To them, as are designated below, alms should be bestowed

> (True poor). Pious, honorable, home poor residing in the three parishes and seven wards, who are not encompassed in the vices delineated above, [who] have also worked, plied a trade and nourished themselves willingly,

---

[87] On the "norms" of peace, unity, and the common weal in civic life, see Rublack, pp. 24–60.

with honor, and have not consumed their belongings extravagantly, but, perhaps through divine destiny, through war, fire, drought, chance, too many children, great illness, age, [or] impossible circumstances, can no longer nourish themselves or work.

Again, most of the criteria are the same as those of 1520. Those poor deserving of alms were moral, pious, honorable, and they were involuntarily poor. Again, residency was reaffirmed; the poor were located physically within the community. Their personal stories, their private tragedies were known. These poor were also located within the human map of the community:

> to such and similar poor folk one should want to distribute these alms for the honor of God and out of brotherly, Christian love, as it has been commanded.

> And whoever would be so weak, woman or man, that they may not themselves go to that place, where [alms] are given out, should have [alms] sent to them.

Here the Poor Law moves beyond the Alms Statute of 1520. Those resident poor who did not choose poverty, indeed whose poverty was against their will, deserved aid. The reason for giving them aid was not simply that they were unwilling victims, but to honor God and help them "out of brotherly, Christian love."[88] Here again we can glimpse something of the nature of the community promulgated by the town council. That community honored God and expressed the love of neighbor that Christ preached. The deserving poor were to be linked to it by bonds of Christian love. This love was expressed not only in giving alms for the care of the poor, but in seeking out those poor who could not ask for aid. The last statement of article eight speaks of a response that was not merely formal and theoretical, but active and communal – to know who those poor were who did not openly seek relief required the familiarity of the neighborhood, of "community."

The poor were also to be distinguished within that community. Their ties, of dependency as well as neighborliness, were to be made public and explicit:

---

[88] The invocation of Christian brotherly love also appears in the poor laws of Nuremberg (Winckelmann, *ARG* 10 [1913]: 259–61, 268, 271–3, 275); Kitzingen (idem, *ARG* 11 (1914): 1–2, 8); and Regensburg (idem, *ARG* 11 (1914): 8–9).

(Sign) And in order that the home poor folk may be recognized, they shall have and wear publicly a stamped or cast metal sign, and if anyone becomes healthy or comes into the possession of goods such that he no longer needs the alms and no longer wants to receive them, he should return the same sign to the guardians again. But if any of them were formerly persons of substance, or males who want to work for the people but who still need alms, then one may permit them not to wear the sign.

These signs served not only to distinguish the deserving poor from the unworthy poor – this residents of their neighborhoods and parishes already knew – but also to make visible to strangers, both local and foreign, the recipients of civic relief. The recipients of public care were to be recognizable; all would know who were the beneficiaries of the poor-relief program.

The demand that recipients of relief wear a sign was standard by the sixteenth century;[89] indeed, that demand had already been expressed in Zurich in January 1523, in a mandate on resident beggars.[90] In the Zurich Poor Law, however, that demand followed immediately upon the invocation of Christian brotherly love. The poor were to be visible, not only as recipients of public relief, but also as objects of Christian love, which would not let the deserving poor remain either unrelieved or invisible. And Zwingli, from the pulpit and from his pamphlets, was invoking that motive, Christian brotherly love, making it explicit and audible.

Certain poor were not to be visible. The distinction between the "shame-faced poor," persons of status within the town who were dependent on the community for aid, and the majority of poor people, who would be publicly designated as recipients of civic relief, was also common.[91] The description of the honorable poor, however, offers one more clue about the poor's relation to the urban community of Zurich. In article eight, the town council spoke of the condition of poverty, when involuntary, as the product of chance or fate. In the next article, the

---

[89] According to Winckelmann, the demand that certain beggars wear a sign can be found as early as 1370, *Historische Viertaljahrschrift:* 193. See, also, the poor laws of Nuremberg (Winckelmann, *ARG* 10 [1913]: 264–5); Kitzingen (idem, *ARG* 11 [1914]: 3–4); and Regensburg (idem, *ARG* 11 [1914]: 11).

[90] EAk, no. 322, article 7.

[91] Richard Trexler, "Charity and the Defense of Urban Elites in the Italian Communes," in *The Rich, the Well Born and the Powerful*, ed. Frederic Cople Jaher (Urbana, 1973), pp. 64–109; also, Amleto Spicciani, "The 'Poveri Vergognosi' in 15th Century Florence," in *Aspects of Poverty in Early Modern Europe*, pp. 119–72.

council also suggested that poverty could be temporary. The council did not treat poverty as the necessary extension of certain kinds of flaws in human character, or as a static condition. For those who did not will it, poverty was an external condition, imposed by outside forces. As such, it could also be transitory. This perception of poverty reaffirms that definition of poverty given by Maschke and others, as fluid in its boundaries, as fluctuating to encompass many who, for the most part, could support themselves and their families. It also accords with Zwingli's view of the involuntary poor.

Article ten banned all begging, in order, as the legislators wrote, that begging be got "off the streets": beggars were no longer to "lie or sit in the streets, in front of the churches," or "before or in houses." No one, resident or foreign, was to beg. There was, as we have seen, an established opposition to begging on the part of civic governments. In part, too, the civic ban of begging reflected Zwingli's, and all reformers', condemnation of all forms of mendicancy. Article eleven made that condemnation explicit, forbidding all mendicants to beg. It also called upon the preachers, as well as the Overseer of beggars, to enforce the prohibition of begging, the one from the pulpit and the other in the streets.

To find in the prohibition of begging the emergence of a new work ethic, or an increase in the values assigned to labor, as R. H. Tawney and others have done, does not fully accommodate the strong link between the ban on begging and the opposition to mendicancy.[92] The opposition to mendicancy was one of the clearest expressions of a more general anticlericalism.[93] As we have seen in Zwingli, moreover, that opposition was rooted in reform theology: For Zwingli, mendicancy represented both the willful choice of a condition God alone bestowed and the arrogant human effort to affect an individual's destiny – mendicancy was false poverty because it was voluntary, and immoral because it was motivated by self-interest.

More recently, Jütte and Lis and Soly have argued that the prohibition

---

[92] R. H. Tawney, *Religion and the Rise of Capitalism* (London, 1926; reprint, Gloucester, Mass., 1962), for example, pp. 240–1, 259–73.

[93] In "Anticlericalism in the German Peasants' War 1525," Cohn has shown that sixteenth century anticlericalism, vocalized most vehemently in the Peasants' War, was also bound up with the enormous economic power of the religious houses.

of begging represented the tightening of social control.[94] This line of reasoning, I think, reduces the interaction between town councils and their poor populations to a single dimension.[95] Clearly, beggars represented an unstable and potentially disruptive element to sixteenth-century urban populations. Begging was a gesture of demand. Analogous to the peasants and artisans who rebelled in 1524–5, beggars confronted burghers with the cry for the redistribution of wealth.[96] Beggars were a vocal and active reminder of poverty. To bring them off the streets was to diminish their visibility and their contact with the rest of the urban population, and to lessen their impact on the collective life. To forbid begging was to silence poverty, to make it less visible, less audible – to make it passive.

Silent, the poor would not be forgotten. Article twelve requested that the presence of the poor be invoked from the pulpit: "the preachers should also admonish the folk in the churches from time to time, to put their alms of all sorts into the chest." From the pulpit, the association with Christian love could be made more explicit. Members of the community were also discouraged from giving directly to the poor. The town council recommended that donors give whatever they wished, "wine, grain, woolen or linen cloth, gold, and the like," directly to the communal stores. The stores, composed originally of the property seized from the religious houses, were to be enhanced through private donations. They were to serve as a medium through which donors could care for the poor. In them all individual gifts were to be collected and from them the council's officers would care for the poor.

The last clause of article twelve suggests both the basis for future donations and the reason why a communal agency was to stand between the donor and the poor: "or each may give, insofar as he himself has grace [*er selbs gnad het*] or is certain in his conscience." This article is the only one that addresses donors, rather than the recipients, and their motivation in giving alms. In this article, the town council sought not only to place its own civic communal agency, the alms stores, between the donors and the poor, but also to invoke the consciences of the donors.

---

[94] Jütte, "Poor Relief and Social Discipline in Sixteenth-Century Europe"; and Lis and Soly, especially pp. 82–96.

[95] As well as ignoring, as town councils did not, the varieties of poverty.

[96] See Lis and Soly, especially pp. 54–63.

The article may have also served to remind the donors that the presence of grace is manifested in Christian love. Perhaps more than any other article in the Poor Law, the language of article twelve invoked Zwingli, both his person and the fullness of his preaching on Christian *caritas*. As one of the best known and most forceful preachers in Zurich, and as one who had already preached on behalf of the poor, he would come to mind with the first sentence of the article. And his formulation of the moral function of collective institutions and the proper attitude of donors resonated in the following lines. Paralleling the institution of tithes as he defined it, the communal stores was to serve as a medium between donors and the poor; and the motivation of the donors was to be anchored in grace or in their consciences, not in self-interest.

The next eight articles deal with specific kinds of poor and the particularities of their relief:

> (8 students) Hereby is it also granted, that in each school no more than 8 school children, who are from the town area, take alms; and the school-masters should take none on, other than those who are sent intentionally for the lesson; and whoever is thus taken on should appear before the officers, and as it is herein requested, the schoolchildren should also wear the beggar's sign.

This is the only provision for poor children. To send poor children to schools was also common in the sixteenth century.[97] Gerald Strauss has suggested that for Luther the function of those schools was not education in the modern sense, but to shape the young members of the congregation into moral and pious members of the Christian community.[98] It is quite possible that the Zurich schools were to socialize the students as well as provide them with formal training, but that function is not explicit here. The article does suggest that the practice of supporting poor children in the schools was already in place, and that the council's concern here was simply to limit the number and to mark the recipients.[99]

The next article returns to the specific problem of foreign beggars. In this article, the town council drew a line excluding from its program

[97] Winckelmann, *ARG* 10 (1913): 267; *ARG* 11 (1914): 6, 10, 12.
[98] Gerald Strauss, *Luther's House of Learning; Indoctrination of the Young in the German Reformation* (Baltimore, Md., 1978).
[99] The effort to limit the number of children may reflect the rural opposition to supporting poor children in schools. See the Grüningen peasants' demands, especially no. 7, in Stumpf, pp. 255–8.

of relief all those who were "foreign" to Zurich: those who had no ties of citizenship or residency to Zurich. Itinerant poor were to receive minimal aid: a meal and, if they arrived after noon, a night's shelter. Under no circumstances were these poor to remain longer than one night in the town, nor were they to return within a six-month period. Perhaps among these "foreign" beggars numbered impoverished members of the rural population of the canton of Zurich, although many of them were familiar in the town and some, like Claus Hottinger, held citizenship.[100] Such an attribution does not accord, however, with Zurich's efforts to extend its influence over the land, nor with the image of the town that the council was seeking to project. It seems more likely that the foreign beggars, "be they pilgrims or others," comprised vagrants, perhaps mercenaries, and those thousands of pilgrims who passed through Zurich, visited its seven churches, and moved on to Einsiedeln. Vagrants were never welcome in towns, and pilgrims would no longer be welcome in a community that had cleansed its churches and reformed its religious life. In any event, the "foreign" beggars were itinerant and they were strangers; they had no place within Zurich. Like all beggars, they were not to "cry and beg on the streets and in front of the churches." They were to be silent and to pass through the town as quickly as possible. The town's attitude toward them may be reflected in their placement in the sequence of special poor: They are followed by the lepers, the most socially outcast

> The lepers, foreign and local, should not beg anymore in the town, but the foreign ones may keep themselves in the leper house just outside the town at Spannweid, as has been the practice until now. Moreover, they may bring in the New Year [*guotjar*] with their singing at Christmas. In any event, their servant may and should collect their alms with their bowls in the town as before.

The Poor Law categorized the poor first according to moral standards, and then according to the kind of care they required. The council differentiated within the body of poor, between foreign and local, children and parents, leprous and other sick, and specified a form of care for each. This attention to detail distinguishes the 1525 Poor Law from

---

[100] See Thomas Schärli, "Die bewegten letzten zwei Jahre im Leben des Niklaus Hottinger, Schuhmacher, von Zollikon, enthauptet zu Luzern 1524," *Zolliker Jahrheft* 7 (1984).

earlier attempts at relief by the town council. It can also be found in the descriptions of the various forms of relief for the poor.

In the following article, the council created a central chest for all the alms that had been traditionally donated to a spectrum of agencies: endowments, confraternities, as well as incomes from cloisters and prebends. The town council sought to extend its authority over a number of agencies and to unify them under its direction: charitable fraternities, monasteries, hospitals for lepers and other sick, certain benefices or prebends, as well as private charity. Equally significant is the transformation of the Dominican cloister into a hospice, "wherein the rooms and several cells are organized into a shelter for the miserable." The decision to turn a mendicant cloister – traditionally the house for the voluntary poor – into a shelter for the involuntary poor was symbolic of a fundamental shift in Zurich's collective life. As we shall see more fully below, it marked the realignment between religious and civic life in the town. The wealth of the religious was to be converted to food and shelter for the urban poor.

Article seventeen designated the Dominican convent of Oetenbach, next to the men's cloister, to nurse certain kinds of sick poor, in particular those with smallpox. The nuns seem to have been more willing to cooperate with the town council's new program of relief; unlike their male counterparts, they were not stripped of their property, but given a role within the new civic program.[101] The town council specified the location, the routine of care, including the amount of wine to be given to each invalid, and designated who would be responsible for the care of these poor. It also stated that a doctor had the authority to override for medical reasons the tradition of eating fish on certain days of fasting.[102]

> The women of Oetenbach have determined to furnish such poor folk, likewise their maidens, with bedding. (Servicemaid). Further a maiden or a nurse should be taken from the hospital, who is also virtuous, who nurses, cleanses, washes, carries food and drink from the cloister, and

---

[101] Pullan discusses another group of women who were to serve the poor, St. Vincent de Paul's Filles de la Charité, in "Catholics and the Poor in Early Modern Europe," pp. 22–4.

[102] The groundwork for this decision had been laid during Lent in 1522. In a private home, in the presence of Zwingli, Christoph Froschauer and others ate sausage, violating the Lenten fast. Froschauer was reprimanded at the time, but not punished, and his reasons for violating the fast, that it had no foundation in Scripture and was impractical for a working man, were not challenged by the town council. See EAk, nos. 233–7.

does everything that is necessary for such poor. To these maidens, one should not be obligated to give anything more than food and drink, like any other maiden in the convent. Nonetheless she herself may spin.

The nun who cared for the sick was to receive no increase in her allotment of food and drink; indeed, she was also to continue her other work, spinning. She was to receive no special recognition, no reward, for her service. Treating the nuns in this way may reflect a general wariness of mendicants, the belief that they had already received far too many privileges for their occasional care of the poor, and that they had abused those privileges. More directly, this treatment of the nuns reflects Zwingli's argument against any personal rewards for acts of Christian love, including charity, because that would be to take credit for work that was essentially God's.

The next article returned to the problem of care for those poor from the countryside around Zurich and sought to ensure their care:

In the Countryside

In order to administer fully to the poor folk in the countryside, it is advised that first, a mandate is sent out to every congregation, that no one supports a foreign beggar longer than one night. Our Lords should as well, through their Overseer or other person, send their own message into each parish, and in the presence of each people's priest and the church warden record what each church, subsidiary or other chapel, which its ancestors built and endowed, has available for annual expenses, or if chaplains were there, so that as one wishes in time, that these same congregations are instructed, to make order among themselves, whereby each congregation administers its own poor and does not send them or let them go to others.

The town council's complex relation to the canton's villages and rural population surfaces in this article. On the one hand, the council mandated the same kind of poor relief as it had formulated for the town, in particular the prohibition of begging and the use of ecclesiastical wealth for the care of the poor. On the other hand, the council placed responsibility for the care of the poor firmly within each community or congregation; care of the poor was to be local and immediate. In doing so, the council was not simply protecting its own resources. It was also reaffirming the importance of local ties. If the poor were cared for locally, the authenticity of their poverty and the degree to which that poverty was involuntary could be known or learned. Perhaps, too, the town council was seeking to draw upon the tighter links of neighborhood, parish, and village to encourage support of local poor. Each community – that is, each Christian congregation – was to care for its own poor.

The next article turned to the poor's legacies:

> Since our lords, for the praise of God and the consolation of our neighbor, have provided the common alms, it is therefore declared that whoever is forced to take alms, whether because of illness, age, or other cause and who has father, mother, friend or other, who according to divine and natural laws are obliged to share with help and nourishment, and who also have the means and are able to do so, (but) who abdicate that obligation, and he must be supported from the public alms, then after that same person's death and decease, they shall not inherit the goods he leaves, but will have them removed from them and paid into the said public alms.

The gift of alms was entailed. The families of the needy were the first resource to which the poor ought to turn for aid. If they, unlike the town council, did not live up to their collective obligations, they could not inherit the estate of the alms recipient. And the town council had the right to seize inheritances, because it did share its resources "for the praise of God and the consolation of neighbor."

In the penultimate article, the town council defined one last group of special poor: women who were both poor and pregnant. Only in this category did the town council clearly demand citizenship, perhaps because the need of pregnant women, and thereby their claim to aid, was considered greater. As the town council acknowledged, these women required more food – "eight heads of wine, broth and bread" – as well as "other help according to circumstances." Perhaps, too, the town council demanded citizenship because these women were less mobile, and they were about to bring forth yet another poor child, yet another demand on the system of relief. This article may well refer to the wives and widows of members of the poorer guilds, whose existence was marginal and whose resources could not accommodate any increased need for food, those who turned to begging in times of scarcity and of increased demands on their resources.

The final article gave warning:

> If some persons were, against the decreed Caretakers' advice, favor, knowledge, and will, to hire for themselves doctors and allow various

costs to consume alms in other ways, the named Caretakers will not execute them, but see to it, that such disruptive persons are punished appropriately. Each knows himself to be directed accordingly.

The Poor Law closed with an admonition against wasting the resources of the program of poor relief; they were not to be "consumed" in private costs and personal attention. Poor relief in Zurich was to be impersonal, public, and frugal. And, as each article reiterated, the town council, along with its designated officials, was the sole decision-making authority.

Poor relief was thus to be administered by one central agency. Some members of the council were responsible for the entire program, others for a particular aspect of relief. The poor were no longer to have a variety of agencies to which they could turn for aid. Instead, they would have clearly recognizable members of the community, such as Ulrich Trinkler and H. Jörg Göldli, to whom they might apply for help. These members, moreover, would have a stake in the care of the poor in Zurich: each one was a prominent citizen whose career and reputation was now joined with the civic program of charity. In so far as the program was efficacious, as the officers' authority was accepted and as relief was perceived to be fair, the reputation of each guardian would become brighter. As members of the Christian community of Zurich, moreover, each officer would find his actions judged against a standard of Christian ethics: Zwingli had preached emphatically of the close link between Christian love and poor relief; to care for the poor effectively was to make visible the Christian love of brother.

Care of the poor was also to be local. The prerequisite of residency ensured that each long-term recipient was known within the community and that his or her contact with the alms office was direct. To have the poor of Zurich monitored within their own wards and parishes was to rely upon existing forms of association and to reinforce them. Outside of Zurich, that same localism placed within each rural congregation the care of its own poor. In returning care of the poor to the local level, in bringing the administration of relief to local hands, the Poor Law strengthened the ties among different members within each civic or village community, and between each community and its poor.

Finally, the Poor Law mandated that ethical and pious standards were to be the foundation both of the administration of relief and in determining the kind of recipient granted aid. Collectively held notions of propriety and morality were to define the parameters within which *caritas* was given form and direction. They were applied to dress, demeanor, behavior, and, most importantly, to will, delimiting the boundaries, both external and internal, of that community in which *caritas* was realized. The community the town council was seeking to shape was demarcated by the motives and desires of its members and by their appearance, their demeanor, their behavior, and it was manifested in the conduct of its least powerful members.

In a way, the poor can be seen as the passive objects of those criteria that were applied in order to delineate them, to give them more distinctive profiles. Patterns of behavior that separated the unworthy from the deserving poor were defined with precision and care in 1520 and 1525, crystalizing in the language of legislation notions that had been in existence in less detailed form for a century or more. At the same time, as the importance of place emerged in the 1520s, the poor who were the objects of communal care became more immediate, more particular, recognized and known as neighbors and parishioners. Worthiness, at least in terms of alms, encompassed not only a moral and pious life, but also a "seemly" life, a life lived in accord with collective morality, Christian piety, and communal notions of propriety. Worthiness also came to encompass residency – place. By 1525, the poor had become known, familiar, concrete to their neighbors. Their begging had been silenced, but the deserving poor had become visible, to their neighbors and, with their signs, to the community and the world. They had become perceptible.

The town council and the poor to 1531

From the time of the Poor Law's publication to Zwingli's death, the town council seems to have been effective in controlling, perhaps even eliminating begging within the town. The records are silent on the subject of beggars through 1531, the year of Zwingli's death; there are no trials, no fines, no incidents.[103] If indeed, the "sturdy" or "false" beggars were no longer drawing upon the town's resources for poor relief, the home poor, those destitute residents of the town who had

---

[103] This holds true for Stumpf as well as for EAk.

given up their begging, stood to receive a greater proportion of aid. More carefully regulated, relief was administered to recipients whose number had been reduced by a detailed screening process.

During the first months after the publication of the Poor Law, the most pressing issue seems to have been the poor in the countryside. The records on the poor speak almost solely of the efforts of the rural congregations to transform their ecclesiastical property into resources for the support of preaching and the care of the poor.[104] It is not surprising that the cantonal population received so much of the town council's attention. During the spring and summer of 1525, the rural population sounded and looked more and more like their neighbors to the northeast and west, who were in open rebellion against their lords. The surrounding villages of Grüningen, Eglisau, Andelfingen, and Neuampt confronted the Zurich town council with a range of demands, for their own preachers, for more just rents, for greater political participation.[105] And in 1525, the Anabaptists, for whom "property signified not a legal right, but a moral obligation to help their fellow men," found broad support among the villagers of the canton.[106] In the end, the rural population did not join the Revolution of 1525. The Poor Law and the community its creators envisioned may help to explain why the peasants and artisans of Zurich remained, on the whole, obedient to the town council: In defining the institution for providing relief to the least powerful in the community, the town council invoked values analogous to their own.

In the months and years following, the predominant concern of the Zurich town council with regard to the poor was increasing the income of the alms office, through the sale of ecclesiastical garments, by taking over the incomes from various benefices, and by encouraging bequests to the alms chest.[107] Between 1525 and 1528, the income of the alms office tripled.[108] In these early years, moreover, it received more than it spent on the poor, in part, because it excluded a number of poor, in

---

[104] See EAk, nos. 626–7, 703.13, and 720.
[105] See EAk, nos. 702–3; and Stumpf, pp. 253–68.
[106] Claus-Peter Clasen, *Anabaptism; A Social History, 1525–1618* (Ithaca, N.Y., 1972), p. 187. See also pp. 186–9 and 330–4, on the Anabaptists' position on poverty and their own relative poverty.
[107] See EAk, nos. 1215, 955, and 1471, respectively; and Stumpf, pp. 334, 351–2. Also, StAZ: C II, 10: Obmannamt.
[108] See Denzler, pp. 43–50. In 1529, the income dropped again, to an amount roughly double that of 1525.

part, perhaps, because it gave them reduced aid, but also, in part, because it was receiving more than enough to support the appropriate poor. The town council had made a fiscal commitment to the poor and their welfare.

The reorganization of relief under a central agency also represented an improvement for certain kinds of poor. It ensured a certain predictability of care absent in traditional ecclesiastical and private sources of relief.[109] By the sixteenth century, traditional sources of relief often turned their resources to building or other uses. In establishing and designating an agency, the sole function of which was care of the poor, the town council had given that care a distinct, public, and stable institutional form, led by certain men, who were charged with the responsibility of caring for the poor.

Some poor came before the town council to request alms. Rudolf Muller received a loan of twenty pounds, "because of his poverty and his illness."[110] The painter, Hans Koewen, received aid in money and kind in 1526.[111] In 1532, the chaplains of the Grossmünster were allowed to receive for one year the income from their former chaplaincies, prebends and fraternities, in order to support the wives and children they had acquired, "because of the Reformation."[112]

The Poor Law also expressed a particular perception of the poor that supported their claim to relief. In distinguishing two categories of poor, the unworthy and deserving poor, the council confirmed the traditional view that certain poor had a right to receive care. In its description of the possible causes of the deserving poor's poverty, the council underlined the involuntary nature of their poverty and found the causes in outside forces – fate, chance, natural disasters – and God. The council

---

[109] See Fischer, p. 144.

[110] "Mine herren ret und burger habent erkennt, dz man h rudoolf müller umb siner armuot und kranckheit willen sol lihen uss den almussen x od[er] xv pf...," StAZ: B VI, 248: *Ratsbuch Natalis* 1525, fol. 263v.

[111] StAZ: F III, la: Almosenamt, 1526, p. 19.

[112] "Der BM, R & die Bürger d. S. Zü beurkunden dass sie, auf Bitten einer Abordnung der Kapläne zu St. Felix und Regula zur Probstei, die grossenteils mit weib und kindern beladen, wegen der Reformation ["Cristenlichen Reformation"], und infolge wegfalls der Opfer und Seelstiftungen nur kümmerliches Auskommen haben und weder kinder erziehen, noch der Familie etwas hinterlassen können, folgends verfügt haben: Es solle der Familie während eines Jahres nach dene Ableben und zwar gerechnet von einem sanct Johannstag zum sunwenden zum andern (24. Juni), alle Einkünfte ihrer Kaplanei, Pfründe und Bruderschaft, entgegen der früheren Satzung, unbehindert vom Almosenamt, verabfolgt werden; Diese Verfügung bezieht sich jedoch nicht auf die anderen Pfründen und Bruderschaften, welche entsprechend der ersten diesbe züglichen Ordnung dem Almosenamt verbleiben," StAZ: C II, 1, no. 855a, dated 9 October 1532.

did not see in the possibility of divine causes any divine moral judgment, as its willingness to care for the involuntary poor attests. Indeed, a number of criminal cases came before the town council in which the defendants claimed poverty as their excuse for theft and prostitution, as well as unpaid debts.[113] Those poor whose poverty was no fault of their own, who had not willed or chosen poverty, had the right to request aid. The council suggested, furthermore, that such poverty could be transitory: health or good fortune could return. Such a perception of poverty implied that anyone could become its victim – the poor differed from other members of the community not in character, but in fortune.

Legislation and the poor: Some conclusions

What were the repercussions of the reorganization of poor relief? Clearly, a limited number of poor, the "deserving poor," benefited from more regulated aid. Yet, in the end, the real beneficiaries were not individuals, nor, probably, the poor themselves, but the two key communal agencies in the town of Zurich: the guilds and the town council. The guilds had previously provided their own relief. Although the town council did not address the guilds directly in the Poor Law, the new civic program of poor relief offered the guilds a kind of protection. For the guilds themselves, the council made available a common fund, shifting the burden from the guilds' own resources. To have a single office for relief also meant that each guild member could expect a certain degree of aid, no matter what his guild could offer him. The poorer guilds would benefit especially from a centralized program of relief administered by the civic authorities; those members who crossed the line from marginality into poverty could turn to the common alms chest, before drawing upon the guilds' limited resources.[114]

In a very different way, the town council of Zurich benefited from the reorganization of poor relief. What did it signify, when the town council took over the care of the poor? First, there were the various agencies from which the council had assumed care of the poor: individuals, the guilds, the confraternities, and the religious houses. In taking

---

[113] StAZ: A26, 2: Diverse Personalien (1526–1540), no. 13, on prostitution; and A27, 4a and A27, 6: Nachgänge, for miscellaneous cases of theft and failure to pay debts.

[114] The records rarely name and never describe the recipients of poor relief, so this remains no more than a logical possibility.

over one part of each's jurisdiction, the council was extending its authority into new territory. Each agency of relief represented an aspect of life within the town walls over which the town council had previously had little or no authority. In moving into this new function, the town council was altering its role and its definition. Let us examine each agency in turn, in order to see more clearly what the council gained in the enactment of the Poor Law.

The council's takeover of poor relief affected individuals, both as inheritors and, more centrally, as donors. It extended its jurisdiction to legacies of poor people. Individuals were encouraged to continue giving alms, but not directly to the poor. The council had placed the alms office between the donors and the poor; a civic institution had become the medium for all relief. Zwingli offered a theological argument for such an arrangement, but it may have also presented advantages to the council. In placing this civic agency between the donors and the poor, the town council became the one agency connected to each wealthier person who gave and each poor person who received, the link between persons of differing status.

As we have seen, the guilds were affected by the reorganization of poor relief. The council's program offered a form of protection beyond the aid available from each of the guilds, rich and poor, for their members. In creating that broader system, in providing a minimum of aid for all deserving poor, no matter what their guild, the council became a kind of bridge between the wealthier and the poorer guilds. In their poverty, the members of the different guilds thus approached a kind of equality, in care if not in status, through the council's alms office.

The confraternities, some of which were allied to guilds, provide a counterpoint. In seizing their property, and thereby effectively dissolving them, the council dissolved smaller circles of association, which, if the civic records are any indication, were private, hidden from the public eye. These confraternities were religious in nature and dedicated to private goals, such as prayers for the dead. They had no place in a town in which the leadership sought to bring all religious activity under its authority. The guilds were the one form of organized association that remained after the reforms in Zurich, and each of them was represented in the town council. No association remained that was not supervised by and connected to the town council.

The most important agency of relief taken over by the town council was that of the religious houses, primarily the mendicants. Not merely the manifestation of general anticlericalism, the takeover of urban mendicant houses was symbolic of a shift in Zurich's collective life. When the civic authority took control of the religious houses, on December 5 and 6, 1524, it crossed the traditional boundary between the civic and religious life in Zurich. This boundary, as Natalie Davis, Richard Trexler, and others have shown, was not the same as the one existing between the secular and the sacred.[115] It was, rather, the line dividing certain jurisdictions, certain functions, by which practices were placed within the scope of one form of human authority or the other.[116] In taking over the care of the poor from the mendicant houses, the town council had assumed a function of particular importance to the mendicants. The mendicants' identity was anchored in poverty; their thirteenth-century founders had chosen, indeed sought, material poverty, and they traditionally cared for those poor who had not chosen their poverty, the involuntary poor. In that identity, both as voluntarily poor and as protectors of the poor, they had found sanctification.[117] In forbidding begging, the town council denied the mendicants their identifying gesture. And in taking over the care of the poor, the town council assumed one function that had brought the mendicants a sanctity and a sanctioned place within each community.

Nor would contemporaries have missed the symbolism of the time in which the council's takeover of the mendicant houses took place: from Advent to Epiphany, or the feast of Christmas. The council had extended its authority over the mendicants during one of the three major liturgical feasts of the Christian year. The feast of Christmas marked the harvest from the old year and the birth of the new, the winter solstice, and a new cycle of religious life. So, too, the events of December 1524 marked a particular solstice in religious life in Zurich. Christmas was the celebration of the central Christian mystery, the Incarnation, when God as Christ crossed the boundary between the divine and the human. In a parallel way, the town council had also crossed an essential boundary,

---

[115] See Natalie Zemon Davis, *Society and Culture in Early Modern France* (London, 1975), and Richard Trexler, *Public Life in Renaissance Florence* (New York, 1980).

[116] Cf. Zwingli, *Von göttlicher und menschlicher Gerechtigkeit, Corpus Reformatorum*, vol. 89: *Huldreich Zwinglis Sämtliche Werke*, vol. 2, ed. Emil Egli and Georg Finsler (Leipzig, 1908), pp. 458–525.

[117] On the special place of the mendicant orders in medieval society, see especially Lester K. Little, *Religious Poverty and the Profit Economy in Medieval Europe* (Ithaca, N.Y., 1978).

one not between the divine and the human, but between the religious and the civic. Finally, the feast of Christmas closed with Epiphany, the date on which the three kings, representing the whole world, paid Christ homage.[118] Here, too, the town council's new role was symbolized: it, along with the people of Zurich, was to "honor God" in the administration of poor relief.

In each case the town council's reorganization represented a shift from separate and fragmented resources to a single public, civic agency, from the disparate to the communal. The town council itself had moved from no role at all in the care of the poor to the sole one. In 1525, the town council had assumed full responsibility for the care of the poor. What role was it seeking? What definition of itself did that new role reflect?

The Poor Law offers some answers to these questions. We have seen that it delineated a community that cared for its own poor through its civic government. That community was defined physically by its walls, by ties of neighborhood and of parish, and inwardly by a standard of Christian ethics. The town council was also redefining the relationship between civic and religious life, linking both through Christian charity and through its own role in the administration of that charity. It had extended its role into areas traditionally under the jurisdiction of ecclesiastical authorities and actively participated in the definition of religious life in Zurich.

The town council justified the extension of its authority and the expansion of its identity in terms of what might be called a Christian economy. Throughout the legislation of the 1520s, the town council set two values in opposition to one another: the genuine need of certain members of the community over against the "extravagance" and "frivolity" of certain agencies, patterns of behavior, religious practices, and ecclesiastical objects. The wealth invested in ecclesiastical art, in pilgrimages, in masses for the dead, in supporting the religious, could be "better used," could be employed both more efficiently and more ethically to provide sustenance and shelter to living men and women. Wealth used "frivolously," be it in the form of church decorations, masses for the dead, or pilgrimage relics, was wealth denied to the needs of one's

---

[118] Robert Scribner, "Ritual and Popular Religion in Catholic Germany at the Time of the Reformation," *Journal of Ecclesiastical History* 35 (1984): 49.

living human neighbor and one's community. "Extravagance," in dress or demeanor, contradicted poverty, not merely its physical destitution, but its psychological repercussions. The truly destitute manifested their physical condition in their demeanor. They not only looked poor in their dress, they behaved in accord with their dependency and destitution – humble and silent.

And here we gain fullest insight into the town council's new role. The town council spent five years delineating which poor it would direct its resources to aiding. The definition of itself that emerged in the early years of the Reformation was reflected in the faces of the poor. The deserving poor, the designated recipients of civic aid, were residents or citizens; they were not strangers, "foreign," but familiar – "neighbors" – members of a community. They were not beggars: Silent, they did not demand aid, but quietly received it. They were "home poor," people whose shame at receiving aid kept them behind doors of houses they may have owned. The poor deserving of public care were involuntarily impoverished, moral in precise ways, and "seemly." These poor acknowledged their dependency, but were ashamed of it; they did not choose their condition, but received aid with gratitude and humility. This was the kind of poverty the cast-metal signs designated. The particular faces of the poor might change, as individual fortunes rose and fell, but the sign was permanent, cast of metal, just as the condition it designated was permanent.

The town council administered to a specific kind of poverty, a poverty whose designation defined it as authentic and proper. That poverty was the recipient of civic aid; it would be fed and housed. Marked with their signs, the poor deserving of public care would make visible the care they received: They would not bear the marks of transiency, of starvation, of homelessness. They were the "neighbors" to whom the Christian love of the community was addressed. As "neighbors," they would reflect that Christian love in their frugal dress, in their humble demeanor, and in their moral and pious behavior. Like the poor in Figure 5, they would manifest that Christian love that could transform appearance, behavior, even nature – a love that had its origin in God and its personification in Christ.

Conclusion

> For from now on, the goods which have been bestowed upon the
> ornaments of the idols such as these, will be turned, if God wills,
> to the poor, who are the true images of God (Zwingli, 1525).

With the performance of the new communion service in April 1525, the
culture of reformed Christianity was essentially in place in Zurich. The
simple table of communion replaced the high altar of the mass. The
churches had been "cleansed," their idols removed, their walls washed
in white. Printed images multiplied in Zurich, filling the eyes of those
who passed the printers' shops, who came to the markets, who purchased
the new Bibles, with their linear representations. The publisher Christoph Froschauer was producing the printed words of the Reformation:
Bibles, the works of Zwingli and other reformers, and dialogues and
diatribes of popular pamphleteers, such as the Zuricher Utz Eckstein.
The first German translation of the New Testament in Zurich had been
printed in 1524; the Old Testament followed in 1525. By 1531, the
Prophezei would produce its own Swiss German translation of the entire
Bible. Reformed preachers were established in each of the parish
churches: Leo Jud at St. Peter's, Zwingli at the Grossmünster, and
Heinrich Engelhard at the Fraumünster. Preaching was to be from
Scripture alone, and a board of censors, headed by Zwingli, was to
ensure the propriety of the printed word in Zurich. Much of the reform
of this culture had been legislated by the town council. It had also
legislated another kind of image for the reformed community of Zurich.
In printed and preached word, in printed images, and in law, the poor
were proclaimed the images of God.

It may be that Zwingli was the first in Zurich to call the poor the true images of God – to contrast them not only as the living images of God to the "stone and wooden idols," but as true images of God, to the "false" images. Whatever their origin, these words found resonance in Zurich. Iconoclasts sought to turn the art of the churches into food for the poor; and the town council turned the wealth of the religious houses to the care of the poor, as well as the support of preaching. By 1525, those images that were "false" – the art of the churches, relics, processions, pilgrimages – had been put away or silenced. Before the eyes of the people of Zurich remained the true images of the reformed Christian community: the cleansed churches, the communion tables, the printed Bibles, the preachers, and the worthy poor.

> And yet, the Lord who had bid people to be invited to the wedding ordered that the poor, sick, blind and lame be called in, Luke 14:21. They had to be clean, however, in the manner in which he demands it. (Zwingli, *Divine and Human Righteousness*[1])

Only a particular kind of poor was to be an "image" in reformed Zurich. Like the images in the churches, the false poor had been removed and silenced. The "true" poor were not "false beggars": They did not choose their poverty; they did not play the community false. The true poor were pious and moral in their behavior, "seemly" in their demeanor and appearance. The gesture of dependency and demand, the beggar's outstretched hand and its accompanying cry, had been replaced by a movable mark of dependency and deference, the cast-metal sign that the town council distributed. And as the sign designated, the "true" poor – the involuntarily dependent and humble – were the "worthy" poor.

What as image did the poor represent? In some ways, they made visible aspects of Zwingli's anthropology. If, for Zwingli, man was no longer a beggar before God, as he had been for Francis and would continue to be for Luther,[2] he was still dependent upon divine favor for his spiritual, as well as his physical, sustenance.[3] The nature of man's

---

[1] *Huldrych Zwingli Writings*, vol. 2, *In Search of True Religion: Reformation, Pastoral, and Eucharistic Writings*, trans. H. Wayne Pipkin (Allison Park, 1984), p. 6.

[2] For Luther, "wir sind wol arme bettler," (WA 45, p. 532; see also, the Tischreden); see Heiko A. Oberman, "Wir sein pettler. Hoc est verum; Bund und Gnade in der Theologie des Mittelalters und der Reformation," *Zeitschrift für Kirchengeschichte* (1967), 232–52; and Lee Brummel, "Luther and the Biblical Language of Poverty," *The Ecumenical Review* 32 (1980): 40–58.

[3] See J. Samuel Preus on Zwingli's insistence on "divine initiative behind every authentic religious expression," "Zwingli, Calvin and the Origin of Religion," *Church History* 46 (1977): especially 191ff.

dependency, for Zwingli, approximated that embodied in the deserving poor. Powerless to nourish themselves, they nonetheless evidenced a "worthiness" in their demeanor and behavior. For Zwingli, and perhaps as well for the town council, that worthiness was an outward sign of divine intervention: moral behavior – behavior that subsumed the self to principles determined by the community and God – was possible only through God's grace. Man was enabled, by God, to behave ethically; or, as Zwingli put it, man was God's "instrument," the agent through which God worked in the world.[4]

Much more explicitly, the poor were to be the images of the civic and Christian community of Zurich. The demeanor and behavior of the worthy poor gave precise expression to the notions of Christian morality and of propriety that the town council articulated for the community of Zurich. The worthy poor were images of Zurich in this additional sense as well: They made visible certain communal values in their very ties to the town. In receiving shelter and food from the town of Zurich as it was represented by the town council, the poor received particular expressions of Christian brotherly love. Fed and housed, they would demonstrate the presence of that love of neighbor that opposed *Eigennutz*, the self-interest that undermined ties between men and opposed all ties of community.

As objects of communal charity, the poor provided the link between the civic and the congregational identities in Zurich's collective life.[5] The town council had redefined the boundaries between the civic and the religious life in Zurich through its appropriation of various jurisdictions in the reform of poor relief. The poor, as objects of Christian brotherly love, bridged the civic and the religious: They were the focus of that most social of Christian ideals. Their well-being was evidence of the presence of the love that was both a religious ideal and a basis for civic harmony. For the town of Zurich, evidence of its presence was also confirmation of the piety and sanctity of the town in its emerging dual identity as *civitas* and *gemeinde*, city and congregation.

In Zurich, the Christian community was to be defined in human terms:

---

[4] Zwingli's "Pestlied." See Siegfried Rother, *Die religiösen und geistigen Grundlagen der Politik H. Zwinglis* (Erlangen, 1956), p. 32.

[5] In fifteenth-century Italy, San Bernardino was preaching "a concept of Christian community, an ideal of a city held together by *caritas* and *dilectio fratris*." Philip Gavitt, "Economy, Charity and Community in Florence, 1350–1450," in *Aspects of Poverty in Early Modern Europe*, ed. Thomas Riis (Alphen aan den Rijn, 1981), p. 81.

in terms of relations between men and in terms of man's relation to God. The standard of man's relation to man was the Christian ideal of brotherly love, which had its origin in God, its personification in Christ, and its affirmation in relations between men. Brotherly love was to link men, and to link the poor to the Christian community. As Zwingli preached to the citizens of Zurich, to the peasants from the surrounding villages, and to all those whose ties to town or village were more tenuous, less visible, what binds the religious to the social and economic, and what infuses social forms with piety, is Christian brotherly love. In expressing brotherly love in their relations with others, the residents of Zurich gave evidence of God's presence in the community; the realization of brotherly love was the sign of God's grace.

Was this vision of the Christian community realized in Zurich? To a certain extent, it seems that it was, in part, because the town council had or acquired the authority to legislate that vision, in part because that vision seems to have held substance much more widely. With the prosecution of Felix Mantz in January 1527, the town council demonstrated that it had the authority to indict, to punish, to expel, and finally, to execute residents who did not follow the outward forms – in this case, infant baptism – of that Christian community.

The town council's ability to act so dramatically against the Anabaptists tells us a great deal about how it came to assume a central role in defining religious life.[6] In part, the town council had at its disposal the traditional authority to prosecute those who acted against the well-being of the community. Its authority, however, was rooted in collective life; its actions, against the mendicants, against the confraternities, and against the Anabaptists were for the most part in accord with the attitudes of the broader populace.[7] When it took over the mendicant houses and turned generations of bequests to the needs of those who were materially deprived, it not only extended its own power, it also expressed a much more widely held view of the community and its pious obligations.

---

[6] In 1528, the town council passed a general sumptuary law that seems to have been unchallenged. *Aktensammlung zur Geschichte der Zürcher Reformation*, ed. Emil Egli (Zurich, 1879; reprint, Aalen, 1973), no. 1,385.

[7] With the marked exception of Kleinbrötli, the town council seems to have been unchallenged in its actions. See, for example, Staatsarchiv Zürich (StAZ): B VI, 289: Nachgänge ca. 1500–25, fol. 68r–v.

The records of the Alms Office provide what little evidence there is for local and popular attitudes toward the civic program of poor relief. The records show an increase over the first few years of the office's operation, settling in the years after Zwingli's death to an amount roughly twice that of 1525:[8]

Year	Income (rounded to whole amounts[9])		
	(in gulden)	(in corn)	(in oats)
1525	3401	754 Mütt	15 Malter
1526	2547	1029	14
1527	5768	1047	61
1528	10498	1013	112
1529	5691	965	116
1530	4668	1244	147
1531	4695	1376	180
1532	6310	1648	182

It is telling that the income in kind, the gifts of oats and corn – the kind of payments made by peasants – consistently increased over the period.[10] Most of the incomes received by the Alms Office were distributed to the poor.[11] The silence of the records on begging, the increase in donations and tithal payments to the communal Alms Office,[12] the expenditures of the Alms Office all suggest that the town council's actions were in keeping with collective attitudes. They also suggest that the poor were receiving consistent care that was perceived for the most part as just, both by the populace who paid the alms and by the poor themselves. Finally, they suggest that the ideal of brotherly love had application in collective life in Zurich. The poor were indeed given a place within its Christian community. It was a place both separate, as symbolized by

---

[8] Hans Hüssy, "Das Finanzwesen der Stadt Zürich im Zeitalter der Reformation," unpublished dissertation, (Zurich, 1946), Supplement 1.

[9] The amounts given in the table are contemporary Zurich measurements: 1 Gulden is the equivalent of a Rhine florin; in nineteenth-century Zurich, 1 Mütt equaled 82.8 liters and 1 Malter of oats equaled 1 Mütt of corn.

[10] The monetary income reflects primarily the sale of ecclesiastical property.

[11] Hüssy.

[12] These payments were not sustained over time. By the 1550s, the Alms Office was no longer able to meet the needs of the deserving poor, who were increasing in number, with the income it received, which was proportionately decreasing. See Hans Ulrich Bächtold, *Heinrich Bullinger vor dem Rat*, Zürcher Beiträge zur Reformationsgeschichte, Bd. 12, (Bern, 1982), chap. 7.

their signs, and linked to the community, through aid that was given only to "brothers in Christ."

> Heini said, like any good companion [*gesell*], he should do the best for another.[13]

Zwingli and the town council had designated the poor as images of the new Christian community. It is hard to say whether or not the people of Zurich accepted the poor as images. Certainly some, such as the iconoclast Claus Hottinger, did. In part, it is the question of the efficacy of rhetoric in shaping conviction; in part, it is a question of the degree to which practice ever matched stated goals. Yet Zwingli and the town council had placed the poor within the matrices of the town's communal identity, demanding of them that they express the community's morality in their dress and demeanor, contrasting them with self-interest and linking them with the ideal of brotherly love. In doing so, they connected the poor with an ideal central to Zurich's emerging identity as a reformed Christian community. It was also the ideal, differently understood, that underlay the notion of Christian community held by artisans in Zurich, villagers in the canton, and more broadly to the north and west.[14]

Was the case of Zurich idiosyncratic, or did other towns also turn to their poor as they redefined religious life? In Wittenberg and Leisnig, Nuremberg and Kitzingen, the reform of poor relief was bound up with a different theology, that of Luther; yet in all, the ordinances invoked the Christian ideal of brotherly love. In Basel, in the years 1519–22, Oecolampad was publishing, first in Latin, then in a German translation, Gregory Naziazanus' sermon on the poor in which Naziazanus reminded his audience that man should love the poor as himself, because he is made in God's image.[15] In Geneva, the iconoclasts invoked the poor as they sought to cleanse the churches of their idols.[16] In Lyon, the city's magistrates and humanists were concerned with the aesthetics of poverty:

---

[13] "spreche heini, er sölt je ein güt gsell dem annderem das best thün," StAZ: A27, 4a: Nachgänge 1524–7, dated March 1526.

[14] See Peter Blickle, *The Revolution of 1525*, trans. Thomas A. Brady, Jr. and H. C. Erik Midelfort (Baltimore, Md., 1981); and *Gemeindereformation: Die Menschen des sechzehnten Jahrhunderts auf dem Weg zum Heil* (Munich, 1985).

[15] *Ein ser Cristliche pre-//dig des heilige Bischoffs Sant Gre-//gorius vo Nazanz*, trans. Oecolampad (Mainz: Johannes Schoffler, 1521), pp. Bir & ff.

[16] Carlos Eire, *The War Against the Idols* (Cambridge, 1985), chap. 4.

how their city would appear to foreigners.[17] In each, the kinds of poor to which the city administered differed, reflecting each town's distinct identity: as a refugee center, Geneva was less concerned with residency than with confessional conformity; as a city seeking a middle path, Lyon did not distinguish between religions.

Analogous to religious images, Zurich's own poor belonged to the community. They had a physical place within parish and neighborhood; familiar, they were located within the matrices of the human maps of the community; and they required pious bequests, collective gifts, and communal charity for their maintenance. In the stead of the old images, the poor were to be the object of pious attention and gift-giving, of the expression of Christian love.

> How I wish all Christians lived in such a way that those who are now called religious might seem hardly religious at all! (Erasmus. Letter to Paul Volz, 1518).

In January 1525, certain poor people in Zurich went about in the robes of the priests. Dressed in the clothes of the old worship, they presented the eyes of the people of Zurich with visible reminders of the transformation of Christian culture. The images were no longer in the churches, but in the neighborhoods. Some were no longer artificial, made by man, but living, created by God: The reformed Christian community was to have living human symbols. And they were symbols of particular definition. Unlike the saints, unlike the mendicants, these human images were not active participants in their sanctification. Their poverty was involuntary, their begging silenced, their dependency specifically designated. The poor in Zurich depended upon the charity of the community just as the people in the woodcut depended upon Christ for *caritas*.

In each of the treatises dealing with images and the poor, Zwingli also addressed the reform of the mass. It was, he argued, not a sacrifice, but a meal, a commemoration of Christ's life and the fellowship of Christians.[18] In Zurich, the reformed preachers metaphorically fed the congregation from the simple communion table; the town council literally

---

[17] Natalie Zemon Davis, "Poor Relief, Humanism, and Heresy in Lyon," in *Society and Culture in Early Modern France* (London, 1975), pp. 17–64.

[18] See Figures 2 and 3 for images of the Last Supper published in Zurich.

fed the poor from the table set up in the former mendicant cloisters. In each, the ritual was at once social and nourishing. In the one, men were fed spiritually, in the other, physically, but in both, the people participated in a feast of *caritas*.[19]

In Zurich, religious culture was redefined according to communal norms. Preachers and the poor were the sole legitimate recipients for pious wealth. The one was to make audible the gospel, to make the Word of God accessible to the Christian community. The other was to make visible the ethic Christ preached in Matthew 22:39. The preachers were to provide the authority by which the community could determine authentic practice and belief. The poor were to replace the old idols and the false worship of the old church.

In the end, the case of the poor in Zurich poses a number of questions. What constitutes "religion"? Is it a rule, as it was understood in medieval Europe, or a more general set of mores by which one governs one's life? Those who wrote and legislated in Zurich sought to make of their town a kind of monastery, encircled by the walls of the town, governed by codes of dress and behavior, and acting in accord with a collective notion of piety. They rejected old notions of worship and replaced them with an understanding of how and where one honors God drawn from the Old Testament and the Gospels and shaped by their own urban experience.

In placing Christ among the poor and common folk, the three title-page prints brought to the poor a special significance. They also presented a social Christ, a Christ who walked among men. Here was not a sacramental Christ, the suffering Christ of the Passion who stood above the altar, but the evangelical Christ who preached to the peoples of Israel an ethic of Christian love: that they should love one another and that the poor would inherit the earth.

Poverty was still linked to Christ, but the relationship had been realigned. Christ was no longer seen as himself the personification of poverty, not as the recipient of *caritas*, but as donor, as the bestower of Christian love and personification of God's love of man. In caring for its poor, the community of Zurich mirrored Christ, as he reached out to the wretched in body and poor in spirit. Like the saints, Francis and Elizabeth, Zurich was to imitate Christ. For the people of Zurich, how-

---

[19] Cf. Adalbert Hamman, *Vie liturgique et vie sociale* (Paris, 1968).

ever, *caritas* was no longer to be located in gestures of humility, in the humbling of themselves, or even in gestures of mercy, but in their ability to see in the faces of the poor their neighbors, their brothers, and their God.

Appendix A

Alms Statute of 1520

"[*Vom almuosen*] Sitmal das allmuosen, uss rechter guotter liebe, meinung unnd barmhertzikeit sinem ebenmenschen erzeigt und mittgeteilt,
ein übertreoffenlich guottfürderlich werk ist, gnad tugent und alle guotte
nütze ding zuo erfolgen unnd alle böse schedliche ding zuo vermiden
unnd gott dem allmächtigen so gefellig unnd angenem, dass er denen
wil geben Das ewig leben die sich damit übent unnd denen den ewigen
tod, die das versument, findt man gar vil menschen, die dester me geneigt
und guottwilliger werent, Ire allmuosen ze geben, wenn sy zuo ziten
glöplich möchtent gdencken unnd hoffen, dass es wol angleit were. Allso
dass die so das allmuosen heischent unnd begerent, dess selbigen notturftig unnd wirdig werent, dwyl doch besser und verdienlicher ist, den
selben ze geben, dann denen, die des nit notturftig und wirdig sind.
Unnd gemeinlich ein jegklicher mensch gneigt ist sin allmuosen uff das
aller nutzlichest und fruchtbarist anzelegen.

Nuon ist wol kuntlich, das man leyder vil lichtfertiger unnd treger
menschen findt, unnder mann und frowen, jung und alt, die dass Ir gar
liederlich überflüssigklich und üppenklich vertuond oder vertan hand. Es
syg mit kostlichen überflüssigen, oder üppigen kleidern, die inen nit
zimment, oder mit kostlichem überflüssigem essen unnd trincken dess
sy nit nottürftig sind oder mit spilen aldandren uppigen unnützen dingen,
oder die sich noch nit geflissen und geschickt hand, und sich ouch nit
schickent und flyssent zuo arbeiten, oder zuo dienen als inen wol möglich
unnd zimlich were, und ouch billich tättent, die selben sol man billich
armuott unnd elend lassen erfaren, und lide und das wasser wollassen
in den mund gan, aber doch nit gar lassen erdrencken und verderben,
dass ander jung dorochte menschen an inen mögent verstan und lernen
sechen und hören, wass und wie sy tuon und lassen söllent, dass inen

sölich armuott und ellend ussgemelten ursachen nit begegneti durch die sy der welt allso verhasst und unwerd werdent, und man wenig erbermd und mitliden mit inen habe und spreche, dass inen das sy geworden, nachdem sy tag und nacht gefochten und geworben hand, das ist prästt, armuott und ellend, die sy billich lydent.

Darwider findt man vil frommer Ersammer lüten, die wol harkommen sind, unnd das Ir nit überflüssiklich oder üppenklich vergüdet und verthan hand, und sich allwegen ir leben lang treülich geflissen hand, sich selber und die iren mit gott und eren, mit ir arbeyt unnd übelzit Erlich ussze-bringen und zuo erneren, die doch nütdestminder zuo ziten uss gött-licher anfechung, verhengniss und ordnung zuo grosser schwerer armuott koment Es syg durch brunst, krieg, misswachs, türi oder durch mengerley kranckheit an inen selber oder an den iren ald durch über-allung vil kinder vonn inen selbs oder vonn iren armen freünden, ald dass sy so alt unnd übelmögent sind worden, dass sy sich selber nit wolme mögent erneren, oder durch ander unversechen zitlich unschick unnd unfäl, die den menschen dick zuo handen gand, durch die sy grossen mangel und presten und schädlichen abbruch in vil nottürfftigen dingen müssent liden, unnd doch so Ersam und schamhafftig sind, dass sy sich des bättles gern erwertind, sover es inen müglich were. Es sind ouch der selben ein teyl, so man Inen ein kurtze zit ettwas stür unnd hilff tätte, dass sy sich des bettels erwerten unnd demnach sich selber möchten erneren unnd ussbringen, unnd by zimlichen eren unnd wesen blyben als sich zuo ziten gibt so es tür ist, oder die lüt nit mögent dienst und arbeit finden.

Es sind ouch der selben hussarmen lüten ettlich allso gsippt, wo sy offennlich müssten bättlen, dass sy selber, und ander lüt mit inen vi-lichter geergert, oder fellig wurdent als wenn jung hübsch frowen, oder jungkfrowen, zuo semlicher not unnd armuott kement, oder dessglichen sich begebe. Ettwan sind auch sölich lüt so kranck und prästhafftig, dass sy nit könnent unnd mögent ussgan, nach dem almuosen unnd öch nieman hand, der Inen zuo trag oder inen rat unnd pfläg tüge, mit heben unnd legen, unnd andren dingen deren sy vast notturfftig werent, unnd an allen semlichen menschen und derglichen were das allmuosen gar vast wol angeleit, unnd ist öch kein zwifel, dass man gar vil guotter frommer lüten finde, wenn sy semlich hussarm lüt wüsstent in sölichen nöten, dass sy fast geneygt unnd guottwillig werent Inen stuor unnd hilff zetuon, wenn sy wüsstent wohin sy ire gab, oder allmuosen gebent, dass es den selben sicherlich, trülich und ordenlich ussgeteilt wurde.

Und darumb sind Ettlich personen, geistlich unnd weltlich die gloubent unnd haltent, dass unnser gnedigen lieben herren Burgermeister und ein rat gar ein guott, glücklich werck täten, wenn sy machten und satztend Ein Ingang und ein ordnung dass ein jettlicher mensch, der sin gab, stür und hilff semlichen frommen hussarmen lüten gern wollte mitteylen, wüsste, wohin er die selben tuon sölte, dass sy den selben sicher trülich unnd ordenlich ussgeteilt wurdent.

Unnd die selb ordnung möcht villichter fuogklich und fruchtbarlich in semlicher mass unnd gestalt zuo wegen bracht werden, dass unnser herren vonn dem rat erwaltent zwen Ersam dapfer pfleger, die dartzuo geschickt und toglich geachtet wurdent und dem volck ouch geoffenbart, die zuo der gült, gab und hab, die unnser herren von dem rat semliche frommen hussarmen lüten verwilget und vergünstet hand vonn mengklichem öch innement güolt unnd gelt unnd was das were, dass jederman semlichen hussarmen lüten zuo stür und hilff wölte geben unnd dass die selben zwen pfleger mangel, presten und anligen semlicher hussarmen lüten (so sy zuo inen kement) verhörtent unnd erfürent, vonn inen selber, oder vonn iren nachpuren oder vonn andren gloubhafftigen lüten, und erfürent ouch in sölicher gestalt, wass ir stät, bruch unnd wesen were unnd wie sy sich biss har gehalten hettent. Unnd dem nach uff ein gestimpte zit zuosammen kement und miteinandern zerat wurdent unnd beschlussent was sy jederman unnder semlichen hussarmen lüten fuogklich möchtent geben alle wuchen, oder zuo viertzechen tagen, einest, nach mass und zal umbstenden unnd gelegenheiten der hab die man zeteylen hette, und der huss armen lüten, Unnd dass sy die selben beschlossnen ansehung schribent in ein buoch dar zuo verordnet, aber doch in semlicher gstalt unnd meinung, dass sy die selben ansehung allweg nach umständen und gelegenheiten der personen und der habe mögent andren, mindren meren nach iren guotten bescheidenheit Und je nach dem sy besser bedunckt getan denn vermitten, diewyl doch die ding vast wandelbar sind und täglich nach den löuffen uff und ab gand. Unnd dass dem nach ir einer nach wysung der beschlossnen und ingeschribnen ansehung die hussarmen lüt ussrichte ein halb jar, In welicher form und gestalt inn aller fuoglichest und zimlichest bedüchte, nach umstenden und gelegenheiten der huss armen luten, dass ist offenlich, uff ein zit miteinander, oder heimlich, jettlichem sunderlich als einem hüt, und dem andern morn im huss oder wo unnd wenne er das aller fuogklichest mag zuo wegenbringen Und diss were für Ersam, schamhafftig huss arm lüt dass schicklicher und zimlicher die sich schempten dass allmuosen ze nemen Und in der selben gestalt müsste der ussgeber allweg ein seckel mit dem selben gelt by im haben Und dass disem nach der ander ouch ein halb jar in jetzgemelter gestalt ussrichte. Unnd dass man den selben zweyen pflegern ein zimlich belonung schapfte unnd stimpte, nach mass, gestalt unnd gelegenheit iro arbeyt Es were denn sach, dass man jeman fund der geschickt und töglich dartzuo were, der umm gotz willen und siner selheil ze tröst semlich arbeit uff sich wölt nemen unnd wölte die sach trülich handlen und ussrichten.[1]

Welche arme lüt vonn disem almuosen söllent ussgeschlossen sin.

Dann namlich söllent si diss almuosen nit ussteylen denen armen lüten, die uff den gassen, im krütz gang, uff den kilchhöffen oder an andren offnen stetten das allmuosen offenlich vordrent oder begerent von den lüten.

Item sy söllent ouch denen nütz da von geben, die ire tag ye cupplery hand getryben, unnd den lüten ire kinder oder gemachel verfürt unnd zuo vall bracht.

Item ouch denen nit, vonn denen kuntlich ist, dass sy dz Ir uppenklich, muottwilligklich, oder überflüssigklich vergüdet unnd verthan hand oder die ire tag nie habent wellen dienen oder flissig arbeiten als doch inen wol müglich und zimlich gesin were, oder die noch so liederlichful und unsorgsam sind, dass sy nit trülich unnd flyssig arbeitend, inen selber, oder ander lüten an diensten, wie inen zimpte.

Item ouch denen nit, die one zwingende oder ehaffte nottdurfft kostlich oder schläckhaftige spys und tranck kouffent, als tür fisch vogel und der glichen unnd des besten winss die sich billich an schlechter spys und tranck liessent benügen.

Item ouch denen nit, die inden wirtzhüsern oder winhüsern unnd trinckstuben in offnen malen oder ürten sitzent und ir gelt verzerent Es were denn uff der stras So sy wandletend von einem end zuo dem andern.

---

[1] In EAk, the "history," given at the end of the Statute, is inserted at this point in the text.

Item ouch denen nit, die da samat syden, silber, gold, oder ander überflüssig zierd, kleider, oder kleinot tragent, deren sy mit eren unnd zimlicheit ires stätss halb wol mögent enberen.

Item ouch allen denen nit, die sich liederlich, uppenklich und ergerlich haltent, Es sy mit buolen, luodren, spilen, oder der glichen, oder die semlich lüt husent, hofendt, oder inzüchent und uffenthaltend oder in ettlicherley wyss, rat, stür und hilff gebent oder tuond zuo semlichen süntlichen dingen.

Item ouch denen nit die da Ee lüt sind, unnd doch one Ehaffte ursach nit by ein andern wonent.

Item ouch denen nit, die das herlich gebett Vatter Unnser und den engelschen gruoss Gegrüsst syest maria, und den glouben unnd die zechen gebott gotz nit konnent oder wüssent, Unnd aber alters halb unnd geschicklikeyt halb die selben wol hettent mögen lernen unnd begryffen.

Item ouch denen nit, die uff suntag unnd fyrtag nit flissig predig, mäss unnd vesper hörent, und doch kein vernünftige redliche ursach habent, die sy dar an hindere.

Item ouch denen nit die nit alle jar zum minsten einest ire sünd bichtent irem eygnen priester.

Item ouch denen nit, die zuo der österlichen zit, nit gand zuo dem heiligen Sacrament, es were denn sach, dass sy das selb uss rat irs eignen priesters ein zit verzugent.

Item ouch denen nit, die indem bann sind, unnd sich uss ir versumlicheit nit daruss lösent.

Item zum letsten ouch denen nit, die da gewonlich gröblich und ergerlich fluochent und schwerent und gott und die heilgen lestrent Und die sich unfridlich und unbillich mit den lüten haltent, oder sy gegen einandern verliegent und vertragent oder verschwätzent, davon sy dick unnd vil zuo grossem ungunst nid und hass und zuo uneinikeyt verwysung, krieg unnd hader koment, das doch ein gross, schantlich übel unnd des tüfels eigen werck ist das die cristenlichen menschen umb kein sach tuon söllent.

Welichen hussarmen lüten dis almuosen sölle mittgeteylt werden.

Sonder söllent sy dis allmuosen allein ussteylen semlichen armen erberen hussarmen lüten, die mit den jetzgenanten lastern, ursachen und hindernissen, nit befleckt oder beladenn sind, unnd sich vast gern wöltent erneren und ussbringen mit ir sorg, und arbeit, wo es in irem vermögen were, und doch so Ersam unnd schamhafftig sind, dass sy sich schement, das allmuosen vonn hus ze hus zuo heischen unnd ze samlen oder so kranck und bresthafftig sind, dass sy dz selb öch nit vermögent[2] wie genuogsam obgemeldt ist von semlichen lüten und von sölichen erberen bekanten menschen, mag man wol glöplich hoffen und truwen, dass sy in den göttlichen emtern unnd vor dem essen und nach dem essen gott trülich und flissig bittent für all die menschen, sy sygent lebendig oder tod, vonn denen inen Barmherzigkeit stür und hilff erzeigt und geschechen ist Als sy das selb durch danckparkeit und durchgöttlich unnd natürlich ordnung billich tuon söllent und schuldig sind.

Unnd darumb dass mengklich dester trülicher und vester möge glouben unnd halten, dass dis allmuosen mit jetzgemeltem unnderscheid fromen erberen husarmen lüten trülich werd usgeteylt, unnd dar durch dester gneigter werde, sin gab, stür und hilff an diss allmuosen ze geben. Wird gar fruchtbar sin und wol erschiessen, das unnser herren vonn dem rät den zweyen pflegern ein eyd ordnetend unnd satztend, der sy krefftiklich verbunde semlich allmuosen uszeteylen frommen erbern husarmen lüten hie hievor bescheiden ist on alle gefärd, vorteyl unnd annemung der personen, früntschafft gsippschafft, gfatterschafft, nachburschafft oder dienst halb, oder andren unbillichen ursachen und gelegenheiten halb, nachdem als sy nach irer bescheidenheit und gewüssenheit meinent unnd gloubent dass es aller billichest und zimlichest syge, nach der hab und zal, notturfft, umstenden und gelegenheit der Ersaen hus armen lüten, oder nach eines gemeinen, wol versamleten rats underwysung unnd empfelchung und das des selben eyds kein pfleger erlassen werd, wie erber oder fromm er sy, dass kein abgang oder missbruch davon möge entspringen unnd er wachsen unnd dis allmuosen hindern.

Es wer vilichter ouch nit übel getan, so es wolfeyl were und nit grosser mangel und presten in den husarmen lüten, dass man ettwas hindersich sparte und behielte, wie Joseph in Egipto tätt, so es tür wurd, dass man dester mer möchte ussteylen unnd geben, man müsste ouch, das volck, so es tür were dester trülicher unnd flissiger ermanen, dass sy sunderlich zuo der selben zit wöltend das best tuon unnd mit liden haben mit den armen lüten.

---

[2] The "history," given following the text of the Statute, is inserted at this point in the manuscript.

Item die pfleger müstend öch ein buoch han, dar inne sy schribent der hussarmen lüten namen unnd dar by wie vil sy beschlossen hettind einem jegklichen zeben, und einem jegklichen des selb ein urkünd geben uff einem permentin zedelin, das er dem usgeber zaigte, (so er das allmuosen wölt nemmen.

Item Sy müsstend ouch ein permentin buoch haben, dar inne man dise ordnung und satzung schribe, nach dem sy volkomenlich unnd entlich beschlossen wurd, und ouch kernen gült, guldin unnd pfünder geltz, unnd annder gab, werschafft, oder barschafft, die biderblüt geben hettint, zuo stifftung merung und uffenthalt des allmuosens.

Item sy müessent ouch haben ein guotten wolbeschlossnen trog dar inne sy sicher möchten behalten, die jetzgemelten bücher gültbrieff unnd annder gabe, und barschafft, die zuo disem allmuosen ghörent.

Dis ist ein anfengklich meinung zuo einem Ingang die man mag mindren, meren, Endren, Unnd bessren Unnd dem selben nach ein recht formklich ordnung, und satzung daruss züchen nach unnser lieben herren willen unnd gefallen und die selben lassen verkünden, aber doch nit entlich unnd blyblich uff perment schriben, vor einem jar, dann der bruch unnd die ordnung der erfarung des ussteylens, möchtent noch wol ettlich nutzbar unnderwysung geben, die vor der sach und erfarung nit allso wol und äben betrachtet und versechen werent, die möcht man dem nach, darzuo setzen und darnach in das permentin buoch vollkomenlich und enttlich [setzen crossed out] schriben.

Actum A partu virginis 1520. Veni sancte spiritus reple tuorum corda fidelium. Et tui amoris in eis ignem accende etc." [Staatsarchiv Zürich: A61.1, nr. 1; printed, with minor and one major textual alterations (see notes), in Emil Egli, *Aktensammlung zur Geschichte der Zürcher Reformation* (Zurich, 1879; reprint Aalen, 1973), [EAk] no. 132].

[The following "history" is bound with the Statute:] "Ein kostliche, tröstliche unnd warhafftige histori allen denen, die diss allmuosen hulffent anfachen, und wie uss eins einigen menschen anfang so lang zit mercklich gross guottät husarmen lüten bewisst ist, das man des selben guotz uff diss mal nit wol zal weisst Allso hat es sich mit gottes Eer schutz und menschlicher hilff on allen abgang gemeret.

In dem jar vonn christi geburt. xiiii.c unnd viii. jar ist zuo Raffenspurg ein Ersamer erlicher burger gsin, ein witling mit namen frick holbein, nit mer denn einen einigen sund und kind habende, der wolt sinem vatter uff einen sontag mitgifft vergeben haben. Unnd als er des morts

durch für sechen gottes unnd siner dienst junckfrowen, die den sun ob
dem hafen by dem für erwust gewarnet, desshalb der sun schnell lan-
trümig ward der vatter durch Ingeben gottes des allmächtigen, bewegt,
den sun ze enterben, Unnd mit verwilligung eins Ersamen rats daselbs,
Ein sölich allmuosen ze stifften Angends ein hüpsch steini hus so einig
ob dem bach stät buwt, dess zuo gedächtnis die herren zuo allen vier
ortten des gemeldten frick Holbeins wäppen malen liessent, das ist ein
schwarzer püffelkopf mit einem ring in der nasen In einem wissen schilt,
Unnd uff dem helm ouch ein sölchen püffelkopf als es noch mengklich
sicht am selben sel hus. Dar inn gebent die zwen verordneten selpfleger
und redlich man vonn ein rat all sontag am morgen nach der predig ob
zwey oder ettwan so es tür ist drühundert behempsch ingeschribnen
hus armen lüten jedem wenig oder vil nach siner nottdurfft. Morndis
am mentag früy gibt man denn ettlichen ancken, haber mäl und salz.
Unnd wenn türi jar infallent als ettwan by unsern ziten gsin sind, (so
stand noch zwen gross mercklich in gmuret kessel im selben hus nebent
ein andern die man all morgen foll wol zügetz habermuoss machet nit
dünn sonder dick dass sick jede person jung und alt on brot ze essen
wol behelfen mocht Unnd so vil ein jeder kind ald folck hett der es
nam, So menge grosse kellen foll gab man im das am grösten in der
türi nit glouplich ze reden ist alt und jung gespyst wurdent Unnd findt
man in diser statt zürich etliche person dess vatter disers huses sel pfleger
und sin schwester und schwesterman lange zit sel meister gsin sind.
Unnd so mercklich hat sich das allmuosen gemeret das es eygne schloss
dörffer höff, hüser, mülinen, und eygen lüt hat, mit grosser rendt und
gült zuo dem allem werdent von allen landbilgri die in das hus koment
über nacht beherbergt etc.

Und darum das ein jettlicher mensch der sin stür und hilff gern wolt
geben an dis allmuosen, semlichs dester fuogklicher und lichter möchte
ze wegen bringen, were guott, dass man all suntag hette etlich erber
andechtig frowen, die in den drü lütkilchenn by den türen stüdent, zuo
den ziten der götlichen emptern, (so man allermeiste in die kilchen gat,
und darus, die das allmuosen vonn den lüten entpfiengent, in beschlossen büchsen unnd demnach den zweyen pflegern brechtent uff ein be-
stimpte zit so sy by ein andern wöltent sin, oder das man in jetlicher
lütkilchen mit vergünstung der geistlichen oberkeit ein stock satzte, an
ein schinbare statt, Unnd dar by mit grossen buochstaben schribe dass
der selb stock fromen, nottdürfftigen hussarmen lüten diente, und dass

man die dry lütpriester flissig bätte, dass sy oder ire helffer alle suntag
ire undertanen ermantend zuo disem allmuosen mit kurtzen wortten,
aber doch dass sy joch zwuren, oder drystent in eim jar ire undertanen
so sy wol versamlet werent trülich und gruntlich underwysstind und
ermantend zuo disem allmuosen mit fürhebung und erlütrung, welcher-
ley armen lüten die pfleger diss allmuosen söllent mitteylen unad welichen
lüten nüt davon sölle werden."

Appendix B

Poor Law of 1525

"Wacht Rodel, Ordnung unnd Satzung die armen und das almuosen betraeffende. 1525.

Ordnung unnd artickel antreffennd das almuossen wie die vor herrenn burgermeister unnd Rat, ouch dem grossen rat der stat Zürich, gehört unnd bestät sind acte am xv. tag Januariy anno Mv. xxv.

[*muoss und brot zuo den predigern*] Des ersten, damit die armen lüt ab der gassenn gebracht, Ist zuo einem anfang angeschen, dass man alle tag, ein kessel mit habermel, gerstenn oder anderem gemüess zuo den predigeren koche, wie hernach folget, Muos, unnd brot, amm morgen, So man die prediger gloggen verlütet hat, gebenn sölle. Söllichs ze tuond und us ze teilen sind verordnet zwen priester, Namlich her Annthoni Walder, unnd her Jörg Sytz, Sampt Annderesenn dem bettel vogt, doch söllend und mögend der obman unnd die ffier nach bestimmpten verordneten, oder ettlich von Inen so es sy guot bedunckt, ouch darby sin, und zuo diser ussteilung ein uf sehen habenn.

[*Vier pfleger und schriber*] Unnd dardurch dis allmuosen zuo gottes lob, unnd zuo trost der armen, heimschen und froembden lüten, für und für zuo nemen und bessere, und dester bestenntlicher unnd langwiriger, Ingenomen, und widerumm den huss armen, oder sunst ellenden lüten mitteilt werde, So sind hier zuo verordnet, vier man uss den kleinen und grossen raeten, Nammlich M. Ruodolf Stoll, J. Jörg Göldli, Uolrich Trinckler, und Hanns Schneberger, wattmann, doch sol her heinrich brennwald probst zuo Embraoch in disem handel ir obman unnd schriber sin, In die Stat zühen, und Imm sin pfruond nüdt desterminder nach dienen zuo welchem obman mengklich so ettwas angelegen ist sin zuo louff habenn, der soll ouch die anderen vier, So es not ist, zuo im

berueffenn, welche ouch als ghorsam erschinen, die selben söllent dan-
nat hin mitteinandernn handlen, und was Inen ze schwer ist, an unnser
herren burgermeister, unnd rat langen lassen.

[*Schlussel*] Der obman und die vier zuo gebnen sol jeder ein besundren
schlüssel halten zuo Irem gemeinen kastenn, darinn sy Ire brief, rödel,
gelt unnd anders behaltend, dessglich zuo den stöcken ouch besuonder
schlüssel habenn, daromit keiner an die anderenn darüber gan möge.

[*Stoeck*] Darby ist ouch beslossen, wenn man über die stöck unnd
kasten gan, und mit dem allmuossen, es sye mit rechnungen, oder sunst
handlen welle, dass allweg zum minsten einer von den dryen lütpriest-
erenn darby sye, umb dass sy dester berichter werdennd, wie und was
an den Cantzlenn von des almuosens wegen ze reden sye.

Des Obmans und der pflaegeren Eyd.

[*Eyd*] Der Obman und die pfleger, So je zuo zitenn zuo disem allmuosen
verordnet werdend, soellend schweren, dass sy die jerlichenn zins, oder
sunst taegliche stür, es sye an gelt, oder anderer hab, So an das almuosen
gebenn ist und füro hin gebenn wirt, Inzühen und empfahen, Sölichs
huss armen lüten, in die drü kilch spel, unnd sibenn Wachten in unnser
Stat gehörennd und den frömbden Wandlenden battleren, Innhalt nach
bestimpter ordunung, trülichen ussteilenn, und hierum kein gferd, vorteyl, annemung der personen, nach purschafft, früntschafft und dero
glichen ursachen nit ansehen, Und umb ir In nemmen unnd ussgeben
jerlich einem burgermeister und rat, oder so dick das an sy erforderet
wirt, rechnung gebenn, alles trülich und ungefärlich.

[*Uf Seher in wachten*] Witter ist demnach beschlossen, als dann sibenn
wachten Inn und usserthalb der Stat Innert den krützen zuo sammen
dienend, dessglich ander usserthalb den krützen so in die dry pfarren
gehörend, und nit eigenn kilch gang habennd, dass dann der obmann
unnd die vier pflaeger uss jeder wacht, einen Ersammen priester, unnd
zuo dem selben einen frommen leyen nemmen und gebenn die soellend
sampt dem bettler vogt, jede in Iren wachten umb gan, ersuochen und
ufzeichnenn, wem das almuosen dienen, wer ouch des vähig und notturfftig sye.

Dessglichen unverzogenlich, darnach all manot oder so dick es notturfftig ist, besichtigenn welche burger syend, dass man die (so fer kein
hinderniss, als hernach volget da ist) zum almuosen uf zeichnen, Ouch

welche uss der stat lanntschafft unnd gebiet, oder sunst nit burger sind,
Sol man jetz zemal das almuosen gebenn, bis uf dem lannd in kilchoer-
inen das almuosen ouch versehen wirt.

[*Nüt burger sind*] Mer welche nit burger sind, noch uss der stat zürich,
sol man fürderlich abwisen.

Man soll ouch mit dem bettler vogt, durch die nach puren fragen,
und erkonnen, das waesenn und gestalt, ouch har kommen deren,
so dann vermeinend das almuosen ze nemmen, darmit das alles wie
obstat, dem obmann, und den vier verordneten werde an zeigt,
daruf sy dester bas ratschlagenn mögen wie vil unnd wass man jedem geben welle.

Uf soelichenn artickel sind uf den siben wachten verordnet und
ussgenommen

Uff Dorf	{	h. heinrich utinger, Custer, hanns kleger.
Zuor Linden	{	her Uorich torman Rudolf Rey
Nüw merckt	{	M. Jacob Edlibach Kaspar Nasal.
Nider dorf	{	peter kistler h. heinrich Städeli zuo S. lienhart
Münster hof	{	her Joss Meyer Jacob Ammann.
Korn huss	{	her hanns Pfiffer Cuonrat kramer.
Rennweg	{	her hanns tormann Steffan Zeller.

**Diesen hienach angezeigten huss armen unnd heimschen
lüten, sol das almuosen nit gebenn werden.**

[*Ubel huss gehan*] Von welchem man kuontlich weisst, es syennd frowenn
oder man, dass sy all ir tag des Irenn üppencklich zuo unnutz über flüssig
vertan, verspilt, vergüdet, ouch verzert, und nie wellen werckenn, sunder
in den wirtzhüseren, trinckstuben, und in aller huory allwegen gelegen
etc., Söllichen unnd dero glichen personen sol man von disem allmuosen

nüt geben, bis sy uff die letstenn not kommen sind, denn sol es erst an einem Burgermeister und rat stan wie man die selben halten welle.

[*Kleider*] Item welcher gold, und silber, Syden, und dero glich zierdenn und kleinoten tragend, den selben sol man ouch nit geben.

[*Kuppler*] Item welche behusend und üppig lüt in ziehend, ennthaltend, zuo sammen kupplend, underschlouff gebennd, denen sol ouch nüt werdenn.

[*Wider das gotz wort unnd zanggen*] Item welche an redlich ursachen nit zuo den predigen gand, das gotzwort, und göttliche aempter weder hoerenn noch sehen wellend, gotz lestrend, fluochennd, schwerennd, mit den lüten zanggend, kriegend, haderend, die gegen einanderen verliegend, zwytracht unnd vyentschafft machend, denen sol man ouch nit gebenn.

[*Brasser*] Welche in offne ürten und trinckstüben gand, spilennd, und kartend, und ander dero glich muotwillen, und licht vertickeitenn bruochend, soellend die allmuosens nit faehig sin. Unnd weliche nit bürger sind, noch uss der statt zürich, die sol man fürderlich abwisen.

Denen Wie hienach angezeigt wirt, sol man das allmuosen mitteilen.

[*recht arm*] Frommen, erberen huss armen lüten in den dryen kilchöerinen, unnd in den syben wachten gesessen, die in den obgemelten lasteren nit begriffen sind, ouch all ir tag gewercket, geworbenn, und sich mit eren gern ernert hettennd, und die das Iren nit üppencklich verbrucht habennd, Sünder unnd villicht uss verhengknuss gottes dürch krieg, brünst, thüri, zuo fael, vile der kinden, gross kranckheitenn, alter, unmögende halb, sich nit mer erneren, unnd arbeitenn moegend, Söllichen und dero glichen armen lütenn sol man dis allmuosen umb gottes eer, unnd uss bruederlicher christenlicher lieby willen, wie es ist geordnet mitteyllen.

Unnd welche so schwach werennd, frowen oder man, das sy selbs an die end, da man es ussgibt, nit gan moechtend, denen sol man es zuo schicken.

[*Zeichenn*] Unnd damit man die selben hussarmen lüt erkenne soellend sy ein gestempft oder gossen zeichen haben, und offenlich tragen, unnd so eins gsünd oder hablich wirt, dass es disers almuosens nit mer notturfftig were, und sölichs nit mer nemmen welte, dass es dann das selbig zeichen den pflaegeren widerumb antwürten soelle, Ob aber ettwan von Iren vorderen eren lüt, unnd manns personen, so den lüten wercken weltind, unnd dennocht des almuosens notturfftig werend, die mag man des zeichens ze tragen wol erlassen, unnd die pflaeger hierinn ze handlen gwalt haben.

[*ab der gassen*] Es ist daruff witer beschlossen, das hinfür aller baettel in der Statt zürich, es syend von heimschen oder von froembden personen, abgestelt sin sölle, also dass weder hussarmen lütenn, froembden noch heimschen werde nach gelassen, an den strassenn, vor den kilchen, ligennd oder sitzend, ouch vor oder in den hüseren, nit bettlen, oder jemantz an höuschen soellend, Unnd so dick einer das übertrit, sol im das allmuosen viii tag abgeschlagen, er mag es oüch so offt triben, imm wurde gar nit me gebenn werden.

[*Stationierer*] Dessglichen sol aller baettel der Stationierer unnd anderer, es sye an der kilchen buw, und sünst wie die nammen habend, In oder usserthalb den kilchen verkünt, noch uf ze nemmen verwilliget werdenn. Soellichs soellennd die predicantenn an der Cantzel verkünden, unnd anderes der baettel vogt ein uf sehen haben, das sölichs werde gehalten.

[*Ermanen*] Es soellend oüch die predicanten je zuo ziten das volck in den kilchen ermanen ir almuosen in die stoeck allenthalb ze tuond, und wer da welt, win, korn, wuollin oder linin tuoch, gelt, unnd dero glichen, den armen mitteilen, der mag soelichs den pflaegeren hie zuo verordneten gebenn, oder ein jeder mag, das wo hin er selbs gnad het, und im sin gwüssne wisst an leggen.

[*viii schuoler*] Hier by ist ouch nach gelassen, das in jeder schuol nit mer dann acht schuoler, So uss der stat gebiet sind, die das allmuosen neminnd, und soellend die schuolmeister keinen an nemmen, dann die zuo der ler, sy gschickt bedunckt, unnd welche sy also angenommen, soellend sy die den verordneten erscheinen, und so die selben hierin verwillgend, soellend die schuoler ouch der baettler zeichenn tragen.

[*Froembd bettler*] Der frömbden bettleren halb, es syennd bilgery oder ander so das allmuosen nemmen wellennd, sol man hie durch die statt lassen, doch Inenn nit gestattenn, das sy an der gassen, vor den hüserenn und kilchen, schryennd und bettlend suonder sollend sy, welcher vor mittag kumpt, jetz zuo mal bis uf witteren bescheid in den spital, zuo herberg han, dem selbigen, unnd ob er kind hat, sol man zuo dem Imbis

muoss, und brot geben, und darnach by der tag zit unverzogenlich von
der Stat hinweg gan, und über die nacht nit bliben.

Ob aber frowen oder man ungefarlicher wiss, nach mittag kemind,
die selben zum nachtmal glicher gstalt, Wie obstat, mit muoss, und brot
gespisst, und die nacht herberg gebenn werden, und demnach amm
morgenn hinweg gan, und dannethin Innert einem halbenn jar, on
mercklich ursachen nit mer in die stat kommen.

Unnd ob einer schon in mittler zit darin keme sol er doch weder
offenlich noch heimlich nit baettlenn, und das allmuosen in der ellenden
herberg nit nemmen, dann welche darwider handletind, die selben soellend, von den pflaegern, und bettler bogt, mit des bettler vogts tuorn,
oder sünst nach gstalt der sach gestrafft werden.

[*Sunder siechenn*] Die sunder siechenn froembd, oder heimsch, soellend in der Statt nit me bettlen, Suonder mogennd die froembden Im
siechen huss vor der Stat an der Spanweyd, wie bis har der bruch gwesen
ist, sich enthalten, doch moegennd sy zuo wienechten mit Irem singen,
das guot Jar In nemmen, nütdesterminder sol und mag ir knecht, mit
der schaellen in der Statt wie bis har, das almuosen sammlen.

[*Spendenn bruoderschafftenn*] In disers almuosen Soellend angends alle
Spenden, bruoderschaftenn, daruf niemand gewidmet ist, und was jetz
von Cloesteren, und pfruonden, für schiessen mag, getan Unnd dem
obman sampt den vier verordneten, angentz unnd unverzogenlich über
antwürt werden.

[*Spital*] Es ist oüch erraten und beschlossen, das man das prediger
Closter zum spital mache, und darmit die stüben und ettliche gmach
zuo einer ellenden herberg verordnen.

Oetenbach

[*Blatterlüt*] Unnd als vor malen den verordneten ouch bevolhen ist, den
armen blaterechten lüten umb ein herberg ze luogen, darin man sy
artznen moecht etc., Habennd sy die frowen an Oettenbach darumb
ersuocht, welche sich guotwillig erzeigt, unnd sich früntlich begebenn
in sölichen minen heren zuo wilfaren. Und ist daruf in dem huss uff
dem hof angesehen die selbenn armen lüt ze artznen, Soellicher gstalt,
das die frowen uss dem kloster, alle tag einem armen mentchen, die
wil er in der artzny und kranck lit, Spiss geben soellennd, wie einer

convent frowenn, ob er so vil bruchen mag, ob aber der artzet je zuo ziten so man fisch Isset, die selben verbutte, sol man Imm andere spiss von eyer, fleisch und dero glich, nach der artzeten geheiss zuo schicken, zuo dem sol man jedem krancken alle tag ein quertli win geben, unnd ob er zuo ziten kranckheit halb so vil nit bruchen moecht, sol man Imm uf zeichnen unnd imm darnach so er win trincken sol oder mag nach volgenn.

Es habennd die frowen in Oettenbach verwilliget, soelichen armen lüten, dessglichen Iren Jungkfrowen mit bett gwand zuo versehen.

[*Dienstmagt:*] Witter soll man uss dem Spittal ein jungkfrowenn oder pflegerin hier zuo tougenlich, nemenn, die soelicher armen lüten, pflege, wüsche, wesche, uss dem kloster, Spyss und tranck zuo trage, unnd alles das Inen notwendig ist, thueje. deren sol man nit witters ze gebenn schuldig sin, dann wie einer anderen Jungkfrowen imm kloster, essen und trincken, doch mag sy ir selbs spinnen.

In der lanntschafft

Die armen lüt In der lanntschafft allenthalb zuo versehen, ist beraten das angends ein gebot in alle kilch spel ussgange, das nieman kein froembden bettler lenger denn ein nacht uffenthalte.

Zuo dem soellend unser heren durch Ire voegt oder sunst ir eigen bottschafft, in alle kilchspel schicken, und da selbs in by sin jedes lüt-priesters unnd kilchen pflegeren uf ziechnet werden, was jede kilch, filial oder sunst Capellen, die ire vorderen gebuwen, und begabet, für ein Jerlich fürschiessend gült habe, oder ob Caplanyen da werend, dero man mit der zit an sin moechte, damit die selben kilchgnossenn un-derwisst werden, ordnung under Inen selbs ze machen, dardurch ein jedes kilch spel sine armen lüt versehe und nit uff ein anderen schicken oder gan lassennd.

[*Die armen ze erben*] Als dann unnser herren, got zuo lob, und den nebend mentschen ze trost das gemein allmuosen an gesehenn, da by ist beredt, wellicher das ze nemmen gezwungen werde, es sye kranckheit, alters oder anderer ursachen halb, der da vatter, muoter, fründ, oder mag hat, die imm von goettlichem und natürlichem rechten hilff unnd narung ze mitteilen schuldig sind, ouch des statt hand unnd vermoegend, So sy es under lassend, und man Inn uss disem allmuosen erziehen muoss, das sy dann nach des selbigen tod unnd abgang, ouch sines verlassnen guotes, es sy dann vil oder wenig, nüt erben, sonder des beroubt sin, und gedachtem allmuosen volgen und werden lassen, darnach wüsse sich ein jeder zerichtenn.

[*Kindbetterin*] So ein arme frow kindes genist die burger ist, und in den wachten sitzt, so ver sy dessin umb gotzwillen begert, sol man Iren viii kopf win gebenn, muoss und brot uss dem allmuosen, darzuo andere hilf je nach gelegennheit der sachen bewisen.

Ob ettlich personen ane der verordneten pflegern rat, gunst, wüssenn, und willen zuo artznen sich verdingend wurdind, und suost in ander weg ettlicher ley kostenns uff das allmuosen gan liessind, den wellend die genonnten pfleger nit ussrichten, besunder verschaffen das soemmlich frefen personen, nach der sach gelegenheit gestrafft werdind, darnach wüsse sich mengklich ze richten." [Staatsarchiv Zürich: A61.1; printed, with minor textural variations, in Emil Egli, *Aktensammlung zur Geschichte der Zürcher Reformation* (Zurich, 1879; reprint Aalen, 1973), no. 619].

Index